Social Marketing Research for Global Public Health

Social Marketing Research for Global Public Health

Methods and Technologies

W. DOUGLAS EVANS, PhD

OXFORD
UNIVERSITY PRESS

OXFORD
UNIVERSITY PRESS

Oxford University Press is a department of the University of Oxford. It furthers the University's objective of excellence in research, scholarship, and education by publishing worldwide. Oxford is a registered trade mark of Oxford University Press in the UK and certain other countries.

Published in the United States of America by Oxford University Press
198 Madison Avenue, New York, NY 10016, United States of America.

Library of Congress Cataloging-in-Publication Data
Names: Evans, W. Douglas, author.
Title: Social marketing research for global public health : methods and technologies / W. Douglas Evans, PhD.
Description: Oxford ; New York : Oxford University Press, [2016] |
Includes bibliographical references and index.
Identifiers: LCCN 2016000593| ISBN 9780199757398 (pbk. : alk. paper) |
ISBN 9780190606459 (updf) | ISBN 9780190606466 (epub)
Subjects: LCSH: Public health—Marketing. | Social marketing.
Classification: LCC RA427 .E92 2016 | DDC 362.1068/8—dc23
LC record available at http://lccn.loc.gov/2016000593

9 8 7 6 5 4 3 2 1

Printed by Webcom, Inc., Canada

Contents

Foreword

Professor Jeff French, PhD, MBA, MSc, DipHE, BA, CertEd
CEO, Strategic Social Marketing

We know that politicians, policy-makers, and public sector officials from around the world are faced with a raft of complex social challenges, many of which require group and individual behavior to be influenced. Social marketing is a long-established, successful, and continuously developing field of research and applied action concerned with the formulation, implementation, and evaluation of such social programs. Social marketing is a systemic, critical, and reflexive process that seeks through the application of marketing principals to enhance social policy selection, objective setting, planning, and operational delivery. Social marketing can help define, develop, and deliver the more citizen-focused and evidence-based social programs that policy-makers now seek.

Social marketing's emphasis on systematic research, strategic analysis, planning, and evaluation make it a natural fit with modern policy development that increasingly emphasizes the application of evidence-based policy-making, efficiency, evaluation, as well as understanding about the lives, wants, and needs of the citizens who are potential beneficiaries of such programs.

Good research lies at the very heart of social marketing and is used at almost every stage of the process, from defining a problem, scoping what is known about it; to developing insight and understanding from participants, groups, stakeholders, and institutions; through to testing interventions, monitoring implementation, and program evaluation. Research helps develop target group insight and understanding and to establish objectives and goals for programs. It also helps with progress checking, day-to-day management, and determining if progress is being made. The goal of social marketing is to increase well-being, not just learn more about an issue or problem. Consequently, social marketing research and evaluation should be used to inform decisions about social programs, budget allocations, and development action plans.

Social marketing seeks to influence human behavior in a way that is ethically and socially acceptable and to produce learning about what works and what does not. This emphasis on evaluation and continuous progressive improvement is a hallmark of best practice. This focus leads to a set of questions that those who practice social marketing continuously ask:

- Is there a need for an intervention?
- Who are the intended audiences and subsegments who need assistance?
- What do we know about the needs, attitudes, beliefs, and behaviors of the target groups?
- What do we know about what has been done before in this field in terms of theory, intervention success, and research?
- Is there a plausible intervention or mix of interventions that could be delivered that will have a significant impact on the problem?
- Is the intervention or mix ethical and acceptable to sponsors, recipients, and the wider public?
- Is the range of interventions affordable and sustainable?
- Are the interventions efficient, and do they represent good value for money?

This book by Doug Evans sets out in a comprehensive and logical way to answer these fundamental questions and describe how researchers, evaluators, policy-makers, and practitioners can address these questions and a number of other related issues in a consistent and systematic way. This book also marks a milestone in the increasing sophistication of social marketing theory and practice. It represents a state-of-the-art review and guidance on social marketing research and evaluation and breaks new ground by including up-to-date information and consideration of a number of rapidly emerging new technologies and methodologies from the digital and social media fields and from the fields of community engagement and empowerment, communications, and behavioral sciences.

Like most modern fields of study, the theoretical basis of social marketing is contested and evolving. In addition to addressing the fundamental research questions set out as discussed previously, Evans also introduces—through the lens of evaluation and research—the big issues related to the theory and practice interface of social marketing. Chapter 1 explores these issues and suggests how they can be addressed through a new continuum model of social marketing research. Chapter 2 builds on this analysis by reviewing research methods and the evidence base for social marketing. Chapter 3 explores the key issues associated with formative research and analysis and why they form the bedrock of effective social marketing practice. Chapter 4 takes a look at how brands can be developed, researched, and evaluated and why they are powerful in the social marketing context. Chapter 5 focuses on how to ensure efficacy in message testing and establish "proof of concept" for campaigns. Chapter 5 also explores the application of both effectiveness and efficacy research and how learning from commercial marketing research methods and the use of new technology can strengthen this aspect of social marketing research.

Chapter 6 sits at the heart of this book sequentially and metaphorically; it focuses on monitoring and evaluation research and provides tools for measuring the performance of programs during and after interventions. It describes in detail methods and measures for both process and outcome evaluation. Chapter 7 reviews social marketing research in the digital age and how new technologies are rapidly reshaping data gathering, analysis, and evaluation. The chapter also reviews potential research opportunities that are being open by new technology. This chapter also makes recommendations on how best to optimize the effectiveness of multiple modalities and the optimization of channel combinations in a digital world of influence. Chapter 8 explores different research and evaluation strategies and models in social marketing and how and when to apply them. Chapter 9 reviews how case study research can and has been used to promote learning and how this learning can be synthesized with other forms of evidence. The final chapter of this book discusses systematic reviews of social marketing based on synthesis of existing evidence to illustrate the range of available programs, research activities, and evidence that exists. This analysis is used to suggest future directions for social marketing research.

As social marketing continues to develop, it is moving into a phase of increasing specialization. This can be seen by the increasing number of new social marketing books and articles that are focused on specific aspects of social marketing research and practice. This book, through its comprehensive analysis, new contributions to theory, and the use of multiple case examples, makes an important contribution to this evolving and increasingly sophisticated understanding of social marketing theory and practice.

It is my view that the social marketing research and evaluation principles explored in this book will significantly contribute to the delivery of more effective and efficient social marketing programs, and in so doing, the book makes an important contribution to social policy delivery, research, and evaluation. In this book, Doug Evans demonstrates that social marketing research and evaluation principles, concepts, and techniques—if systematically and reflexively applied—can add considerable value to both the development and the implementation of social programs that seek to influence human behavior.

Preface

W. Douglas Evans

Introduction

Social marketing has existed as a defined field of activity at least since Kotler and Zaltman's (1971) seminal article, with its roots going back to Wiebe's (1951) question: "Why can't we sell brotherhood like we sell soap?" There have been many useful definitions of this diverse, multidisciplinary field, many of them summarized by Kotler and Lee (2008). The one we focus on for purposes of this book is the following: Social marketing is a process that uses marketing techniques to influence target audience behaviors that will benefit society as well as the individual. The key phrase here, for our purposes, is that "social marketing is a process."

If social marketing is a process, the natural questions are Does it work? and, if so, How does it work? That is where research and evaluation come in. This book is about describing, applying, understanding, and advancing the state of social marketing research and evaluation. That means articulating a basis in theory and practice for specific social marketing initiatives, developing processes by which social marketing can be implemented in the real world, and conducting evaluation research to determine if those processes are effective in achieving their objectives (behavioral and social change) and if so how they achieved them (whether the underlying theory and practices explain their success).

Goals and Objectives of This Book

The aim of this book is to describe the state of the art in social marketing research and evaluation methods. In recent years, there have been significant developments in theory, measurement, data collection, and analytical methods to conduct research aimed at designing social marketing programs and campaigns and to evaluate their efficacy and effectiveness. In particular, the rapid growth and widespread use of new technologies, such as mobile digital devices and social media and improved knowledge about experimental methods in developed and developing countries, provide significant new opportunities for research, including experiments and quasi-experiments in which researchers can measure participants' exposure to marketing and media stimuli. Much has been learned in recent years about which message strategies, such as appeals to individual and group norms, and marketing strategies such as stealth and viral marketing are most effective and in which topic areas in the health and social sectors. This book explores these new methods and evidence, how new technologies have influenced social marketing programs and research on them, what has been learned from the commercial sector to inform social marketing, and where the field is headed.

The overall trend of translation and application of commercial marketing strategies into public health is the most important in social marketing. Marketing research principles have been translated into the public health space, and evaluation of program effectiveness is rapidly evolving with the advent of new technologies, such as Internet panel studies, research with handheld devices, and social networking sites as natural laboratories for communication and marketing studies. This book aims to capture the application of research and program evaluation in this domain.

Purpose and Objectives of This Book

Audience

This book aims to meet many of the "T"-shaped needs of the social marketing researcher (the T representing a need for breadth and generalizability and for depth into a social marketing program), regardless of your discipline or background and whether this is your first day on the job or your fifth year. Chapters are structured to present research questions and challenges over the course of an intervention. Each chapter sets forth the scope of options facing the researcher and outlines steps to follow to conduct the research. References point you to studies that have implemented those steps. This book, along with coaching from more experienced researchers, can move you from feeling overwhelmed by the enormous demands placed on social marketing researchers, to understanding and action.

The primary audience for the book is public health professionals, health communicators and social marketers, and researchers working in these fields.

The intended audience is professionals who design, implement, and study programs in social marketing. It also acts as a reference book for advanced (master and doctoral level) courses in social marketing, marketing, public health, and related social science disciplines, such as social psychology and communications.

The book aims to be a valuable resource to research professionals and managers and other practitioners who need to be educated consumers of social marketing research methods and results. It will be suitable as a text in an intermediate-to-advanced undergraduate- or graduate-level course in a business, marketing, or public health school. It would cover basic and advanced methods (and so be suitable for higher and lower course levels), study designs, and analysis methods; review of evidence in field; and contain numerous case studies. It would also go in depth into research using new and social media (online studies, use of social networking as a research tool and venue, etc.). The book is aimed at social marketing and health communication professionals and researchers and as a text for use in advanced graduate-level courses.

In addition to a broad professional and academic audience, the book provides an introduction for those already working in these settings and for policy-makers and managers wishing to understand social marketing. The book summarizes the evidence from extant research, current state-of-the-art methods, and new and emerging methods and will thus be a resource for researchers and program evaluators, as well as consumers of research and evaluation.

Scope

The book reviews and clarifies the concept of the "full spectrum" or "continuum" approach to social marketing research and evaluation. The social marketing research continuum represents the breadth of research questions, methods, and measures from initial conceptualization of a campaign and its initial design, through in-depth testing, including experimental message testing, and after campaign launch to process and outcome evaluation. Research begins with the definition of a vulnerable population in need of intervention or behavior change and spans the full spectrum of social marketing activities to have an impact on evaluation of morbidity and mortality outcomes.

The book begins by defining and describing this spectrum of activity, using global case examples to illustrate stages of research from formative research to process, outcome, and impact evaluation. It describes the relationship between the commercial and social sectors and the actual and potential translation of methods and measurement between the sectors. It then describes design, measurement, data collection, and analysis strategies and specific methodologies, again illustrated by numerous global case studies and findings from recent studies across global settings. The book concludes by examining new and emerging methods, including new and social media research methodologies, and outlines an agenda for 21st century social marketing research and evaluation.

Major Themes

There are several major themes in the book. First, chapters consistently focus on the intimate connection between social marketing campaign development and the research enterprise. Social marketing research is an applied methodology that serves two main functions. Initially, it is about identifying likely *determinants of behavioral choice.* Beneficiaries of social marketing programs choose to engage in a behavior, such as consistently using condoms, due to market factors such as price, availability, social norms, and other relevant knowledge, attitudes, and beliefs they have and form about the behavior. Social marketing research is concerned with identifying and analyzing those determinants of behavioral choice and working hand in hand with social marketers to design and improve the marketing plan and execution. Thus, it represents a kind of formative research.

Social marketing research is also very much concerned with evaluating the *outcomes of campaign activities.* Individuals who use condoms (as a category of behavior), or use individual condom products, will with some probability have different health outcomes than those who do not. What effect does exposure to social marketing activities, to the executions of the 4Ps (place, price, product, and promotion) in a campaign, have on individual health outcomes? Social marketing research, in its outcome evaluation function, is concerned with this question. In particular, it is concerned with the effects of campaigns on *communication objectives* of campaigns and their role as *mediators* of health outcomes. Social marketing aims to use the 4Ps to change behavior, promoting smoking cessation or increasing physical activity, through a theory of change for the specific campaign. In other words, by achieving certain proximal outcomes such as changes in social norms, self-efficacy, or outcome expectations for engaging in a behavior, longer term outcomes such as increases in daily exercise or smoking quit attempts will result.

Campaigns are designed based on such theories of change. Evaluation studies model those theories and measure the extent to which achieving communication objectives, such as increasing social norms among adolescents to avoid junk food, leads to behavioral outcomes, such as less junk food consumption. Beginning in Chapter 1 on the social marketing research continuum, this book examines outcome evaluation from several different perspectives and provides detailed case studies of the principles, methods, and case studies of relevant evaluation studies.

Second, the book addresses research questions, methods, design, measurement, and analysis at each of the stages of campaign development. Beginning with initial formative exploration of behavioral determinants, chapters explore how social marketing research is built to address each stage of the research continuum. In the formative research stages, Chapters 2 and 3 explore the different purposes and objectives of social marketing in its first application, to assist in developing campaigns. These chapters identify and explore three phases of formative research—exploratory, concept testing, and pretesting—that lead to the completion of a campaign plan. Qualitative and quantitative methods and mixed methods can be applied in each of these phases, as illustrated by case studies.

Third, new, digital technologies such as the Internet, mobile phones, and social media are playing an increasingly important role in the design, implementation, and research and evaluation of social marketing programs. New technologies can be both *channels* for delivery of social marketing and *platforms* for conducting research. As channels, digital technologies have certain distinctive features that have major implications for social marketers. For example, the ubiquity of mobile phones and the fact that they are almost always with many users makes them well suited to social marketing using any of the 4Ps. Think of promoting physical activity messages through text messaging (promotion) and healthy eating messages through a mobile app close to dinner time (place). Or, consider how social media allow for new ways to influence social norms through social networking effects. These features of new technologies have changed and continue to change the way social marketing is done and expand opportunities for behavior change. Chapter 6 explores research with new technologies in depth.

At the same time, social marketing research has new opportunities to collect data, new ways to design and implement studies, and new ways of answering research questions. The Internet creates opportunities for experimental research on behavior change messages that did not exist previously. This is powered in part by the existence of Internet-based research platforms, such as large consumer panels, which recruit and retain participants who have expressed interest in research participation. The existence of large, and in some cases nationally representative, samples of individuals within a country, region, or worldwide creates opportunities to experimentally control exposure to social marketing and to compare the effects of exposure, or higher and lower levels of stimulus, to control or no exposure conditions and examine effects on behavioral determinants and behavior over time. Chapter 7 explores message testing and case studies in experimental social marketing research.

Fourth, the book addresses important but relatively underappreciated methodologies and social marketing techniques such as branding and brand research. Chapter 5 covers the topic of branding and its role in social marketing efforts. Brands seek to build relationships between consumers and products, services, organizations, and increasingly healthy behaviors. Brands can be measured by the mental representations, the associations that individuals form with the brand. This construct, often called *brand equity*, is the key metric for brand research, which serves both formative research and outcome evaluation functions. There is a growing literature of published brand research studies, and Chapter 5 explores the evidence, methods, and case studies in this crucial domain and technique of social marketing.

Finally, the book covers social marketing research from a global perspective. Chapters 8 and 9 delve into a series of in-depth case studies in developed and developing countries. These chapters compare and contrast social marketing and research and evaluation activities in relatively resource-rich and -deprived contexts. New technologies offer great promise for increasing the effectiveness of social marketing in both contexts and have potential to overcome long-standing barriers to delivering and evaluating campaigns in developing countries. A wide range of case studies in infectious and chronic disease illustrates the breadth of social marketing and the evidence base and research on its development and effectiveness.

The book concludes with an examination of where social marketing research goes next. In many ways, existing theory and practice guide the way. Social marketing research is by nature applied and is about not only evaluating effectiveness of campaigns but also having continuous improvement and feeding back lessons learned in a continuous loop to improve practice. Chapter 10 examines these ideas, how they have in some cases been successfully applied and in others failed, and how the emergence and growing role of new digital technologies affect the basic principles and use of social marketing research.

References

Kotler, P., & Lee, N. (2008). *Social Marketing: Influencing Behaviors for Good* (3rd ed.). Los Angeles: Sage.

Kotler, P., & Zaltman, G. (1971). Social Marketing: An Approach to Planned Social Change. *The Journal of Marketing*, 35(3), 3–12.

Wiebe, G.D. (1951–1952). Merchandising Commodities and Citizenship on Television. *Public Opinion Quarterly*, 15, 679. doi:10.1086/266353

1

Introduction to Social Marketing Research

W. Douglas Evans

Summary Points

- Social marketing is a process, an approach to behavior change rather than a distinct discipline, that has grown tremendously, and there is a need for more research and guidance on best practices.
- Social marketing research also is a process with multiple stages.
- This chapter provides a continuum of social marketing research activities.
- Just as the needs of a campaign should be considered in recommending which of the 4Ps (place, price, product, and promotion) to apply, so should the mix of research methods also be considered in recommending how to research and evaluate a campaign.

Social Marketing, Research, and Evaluation as Interactive Processes

Social marketing is a process, rather than a distinct discipline unto itself (Kotler & Lee, 2008). It is a process that "uses marketing techniques to influence target audience behaviors that will benefit society as well as the individual" (Kotler & Lee, 2008, p. 5). In this sense, the field represents a toolkit of marketing techniques, specific goals and objectives for behavioral and social change, and multidisciplinary approaches to design, test, implement, evaluate, and improve future practice to those ends (Andreasen, 1995; Lefebvre & Rochlin, 1997; Maibach, Abroms, & Marosits, 2007).

The idea of social marketing as a process is illustrated in the well-known benchmark criteria, first introduced by Andreasen (2006) and later amended by French and colleagues (2010). (There have been other amendments, but for now we will stick to these published versions.) These criteria include use of the entire marketing mix, or all four of the "Ps" of marketing (i.e., place, price, product, and promotion) (Borden, 1964), creating attractive and motivating exchanges of value for consumers and paying careful attention to the competition, to name a few. The benchmark criteria are discussed in more depth in Chapter 9.

These criteria apply at each stage of social marketing planning and execution. Major social marketing organizations, such as the Centers for Disease Control and Prevention in the United States, describe a step-by-step process for social marketing activities. For example, the basic steps may be summarized as (1) problem description, (2) formative research, (3) strategy development, (4) intervention design, (5) evaluation, and (6) implementation (see, e.g., http://www.cdc.gov/nccdphp/dnpa/socialmarketing/training/basics/planning_process.htm). Clearly, strategy development, intervention design, and implementation, just to name three of these steps, involve the application of 4P approaches (e.g., Which channel to use? To promote which message? With what requirements from the audience? and Where?), an exchange of value, and consideration of the value offered by the competition. At the conceptual level of the benchmark criteria and at the practical level of planning and implementation, social marketing is a process of applying techniques from multiple disciplines to execute a program of activities, a *campaign*, with a specific set of measurable behavioral or social change objectives and outcomes (Hastings, 2007). This book frequently refers to social marketing activities using the general terminology of a campaign as the frame of reference.

At the same time, it is worth recognizing that the benchmark criteria described by French and colleagues (2010) and the social marketing planning process referenced previously each include major elements of research. For example, segmentation, audience research, and process and outcome evaluation feature in these basic descriptions of social marketing. So, it is clear from the start that social marketing practice and research are interwoven and complementary processes.

Social Marketing Research as a Complementary Process

Social marketing research is an overarching subject area that includes the study of marketing campaigns intended to promote or change consumer behavior, to bring about social change (e.g., through government policies), and to assess educational and entertainment media and the effects of news media on public discourse and policy (Siegel & Lotenberg, 2007). For example, both the American Stop Smoking Intervention Study (ASSIST), with its emphasis on tobacco control policy change at the state and local levels (Stillman et al., 2001), and the Heart Truth campaign to increase women's awareness that heart disease is the leading cause of death among adult women (Long et al., 2011) each represent social marketing, and evaluations of the implementation and outcomes of these efforts are social marketing research.

This chapter introduces a perspective and overall approach to research and evaluation of social marketing campaigns with an emphasis on their role in changing health behavior. In this respect, social marketing research is distinct from other forms of health promotion research and evaluation in that it focuses specifically on behavior change through social marketing processes—the use of 4P strategies—and promotion of health behavior or avoidance of unhealthful behaviors. Chapter 2 presents initial examples of distinct designs, methods, and measurement in social marketing research, and following chapters provide details on analysis, results, and implications for future research and practice.

The future of development of social marketing will be shaped in large measure by several developments: (1) growth in the evidence base through more rigorous formative and outcome evaluation research; (2) more evidence-based programs targeting health risk behaviors and health inequalities; and (3) increasing use of digital, social, and mobile media technologies to target and tailor messages for diverse audiences (Evans, 2013). Each of these domains is addressed in this book.

Social marketing scholars have synthesized the evidence base through systematic reviews of the literature to identify effective behavior change messages and campaigns across domains of public health. Systematic reviews and case studies produced by the Task Force for Community Preventive Health Services (Robinson et al., 2014), the National Social Marketing Centre in the United Kingdom (http://www.thensmc.com), as well as academic researchers such as Snyder and LaCroix (2013) and Evans and colleagues (2014) generally show that social marketing campaigns are effective and provide broad outlines of the types of 4P strategies that work and their strengths and limitations. In particular, they point out the generally small-to-moderate effect sizes and variability in how social marketing is described, how campaigns are implemented, and research and evaluation methods used to study their development and effectiveness.

The development of new technologies, including the Internet, social media (e.g., Facebook, Twitter), and mobile health (mHealth), is equally transforming social marketing practice and research. The development of mHealth, or the use of mobile devices as tools to change health behavior and promote healthcare, is rapidly expanding and offers tremendous opportunities to reach populations using the one technology they use most—mobile phones. The widely cited systematic review article on text messaging programs by Cole-Lewis and Kershaw (2010) indicates that mobile solutions are generally effective in promoting health behaviors and healthcare treatment and adherence outcomes. In recent years, the use of mobile phone technology for health and healthcare has grown rapidly as a strategy to increase patient adherence to care protocols for chronic conditions. Mobile phones allow patients to monitor and take control of their own health (Abroms, Padmanabhan, & Evans, 2012).

Social media and mHealth also represent a kind of "leveling" technology that is accessible to almost everyone and thus represents a major opportunity to address health disparities. For example, the *text4baby* program is a service facilitated by a public-private collaboration (Jordan et al., 2011). The service (described at https://www.text4baby.org) delivers text messages promoting prenatal care behaviors to improve maternal and child health behavioral outcomes. It is primarily aimed at the Medicaid-eligible population in the United States and at increasing their healthcare utilization, reducing smoking during pregnancy, taking prenatal vitamins, and improving nutrition and related behaviors. By targeting low-income women with mobile technology readily accessible to them, text4baby seeks to reduce health inequalities facing racial/ethnic groups, including low-income Hispanic and African American populations. The text4baby program represents an innovative social marketing model to combat health disparities using mobile phones and the mobile phone infrastructure to address large-scale health and healthcare challenges.

Social marketing research generally follows the methodologies widely utilized in the study of health promotion programs, with specific methods, metrics, and analytical techniques related to campaigns and their design, implementation, and outcomes (Chapman, 2010). Research and evaluation in this field also presents special challenges, applies methods specific to the intervention modality, and faces a number of design and measurement considerations. Social marketing research methods and theories are interdisciplinary in nature, drawing from the social and behavioral sciences, business and marketing, and health and public policy arenas. Major domains of theory in communication and marketing include exposure theory, message theory, behavior change theory, and marketing theory. Methods include using behavioral theory to influence behavior that affects health; assessing factors that underlie the receptivity of audiences to health messages; and both traditional mass communication of messages that aim to change the behavior of target audiences and new media technologies, such as mobile and social media, and their use in research and evaluation.

Closing the Loop: The Role of Evidence in Social Marketing Decision-Making

Social marketing practice and research are interwoven and interdependent activities. Yet, the practical integration of the work done by campaign designers and researchers is often challenging. Campaigns are developed by marketers working in marketing organizations, and the marketing mix is a product of creative developers and practitioners whose primary focus is on delivery of the best 4P strategy possible. While research is integral to the development process, as seen in the literature, resources, attention, and real use of research that results in the design, implementation, and ongoing continuous improvement of campaigns are often in short supply.

There are several reasons for this situation. Unlike most commercial marketing activities, which operate on a long-term basis to promote brands that may have many years or decades of sales history behind them (Mazur, 1996), most social marketing interventions are of limited duration (perhaps 3–5 years at most); thus, time is a serious constraint. Research typically operates on a much slower time frame and requires analysis and interpretation, which may not fit the fast timeline of a campaign operating on a schedule and time-limited budget. Marketers are often not trained in research and may not recognize the value provided by research insights, and researchers may not appreciate the nature of marketing decision-making, leading to a lack of connection between the two worlds (Evans, 2013). Finally, knowledge about research methods, resources to help conduct the research process, and decision-makers' knowledge and understanding of research and its role in decision-making are all significant constraints for influencing marketers' decision-making with research results.

As discussed throughout this book, the integration of social marketing practice and research is a delicate balance that has implications for both the success of campaigns and the growth of the evidence base. First, practitioners and researchers need a common basis in education, language, and understanding of the role and importance of the benchmark criteria and the growing evidence that fully integrated campaigns using all the tools in the social marketing toolkit are typically most successful (French et al., 2010). Practitioners often have public health, business, communications and marketing, social work, or other backgrounds related to implementation, while researchers have backgrounds in the social sciences (Evans, 2013). Bridging this gap requires workforce professional training and development programs both for practitioners on the importance and use of research and for researchers on how to understand and integrate marketing concepts and activities into their study designs and measures (Evans, 2013). For social marketing practice and research to be *synergistic* as the benchmark criteria imply, all parties to the enterprise need to share a common knowledge base. This will lead to better research based on valid and reliable measures of campaign activity, which has been a challenge in previous campaigns, from tobacco control to HIV/AIDS prevention (Evans, Davis, & Farrelly, 2008), and better use of research in the continuous improvement of practice. Examples of this challenge, and situations for which it has been successfully overcome, are discussed in Chapters 2, 6, and 9 of this volume.

Second, for social marketing as a field to achieve its long-term potential of achieving social good through behavior change, evidence must be integrated into practice. This is the basic goal of the PRECEDE-PROCEED model (Green & Kreuter, 2005): to close the translation loop from program theory to development, implementation, evaluation, and integration of resulting evidence of what works back into improved future practice. This is a long-recognized and central challenge for all health promotion programs (Green et al., 1980) and has been reinforced by recent models, such as the RE-AIM (Reach, Effectiveness, Adoption, Implementation, and Maintenance) model, which calls for increased translation of research to demonstrate efficacy of programs under controlled conditions into field-based effectiveness studies under real-world conditions, leading to improved practice (Glasgow, Lichtenstein, & Marcus, 2003).

Social marketing shares this same challenge with the broad field of health promotion, in part because of the disciplinary and educational differences between practitioners and researchers noted previously. There are examples of successful partnerships between social marketing practitioners and researchers on large-scale programs in tobacco control and drug use prevention, as discussed in Chapter 9. These examples stand out in that they achieved a high degree of research-to-practice translation, and shared the common characteristics of integrating multiple components of the social marketing benchmark criteria and planning process into a single campaign. The gap that remains to be closed, and discussed further in Chapter 9, is *how to promote translation*

and integration of research and practice from the beginning of a project. This remains a central challenge to realizing the potential of social marketing.

The Social Marketing Research Continuum

This chapter introduces the idea of social marketing research and its integration into the social marketing process as a whole. Use of research at the design, development, implementation, and evaluation stages of social marketing is part of the benchmark criteria (Chapman, 2010). These areas of use represent stages in a time sequence over the life span of development of the campaign, our rubric for speaking about social marketing practice in this book. Each of these stages represents an important part of the evidence creation and decision-making process for social marketing. The key to gathering valid, timely, and actionable evidence is recognizing what place on the social marketing research continuum a project currently stands when planning research. Figure 1-1 (reproduced from Evans, 2015) illustrates the continuum concept.

Figure 1-1 illustrates a basic model of social marketing research based on the key questions researchers seek to answer. These follow the continuum from left to right and define a process moving from marketing design and development (Brown, 2009) through implementation, monitoring, and evaluation. The following are social marketing researchers' basic questions:

1. What should the marketing campaign be?
2. Are its strategies and messages efficacious?
3. Is it implemented as planned?

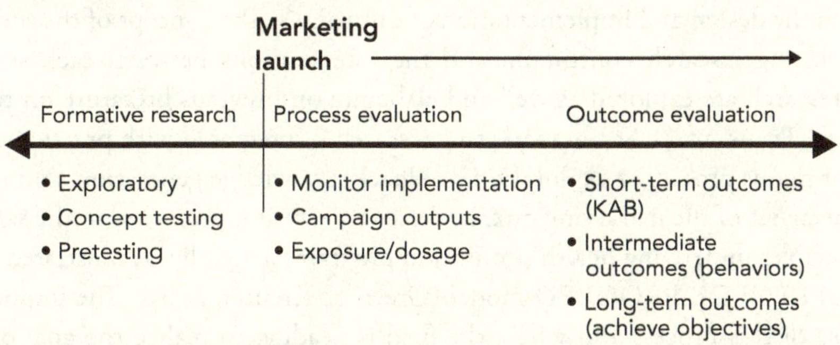

FIGURE 1-1 The social marketing research continuum.

Source: Evans, W.D. (2015) A Social Marketing Research Paradigm. In *Social Marketing: Global Perspectives, Strategies, and Effects on Consumer Behavior*, W.D. Evans (Ed.). Hauppauge, NY: Nova Science; Chapter 1.

4. Does the audience receive and adopt the intended knowledge, attitudes, and beliefs (KAB)?
   a. Are the campaign **communication objectives** achieved?
5. Does the audience know/adopt key messages?
6. Does the audience adopt and maintain intended behaviors?
   a. Are the campaign **behavioral objectives** achieved? These behavioral endpoints are either buy a socially marketed product or service or engage in health-promoting or disease-preventing behaviors.

Based on this basic process flow and distinct stages of research questions and objectives, there are several familiar methods of research used in social marketing, including the following:

- Formative research—What affects the targeted behavior of interest? How does the audience think and feel about the targeted behavior? What should be the marketing mix (4Ps)?
- Message testing research—Do messages achieve their communication objectives?
- Process evaluation—How is the marketing delivered?
- Outcome evaluation—What are behavioral effects of the message on audiences?
- Impact evaluation—What is the long-term effect of the message on health promotion and disease prevention (morbidity and mortality)?

The following chapters explore and elaborate on each of these research methodologies and how they are applied in social marketing. Each method is explicated using results from social marketing research and case examples from the design and implementation of campaigns. The concept of the social marketing research continuum and the interrelations between each stage of research are explored as well and elaborate on previous literature on this topic (Evans, 2015). Social marketing research is integrated with practice as a continuous process of exploration, feedback, knowledge generation, and improvement of the marketing mix. In these respects, it is grounded in the same principles underlying health promotion programs generally, as illustrated by the PRECEDE-PROCEED model (Green & Kreuter, 2005). The implications of this process and where the field is heading to realize the goal of a closed loop of translation from research to practice is discussed in detail in Chapter 10.

Additional Resources: Web Based

- Developing Health Communication Campaigns: http://www.nccmt.ca/registry/view/eng/75.html
- Making Health Communication Programs Work: http://www.cancer.gov/publications/health-communication/pink-book.pdf
- Oxford Bibliographies Online: Health Communication: http://www.oxfordbibliographies.com/
- Theory at a Glance: A Guide for Health Promotion Practice: http://www.sneb.org/2014/Theory%20at%20a%20Glance.pdf

Additional Resources: Literature

- Holden, D.J., & Zimmerman, M.A. (2008). *A Practical Guide to Program Evaluation Planning: Theory and Case Examples*. Thousand Oaks, CA: Sage.
- Lefebvre, R.C. (2014).
- Valente, T. (2002). *Evaluating Health Promotion Programs*. Oxford, UK: Oxford University Press.

References

Abroms, L.C., Padmanabhan, N., & Evans, W.D. (2012). Mobile Phones for Health Promotion. In *eHealth Applications: Promising Strategies for Health Behavior Change*, S. Noar & N.G. Harrington (Eds.). New York: Routledge; 147–166.

Andreasen, A. (1995). *Marketing Social Change: Changing Behavior to Promote Health, Social Development, and the Environment*. San Francisco: Jossey-Bass.

Andreasen, A. (2006). *Social Marketing in the 21st Century*. Thousand Oaks, CA: Sage.

Borden, N. (1964). The concept of the marketing mix. *Journal of Advertising Research*, *4*(6), 2–7.

Brown, T. (2009). *Change by Design: How Design Thinking Transforms Organizations and Inspires Innovation*. New York: HarperCollins.

Chapman, S. (2010). Evaluating Social Marketing. In *Evaluating Health Promotion*, M. Thorogood & Y. Coombes (Eds.). Oxford, UK: Oxford University Press; Chapter 7.

Cole-Lewis, H., & Kershaw, T. (2010). Text messaging as a tool for behavior change in disease prevention and management. *Epidemiologic Reviews, 32*(1), 56–69.

Evans, W.D. (2013) Branding Social and Health Behavior: An Education and Research Agenda. In *Psychology of Branding*, W.D. Evans (Ed.). Hauppauge, NY: Nova Science; 133–148.

Evans, W.D. (2015) A Social Marketing Research Paradigm. In *Social Marketing: Global Perspectives, Strategies, and Effects on Consumer Behavior,* W.D. Evans (Ed.). Hauppauge, NY: Nova Science; Chapter 1.

Evans, W.D., Davis, K.C., & Farrelly, M.C. (2008). Planning for a Media Evaluation. In *A Practical Guide to Program Evaluation Planning,* D. Holden & M. Zimmerman (Eds.), Thousand Oaks, CA: Sage; Chapter 6.

Evans, W.D., Pattanayak, S.K., Young, S., Buszin, J., Rai, S., & Wallace, J. (2014). Social Marketing of Water and Sanitation: Systematic Review of Peer-Reviewed Literature. *Social Science & Medicine.* doi:10.1016/j.socscimed.2014.03.011

French, J., Blair-Stevens, C., McVey, D., & Merritt, R. (2010). *Social Marketing and Public Health.* Oxford, UK: Oxford University Press.

Glasgow, R.E., Lichtenstein, E., & Marcus, A.C. (2003). Why Don't We See More Translation of Health Promotion Research to Practice? Rethinking the Efficacy-to-Effectiveness Transition. *American Journal of Public Health,* 93: 1261–1267.

Green, L.W., & Kreuter, M.W. (2005). *Health Promotion Planning: An Educational and Ecological Approach* (4th ed.). New York: McGraw-Hill.

Green, L.W., Kreuter, M.W., Deeds, S.G., Partridge, K.B. (1980). *Health Education Planning: A Diagnostic Approach.* Mountain View, California: Mayfield.

Hastings, G. (2007). *Social Marketing: Why Should the Devil Have All the Best Tunes?* Oxford, UK: Elsevier.

Jordan, E.T., Ray, E.M., Johnson, P., & Evans, W.D. (2011). Early Results: Text4baby Program Reaches the Intended Audience. *Nursing for Women's Health,* 15(3): 206–212.

Kotler, P., & Lee, N. (2008). *Social Marketing: Influencing Behaviors for Good* (3rd ed.). Los Angeles: Sage.

Lefebvre, R.C. (2014). Social marketing. In *Oxford Bibliographies Online: Public Health.* Oxford, UK: Oxford University Press.

Lefebvre, R.C., & Rochlin, L. (1997) Social marketing. In *Health Behavior and Health Education: Theory, Research and Practice,* K. Glanz, F.M. Lewis, & B.K. Rimer (Eds.). San Francisco: Jossey-Bass; 384–402.

Long, T., Taubenheim, A.M., McDonough, S., Austin, P., Wayman, J., & Temple, S. (2011). Delivering *The Heart Truth®* to Women Through Community Education. *Social Marketing Quarterly,* 17(4): 24–40. doi:10.1080/15245004.2011.620682

Maibach, E., Abroms, L., & Marosits, M. (2007). Communication and Marketing as Tools to Cultivate the Public's Health: A Proposed "People and Places" Framework. *BMC Public Health,* 7: 88. doi:http://www.biomedcentral.com/1471-2458/7/88

Mazur, L. (1996). Marketing madness. *E Magazine: The Environmental Magazine,* 7(3–8).

Robinson, M.N., Tansil, K.A., Elder, R.W., Soler, R.E., Labre, M.P., Mercer, S.L., Eroglu, D., Baur, C., Lyon-Daniel, K., Fridinger, F., Sokler, L.A., Miller, T., Dearing, J.W., Evans, W.D., Snyder, L.B., Viswanath, K., Glik, D.C., Beistle, D.K., Chervin, D.D., Bernhardt, J.M., Johnson, L., Salmon, C.T., Green, L.W., Rimer, B.K., Task Force on

Community Preventive Services. (2014). Health Communication Campaigns That Include Mass Media and Health-Related Product Distribution: A Community Guide Systematic Review. *American Journal of Preventive Medicine*, 47(3): 360–371.

Siegel, M., & Lotenberg, L.D. (2007). *Marketing Public Health.* Sudbury, MA: Jones & Bartlett.

Snyder, L.B., & LaCroix, J.M. (2013). How Effective Are Mediated Health Campaigns? A Synthesis of Meta-Analyses. In *Public Communication Campaigns*, 4th ed., R. Rice & C. Atkin (Eds.). Thousand Oaks, CA: Sage; 113–129.

Stillman, F., Cronin, K., Evans, W.D., & Ulasevich, A. (2001). Can Media Advocacy Influence Newspaper Coverage of Tobacco: Measuring the Effectiveness of the American Stop Smoking Study's Media Advocacy Strategies. *Tobacco Control,* 10: 137–144.

2

Research Methods and Evidence For Social Marketing

W. Douglas Evans

Summary Points

- Social marketing has a growing evidence base.
- There are challenges in reviewing the literature due to inconsistent reporting and description of programs.
- Gaps in the current evidence base should be filled using innovative methods and by harnessing new technologies, such as social media and mobile devices.

THIS CHAPTER BEGINS to explore the social marketing research continuum introduced in Chapter 1. Each of the steps in research methods, and their purpose in the social marketing process outlined in Chapter 1, is based in theory, practice, and evidence and has been widely used in the field. The overall goal of this chapter is to provide a brief, not exhaustive review of current methods and evidence in the field. Challenges in assessing the social marketing evidence arise due to issues of how programs and campaigns in the field are described and reported, and the chapter highlights these issues and ways that researchers have attempted to overcome them. Finally, the chapter addresses opportunities for innovation, such as new technologies for social marketing research, how these are currently being to be applied in the field, and how they are evolving.

Overview of the Evidence

There is a growing body of evidence, especially from public health subject areas such as tobacco control, nutrition and physical activity, and HIV/AIDS, to suggest that social marketing can change behavior and is a broadly effective social change strategy that can be applied to modify behaviors across multiple subject areas (French et al., 2010; Abroms & Maibach, 2008). A recent systematic review by the US Preventive Services Taskforce of 23 campaigns that used products (e.g., bicycle helmets) to promote health and prevent disease and injury concluded that communication and social marketing campaigns using these techniques were effective (Robinson et al., 2014).

There is also growing evidence that social marketing is effective in programs aimed at other types of behavior change, from increasing environmental conservation (McKenzie-Mohr, 2011) to promoting community participation (Dutta-Bergman, 2003). The best evidence of social marketing effectiveness comes from media campaign evaluations, typically studies of large mass media campaigns or laboratory experiments where messages are tested under controlled conditions (Snyder & Hamilton, 2002; Evans, Uhrig, et al., 2009). Recently, however, mobile phones, social media, and other new technologies have been studied for behavior change as well (Abroms, Padmanabhan, & Evans, 2012).

Recent evidence reviews indicate that social marketing through mass media is effective in changing health behaviors on a population level. In general, these studies show that social marketing has been effective in changing health behavior (e.g., those related to smoking, physical activity, and condom use) and behavioral mediators, such as knowledge, attitudes, and beliefs related to these behaviors. However, most of these studies have shown effect sizes of less than 10% (Snyder & Hamilton, 2002).

In their widely cited study of 48 US social marketing campaigns based on mass media, Snyder and Hamilton (2002) found that the average campaign accounted for about 9% of the variation in health risk behavior outcomes but with heterogeneous results. A study of 17 recent European media campaigns on a range of topics, including promotion of HIV testing, myocardial infarction admissions, immunizations, and cancer screenings, found similar effects in the range of 5% to 10% (Grilli, Ramsay, & Minozzi, 2002). Evans (2006) points out that single- or few-time behaviors can be easier to promote than behavior requiring repetition and maintenance over time. Some behaviors that do not require long-term maintenance, such as vitamin A promotion and switching to 1% milk, have shown greater effect sizes and generally appear to have higher rates of success (Hornik, 1997; Reger, Wootan, &

Booth-Butterfield, 1999). Media campaigns have thus been used to modify both complex behaviors, including those involving multiple lifestyle risk factors (e.g., HIV risk behavior) and simpler behaviors (e.g., choosing a food product). Because of the wide applicability of media campaigns to behavior modification, it may be that such an approach would be effective in changing civic behaviors, such as mailing back a census form.

The most effective mass media campaigns have generally been those with substantial financial resources and thus the ability to generate high levels of audience exposure and recall or recognition of messages and advertising executions. For example, among the most successful media campaigns to change health behavior have been tobacco countermarketing campaigns aimed at preventing youth smoking initiation, such as the American Legacy Foundation's (http://truthinitiative.org/) *truth*® campaign. Legacy spent several hundred million dollars in the campaign's early years, from 2000 to 2002. Farrelly and colleagues (2005) showed that from 1999 to 2002, US youth smoking prevalence declined from 25.3% to 18.0%, and the *truth* campaign accounted for approximately 22% of that decline. While this is a relatively small effect size by clinical standards, it demonstrates that media campaigns can have a big impact on population-level health. For example, in the case of *truth*, the campaign-attributable decline in youth smoking equates to some 300,000 fewer youth smokers and thus millions of added life years, as well as tremendous reductions in healthcare expenditures and other social costs.

There is evidence that media campaigns are effective in targeting other behaviors, such as financial education and literacy. The Mediae Financial Education project in Kenya aimed to improve knowledge, attitudes, behaviors, and practices in terms of financial capability (World Bank, 2012). This initiative focused on banking, budgeting, savings, and investments to increase levels of financial education in the country. The campaign's primary objective was to encourage people to manage their finances in a sustainable manner more likely to lead to financial security. The basic approach integrated financial education content into an entertaining television program, *Makutuno Junction*, featuring characters that people could identify with. Outcome evaluation was conducted through a pre and postintervention cross-sectional survey of viewers and nonviewers. Prior to the airing of the episodes involving financial topics, 57% of the baseline survey respondents claimed to have "seen/heard information about the four target financial topics from sources in their environment"; among viewers, this number jumped to 67% after the show. For nonviewers, there was no increase in awareness or knowledge, suggesting a potential treatment effect of *Makutano Junction* (World Bank, 2012).

Evidence for New Technologies and Behavior Change

Randomized trials of text messaging programs have shown behavioral effects among adolescents and adults, among minority and nonminority populations, and across nationalities (Cole-Lewis & Kershaw, 2010). With mobile phones, the majority of published research has been on short message service (SMS), or text messaging. There is evidence that supports text messaging as an effective behavior change strategy in smoking cessation, weight loss, physical activity, and diabetes management (Cole-Lewis & Kershaw, 2010; Fjeldsoe, Marshall, & Miller, 2009; Whittaker et al., 2009) and to a lesser extent for sexually transmitted disease (STD) prevention and treatment (Lim et al., 2008) and for treating hypertension (Logan et al., 2007).

Relatively little is known (although many new studies are being implemented at the time of this writing) about the utility of smartphones and their associated applications (or "apps") for health promotion. Recent reviews of the literature found no studies that examined the efficacy of smartphone apps for health promotion or disease management, although a few studies have evaluated the quality of apps for smoking cessation (Abroms et al., 2011), weight loss (Breton, Abroms, & Fuemmeler, 2010), and diabetes self-management (Ciemens, Coon, & Sorli, 2010), as well as their usability for diabetes self-management (Rao et al., 2010).

In summary, media campaigns have been shown effective across a wide range of subject matter, with the majority of evidence coming from health and healthcare fields. Because media campaigns have been effective in affecting a range of behavior changes—including complex hard-to-change health behaviors and simpler knowledge and awareness raising and consumer choices—the collective evidence suggests that they may also be effective in promoting survey participation and civic behaviors, such as returning census forms. The 2010 Integrated Communication Campaign (ICC) is perhaps the largest example of a paid media campaign designed to promote participation in a census.

Challenges in Synthesizing Social Marketing Evidence

Assessing the social marketing evidence is complicated by some of the challenges in compiling and synthesizing it. A major limitation of systematic reviews of social marketing, and specific subtopics such as tailored campaigns (Noar, Benac, & Harris, 2007), branding (Evans, Blitstein, et al., 2014), and use of specific 4P (place, price, product, and promotion) strategies, is the absence of well-recognized keywords that can be used to identify relevant literature (McDermott, Stead, & Hastings, 2005).

As noted by multiple studies (Evans, 2008; McDermott, Stead, & Hastings, 2005), reviews of social marketing evidence have a number of limitations. Methods have not always been systematic, and there is often insufficient information on the search strategy and inclusion criteria. In particular, reviews often fail to state explicitly how social marketing interventions have been defined and conceptualize social marketing in widely differing ways. For example, in family planning reviews, social marketing is often taken to mean, primarily, free distribution of condoms. In others, social marketing is misconstrued as simply social advertising or communications (e.g., Alcalay & Bell, 2000), which represent only the "promotion" P and miss the other thee (place, price, and product).

One difficulty has been the lack of an agreed and easily operationalized definition of a social marketing intervention. Generic definitions, such as Andreasen's previously discussed definition, are not precise enough to help decide whether a specific intervention does or does not qualify as social marketing. One solution to the difficulty is simply to select interventions that are labeled social marketing programs by their managers or evaluators. However, relying solely on the label is a problematic approach. First, it excludes many interventions that are not labeled social marketing but appear to incorporate social marketing principles. Second, it includes interventions that, despite their label, are poor examples of social marketing or are not social marketing at all. For example, the misperception that social marketing equals advertising means that many interventions that are essentially media campaigns are erroneously described as social marketing (Stead & Hastings, 1997). The resulting evidence base, if a search is restricted only to interventions called "social marketing," is likely to be limited and flawed.

The basic solution to this problem as recognized in recent literature, and applied in a recent systematic review (Evans, Pattanayak, et al., 2014), is to utilize the full set of social marketing benchmark criteria (French et al., 2010), presented in Table 2-1. Programs meeting these criteria represent robust examples of social marketing. Next, let us consider the methods used to gather evidence for each step of the social marketing process.

Table 2-1 Social Marketing Benchmark Criteria

Benchmark Criteria	Description
Methods mix	The marketing activities used a 4P strategy.
Customer orientation	The marketing was designed to serve a specific group of consumers.
Insight	Formative research to understand the consumer was used in designing the marketing.
Behavioral goals	The marketing had specific behavior change goals or objectives.
Segmentation	Specific promotional strategies were designed for a targeted subgroup of the population (e.g., individuals with a high need for sensation—"sensation seekers"; Palmgreen et al., 2002).
Exchange	A cost-benefit exchange was explicitly part of the marketing strategy.
Competition	Market-level competition for the behavioral choice was included in the social marketing.
Theory	Validated and reliable behavioral theory was used in the social marketing.

Source: French, J., Blair-Stevens, C., McVey, D., & Merritt, R. (2010). *Social Marketing and Public Health*. Oxford, UK: Oxford University Press.

Overview of Social Marketing Research Methods

The decision-making and evidence-gathering process illustrated in the research continuum (Figure 1-1 in Chapter 1) represents six basic questions:

- What should the campaign be?—**formative research**
- How do audiences respond to campaign messages?—**message testing**
- Is it implemented as planned?—**process evaluation**
- Does audience receive and adopt intended knowledge, attitudes, and beliefs?—**communication objectives (outcome evaluation, short term to intermediate)**
- Does audience adopt and maintain intended behaviors?—**behavioral objectives (outcome evaluation, long term)**
- What long-term effects do achievement of behavioral objectives have on indicators of social well-being (e.g., morbidity and mortality in public health)?—**impact evaluation**

This chapter explores the evidence, and purposes of the evidence, gathered to answer each of these questions during the social marketing research process. These questions map onto the stages of social marketing research identified in Figure 1-1, the social marketing research continuum. We explore these stages of research in overview format here and in more depth further in the book. The main categories of research activity are as follows:

- Formative research—What affects target behavior? What are the message and product?
- Process evaluation—How is the message delivered?
- Message testing—How do recipients respond to the message?
- Outcome evaluation—What are the behavioral effects of the message on audiences?
- Impact evaluation—What is the long-term effect of the message on health promotion and disease prevention?

Because impact evaluation typically requires a long time period that typically extends beyond the scope of an individual research or evaluation study on a campaign, we do not focus on that category in this book. But, in

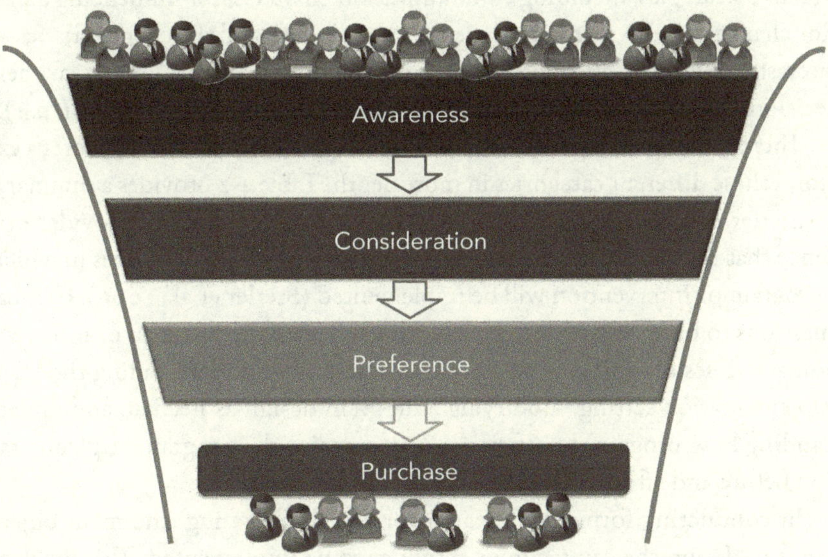

FIGURE 2-1 Simple illustration of consumer choice process: research at each stage.

Chapter 7, on outcome evaluation, resources are provided for further consideration and research on campaign impact.

Figure 2-1 provides a simple illustration of the process of consumers' intake and response to promotional information. While the messages, consideration, preference formation, and choices involved in social decision-making, such as an adolescent choosing whether to smoke or an adult choosing to recycle, are different, this underlying process applies. Each stage of the process involves research activities ranging from design to implementation and outcomes. We examine methods along this pathway to behavior and population-level effects on the consumers.

Formative Research

For purposes of this chapter, *formative research* is research that occurs before a program is designed and implemented. Some authors and sources will include *implementation* in their definition of formative research, while others treat implementation as part of the evaluation. We follow the latter definition and treat research on implementation of programs as part of "process evaluation" as reflected in the distinction between research before and after a campaign launch as shown in Figure 1-1. The California Department of Public Health defines it this way: "[Formative research] is the basis for developing effective strategies, including communication channels, for influencing behavior change. It helps researchers identify and understand the characteristics—interests, behaviors and needs—of target populations that influence their decisions and actions" (California Department of Public Health, 2001, p. 1).

There are several stages of formative research to consider, and Chapter 3 explores these different categories in more depth. Table 2-2 provides a summary.

Stetler and colleagues (2006) note that formative research provides evidence that is critical to understanding the design and circumstances in which a program or intervention will be implemented (Stetler et al., 2006). Critical questions to be answered include assessing whether the program or intervention addresses a significant need of the population, understanding the local implementation setting, modifying a program design as needed, and understanding how program beneficiaries may perceive the program implementation before and after it is launched.

In conducting formative research for social marketing, the main objective is to design the campaign or activities to be implemented. This involves understanding the intended recipients (or audience) for the campaign; the

Table 2-2 Categories of Formative Research

Audience analysis/environmental scanning	• What do we know about the audience's relevant behaviors? • How does social and physical environment matter? • How can we best reach them?
Exploratory research	• What affects the target behavior (attitudes/beliefs)? • What are barriers or supports to adoption of behavior?
Concept testing	• What messages appeal to the audience? • What channels are likely to be effective/ineffective?
Pretesting	• How does the audience receive the message? • What channels are effective? • What did we forget in the message strategy?

determinants of their behavior (e.g., attitudes and beliefs, cultural norms, social and physical environmental factors such as their community that may affect their behavioral choices); how they are likely to respond to what the social marketing campaign "offers" them (i.e., the product); how and where the offer is made (i.e., the place); and how the offer is promoted (i.e., the promotion). These factors form part of the "creative brief," the document that summarizes planning behind a marketing effort and serves as an overarching guide to design and development of campaign components and as a roadmap for implementation (Kotler & Lee, 2008). Formative research efforts in the end are intended to help develop, refine, and validate the final creative brief prior to campaign launch.

The key questions to be answered in formative research can be summarized then as follows, with these steps suggesting the sequence of steps in formative research:

1. Who is the target audience, and what are they like?
2. What are the actions we would like them to take?
3. What are the benefits of engaging in the actions?

4. What makes the audience believe they can perform the action and achieve the benefit (support)?
5. What are the "places" (times, openings, states of mind) when audiences will be most attentive to and able to act on messages?
6. What is the image (or "look and feel") communications should convey?

The combination of these strategies could be conceptualized as the "brand" for a campaign (Evans et al., 2002). We explore the concept of, and research on, branding behaviors and behavior change in social marketing in Chapter 4 of this book.

Consider a case example of formative research and the elements of a research plan to design a campaign addressing childhood obesity prevention and control in the US state of Georgia.

Case Example: Formative Research Plan for a Campaign Addressing Child Obesity in Georgia

Research Questions and Audience Segments

To develop an effective social marketing campaign addressing child obesity in Georgia, exploratory market research will be conducted in three rural Georgia counties: Terrell, Jefferson, and Burke. These counties were selected based on a high presence of child obesity risk factors, such as high rates of adult obesity, primarily rural area, large percentage of minority, low-income households, as well as low levels of physical activity (County Health Rankings and Roadmaps, 2013). Research questions that emerge from the environmental scan will be addressed to adequately segment target audience(s) and assess factors that may influence the prevalence of child obesity within the environment.

First, it is important to assess the level of awareness of the prevalence of childhood obesity within the community and knowledge or awareness of risk factors contributing to obesity and of resulting health consequences and comorbidities of obesity. Given that parents were identified as some of the primary influencers on children's nutritional and physical activity behaviors, the study explores their knowledge, attitudes, and beliefs regarding their child's weight, nutrition, and physical activity. The health belief model (HBM), which posits that health-related action depends on an agent's perceived susceptibility, perceived severity, perceived benefits, and perceived barriers to the desired action, will be utilized to guide some of these research questions (Rosenstock, Strecher, & Becker, 1988). Using HBM constructs, researchers will assess the following parental perceptions regarding their child to assist in the development of the most relevant campaign concepts and messages:

1. **Perceived susceptibility**: Do parents believe that their child is susceptible to either becoming obese or suffering the health consequences and comorbidities of obesity?
2. **Perceived severity**: How do parents perceive the severity of child obesity and its comorbidities?
3. **Perceived benefits**: Do parents believe that promoting nutrition and physical activity within the family unit will have a positive impact on their child's health?
4. **Perceived barriers**: What do parents see as costs to healthy eating and physical activity among their children?

The initial research also caused emergent questions based on the family, community, and school environments of children living in rural communities in Georgia that may have an impact on obesity risk behaviors. The study will evaluate

1. Family norms among children in these communities;
2. Protective environmental factors within these communities; and
3. School-based social norms or common activities that may propagate unhealthy behaviors.

Proposed Methods: Quantitative and Qualitative

To develop the most effective, relevant, and audience-centric social marketing campaign, the formative research will use both quantitative and qualitative methods. Quantitative methods are an objective approach that will allow for reliable analyses of the relationships between variables that are generalizable to each of the high-risk communities. They will also allow us to measure baseline data as well as benchmark progress and outcomes once the program is launched. Qualitative and observational analyses will provide perspective and context that will allow for a better understanding of quantitative observations. Previous literature has underscored the value in using quantitative and qualitative methods, as well as the importance of integrating demographic, health status, and psychosocial data in audience segmentation (Boslaugh,

2005). In the context of childhood obesity, for which multiple behavioral, attitudinal, and environmental factors affect outcomes, it is valuable to use this mixed-methods approach.

Methodologies and Sample Sizes

A mixed-methods approach will include online surveys, focus groups, and school observations. Data collected through these methodologies will provide necessary information for audience segmentation and target audience(s) selection. Online surveys will yield both quantitative and qualitative information that will be analyzed for consistencies across participants and help develop a tailored campaign with a broader reach. Using principles of sound research, researchers aim to recruit at least 200 participants per county for the surveys. Focus groups will consist of 8 to 10 parents with children in preschool, kindergarten, or elementary school and allow parents to express their wants, needs, opinions, challenges, competing behaviors, and other qualitative information related to child obesity. School observations will take place in lunchrooms, during physical education, or during after-school programs. Observations will glean whether class parties or similar events propagate unhealthy eating behaviors (i.e., they provide cupcakes and soda while lacking healthy options) and whether bullying is present that may cause low self-esteem or a lack of motivation to be active (i.e., to play with other children during recess or after school). Overall, the observational approach will yield a better understanding of school-based norms, student attitudes and behaviors in their natural environment, as well as insights into potential barriers to healthy eating or physical activity. The goal is to observe at least 30 students per county when using this method.

Recruitment and Screening

Researchers will use multiple recruitment methods to invite parents to participate in the questionnaire and focus groups. Given that the target is childhood obesity, reaching parents through their children's schools will be vital. Where possible, researchers will request the schools to send out an email "blast" to parents about the study, asking parents to participate in research on childhood obesity in Georgia. In addition, and in case schools do not have access to email addresses or parents do not use email frequently, researchers will ask schools to send the children home with paper notices from the school for the parents. Researchers will also ask teachers and administrators to use parent-teacher conferences to inform parents of the opportunity to participate in surveys and focus groups on the topic.

To reach parents in places they might frequent, online survey recruitment flyers (with tear-off tabs) will be posted in grocery stores, community centers, and churches. Researchers will also set up recruitment stations in these locations to directly approach parents about participating in the study, screen participants, and explain our purposes in the process.

Last, participants who complete the online survey will be asked to provide their email address on the survey instrument if they are interested in participating in a focus group. Monetary incentives for completing the online survey as well as participation in a focus group will be provided in the form of a raffle for one of nine $50 Visa gift cards (three per community).

Research Instruments

The study will employ multiple tools to conduct observational research, online surveys, and focus groups. A screening tool will be included at the start of each online survey to ensure that information is gathered from an audience that previously identified as a having high-risk factors for childhood obesity in the community. Observational research tools will aim to record children's choices in the lunchroom as well as their physical activity during the school day.

An online survey will assess demographics, such as age, ethnicity, county, children's ages and schools, as well as the height and weight of both children and parents. The target audience for this survey will be parents of children in Terrell, Jefferson, and Burke counties. Parents are the family members purchasing most of the food consumed by their households, and obtaining parental consent to survey children could have an added barrier if the response rate in reaching parents was low. Therefore, the primary focus of the online survey will be to assess parental influences related to children's eating and activity behaviors, as well as parents' behaviors and attitudes on health outcomes related to these behaviors. Questions related to family and community norms will inquire whether parents with overweight or obese children are inclined to eat at fast-food restaurants or fail to discourage excessive screen time or other sedentary behavior. The survey questionnaire was developed by adapting several validated and previously used tools: the Centers for Disease Control and Prevention (CDC) Youth Risk Behavior Surveillance System (YRBSS), the Maternal, Child, and Adolescent Health (MCAH)Community Health Assessment Survey, the Comprehensive Feeding Practices Questionnaire, as well as questions assessing knowledge, attitudes, and beliefs about nutrition and child obesity from a previous study (CDC, 2013; MCAH Community Health Assessment Survey, 2003; Musher-Eizenman & Holub, 2007; Adedze et al., 2011).

Through focus groups, the study will delve into the reasoning behind lifestyle choices and the family environment that will inform creative concept and message development, as well as where the audience acquires information to help determine the most relevant media or other channels to convey information. The focus group moderator's guide will mirror certain questions from the online survey but enable a more in-depth conversation about childhood obesity in Georgia. A trained moderator will ask questions and lead discussion for 1.5 hours, during which focus group participants will provide qualitative information on parental attitudes and beliefs surrounding their children's health and weight. Surveys and focus groups will also enable researchers to assess whether protective factors exist in the community, such as grocery stores with nutritious food, availability of parks and sidewalks, safe neighborhoods, transportation to healthcare services or recreation centers, as well as physician awareness and support.

Data and Insights

Through focus groups, online surveys, and observational sessions, researchers will obtain a wide variety of data that will include demographics, perceptions, attitudes, beliefs, knowledge of obesity, barriers, and local norms. Focus groups will be either video or audio recorded, and a research assistant will develop a transcript that will then be analyzed using qualitative data analysis software, such as ATLAS.ti. Focus groups and survey data will provide insights into the attitudes and behaviors across the individual as well as group levels. Observational checklist data will be quantitatively analyzed by calculating the percentage of positive, healthy behaviors versus negative, unhealthy behaviors. This will help attribute how much influence the school setting has on a child's obesity risk factors. We plan to code the data collected through the focus groups, surveys, and observations and interpret commonalities or outliers. Through these findings, researchers will gain insights into parental attitudes, beliefs, and behaviors and how they affect children's overall health at home as well as at school.

Insights to Plan Campaign

Insights obtained from this research will inform several important processes for campaign development. First, results will enable appropriate segmentation of the target audience(s) by demographic and psychographic characteristics based on focus group discussion and survey responses. Second, this information will help to establish the four P's of our marketing program: product, price, promotion, and place, which will be tailored for Terrell, Jefferson, and Burke counties in GA. Third, through assessing current knowledge, attitudes, and beliefs, the formative research will inform the design of a product and message that is most relevant to the target population. Lastly, insights from the data will also inform how to adequately address community needs and lower the price of desired behavior, as well as the most relevant placement and promotion of materials, messages, and community engagement efforts.

Limitations

Some limitations of the proposed sampling and data collection methods include the risk of an insufficient sample size and the potential for not obtaining information on the population hypothesized to be high risk. A lengthy online survey could have a low response or completion rate that may have an impact on the validity and generalizability of results. Although the study will use a mixed-methods recruitment approach, there is still a risk for response bias. There may also be desirability bias in survey responses and focus group responses because the population may be generally aware that childhood obesity is a problem in their community. By also conducting face-to-face focus group interviews, the goal is to decrease the desirability bias that may be present in survey responses. However, conducting focus groups may have limitations as well. For example, certain focus group participants may feel too self-conscious to speak candidly or may be less motivated for discussion, and responses may be biased by more dominant speakers. The use of credible moderators who will use a guide and be thoroughly trained prior to conducting the focus group interviews may mitigate this limitation.

Message Testing

A message testing study in health communication and social marketing (sometimes described in the literature as an "efficacy" study) is designed to evaluate the effects of a message or campaign under optimum conditions, whereas an effectiveness study evaluates the effects of a message or campaign under real-world conditions (Evans, Uhrig, et al., 2009). In medical research, efficacy studies are regarded as necessary in the development of a new drug, treatment, or technology (Flay, 1986). As a result, when medical researchers conduct an effectiveness study, it is only after the intervention has been shown to be efficacious. In contrast, in health communication and marketing evaluations, effectiveness studies are often conducted without previously determining whether the campaign messages are truly efficacious. Rather, the messages are tested using qualitative, formative research methods, implemented in the campaign, and then evaluated as part of an effectiveness study.

Without first determining the efficacy of the campaign messages, results of effectiveness studies can be more difficult to interpret (Flay, 1986). For example, if a campaign produces negative or null results, is it because the campaign was implemented in an ineffective way or because the campaign messages were not efficacious? If efficacy was not established prior to the effectiveness study, this question is difficult to answer. A well-done process evaluation would provide information on implementation fidelity, but it would not provide a good answer to the question of whether and, if so, how the message failed in terms of audience reaction and receptivity. Efficacy studies help to address this gap in the evidence base.

Efficacy studies permit researchers to assess message effects under controlled experimental conditions. This leads to high internal validity, facilitating much stronger causal inferences than typically possible in effectiveness studies. On the other hand, efficacy studies typically have lower external validity than do effectiveness studies. This is because efficacy studies have traditionally been implemented in person, in laboratory settings with small samples. Also, they do not allow researchers to make conclusions about the effectiveness of the campaign messages under real-world conditions or to make population-based estimates of actual awareness of or exposure to campaign messages that are possible with effectiveness studies.

Chapter 5 in this volume explores message-testing research in much more depth. Some good recent examples of message testing studies include the following:

- Efficacy testing of the Parents Speak Up National Campaign (PSUNC; Evans, Davis, et al., 2009): In this online randomized trial, parents of children age 10–14 were randomly assigned to receive messages (video and radio ads) from the PSUNC or not (control). Mothers were randomly assigned to a higher dosage of messages at a 6-month follow-up to test for dose-response effects. Messages tested were found efficacious in increasing parent-child communication about sex and related parental actions, such as searching for information online, to improve sexual communication with their children.

- Framing of human papilloma virus (HPV) vaccine acceptability (Gerend, Shepherd, & Monday, 2008): In this framing experiment, investigators examined whether behavioral frequency (i.e., the number of HPV shots required) moderated the effect of framed health messages on women's intentions to receive the HPV vaccine and mediators of message effects on this outcome. This study compared frames and frequency and found an interaction: Loss-framed messages led to greater vaccination intentions than did the gain-framed message in the one-shot condition. Perceived susceptibility to HPV infection mediated framing effects.
- Message framing and cigarette warning labels (Mays et al., 2014): In this framing experiment conducted online, investigators showed young adult smokers gain- and loss-framed cigarette warning messages with and without graphics and examined their smoking cessation motivations. The study found a framing-by-packaging interaction in which gain-framed warnings on plain packs generated greater motivation to quit for lung disease, cancer, and mortality warnings. The study concluded that combining pictorial warnings with text-based risk messages may increase motivation to quit.

Process Evaluation

Process evaluation (also called monitoring or implementation evaluation) concerns the activities that occur after the launch of a campaign and attempts to determine the extent to which its strategy, as defined in its conceptual framework or logic model, was implemented (Weiss, 1997). Process evaluation focuses on the initial components of a conceptual framework or logic model—the resources, 4P marketing strategies, and immediate outputs—of the campaign. Process evaluations allow evaluators to make the important distinction between implementation failure and theory failure (Hornik & Kelly, 2007). Implementation failure is when expected campaign results are not achieved (e.g., formation of intended beliefs and increase in a targeted behavior) due to the campaign not being implemented as planned, such as by a lack of exposure to messages delivered through social media. By contrast, theory failure is when the campaign is implemented according to strategy but expected outcomes are not found, meaning the theory that linked the activities to expected outcomes is incorrect or some other factors not accounted for in the theory (e.g., moderating variables) are present (Saunders, Evans, & Joshi, 2005). For instance, the widespread dissemination of a smoking cessation message via a text messaging campaign coupled with unchanged quit motivations or attempts to quit smoking would be a theory failure.

Beyond the importance of identifying why the campaign succeeded or failed due to implementation or theoretical reasons, process evaluation is important both to document campaigns for future use or adaptation and to obtain data that is also of use in outcome evaluation. First, it is important to document what is actually decided and implemented and the immediate outputs of campaign implementation for future use. Decisions such as segmentation; resources allocated to specific place, price, product, and promotion strategies; staffing; and environmental factors (e.g., other supporting programs or counterinfluences present) need to be understood for future social marketers to adapt campaigns and for researchers to interpret results of evaluations.

Second, process data are useful not only in monitoring campaign implementation but also for measuring dosage of the campaign and other variables that may serve as moderators in outcome analysis. Measuring exposure to campaign activities such as messages delivered through TV advertising or social media or community-based events intended to raise awareness of a social marketing brand are important process measures. These can be used both to assess implementation success (e.g., Did the campaign reach the intended numbers of the target audience?) and to assess outcomes (e.g., Are higher levels of campaign exposure associated with better intended outcomes?). Other variables, such as noncampaign messages prevalent in the community (e.g., smoking advertising present in a community receiving a smoking cessation campaign), are important to account for in outcome analyses but would be collected initially as part of the process evaluation.

Process evaluation questions include both components of initial campaign planning and the implementation of plans. For example,

- Planning
  - Were resources well spent?
  - Was the timeline met?
- Implementation
  - How many people did we reach?
  - Did the people we reached share our messages with others (networking)?
  - Who did we reach?

- How did they respond?
- Did we generate media coverage?

In addition, process evaluation questions and measures cover each of the 4Ps. For example:

- **Place**
  - What materials are disseminated?
  - What is the distribution?
- **Product**
  - What beliefs and behaviors are changing?
  - Are messages understood?
  - What is needed next?
- **Price**
  - What are barriers to change?
  - Is the behavior inconvenient, hard to do?
- **Promotion**
  - How aware is the audience?
  - Are there unexpected outcomes?
  - What is the demand for materials, programs, or messages?
  - Is there diffusion of the message to other audiences (networking)?

Case Example: Ask Medicare Process Evaluation

The AskMedicare program, initiated in 2008, provides a simple example of process evaluation and measurement. The Centers for Medicare and Medicaid Services (CMS) of the US Department of Health and Human Services (USDHHS) designed a website as a resource for individuals caring for others, such as family or friends, in need of healthcare support. The site provides resources and information for specific conditions and helps caregivers provide the most effective possible care and assist in both self-care and navigating the healthcare system. Figure 2-2 is a screenshot from the website.

The rollout of the website, its utilization by the public, news coverage, and dissemination and networking related to the site were tracked by CMS. During the first month after the site's launch, CMS captured the following implementation statistics:

- Webcast launch: 870 viewers
- Web page: 30,036 page views

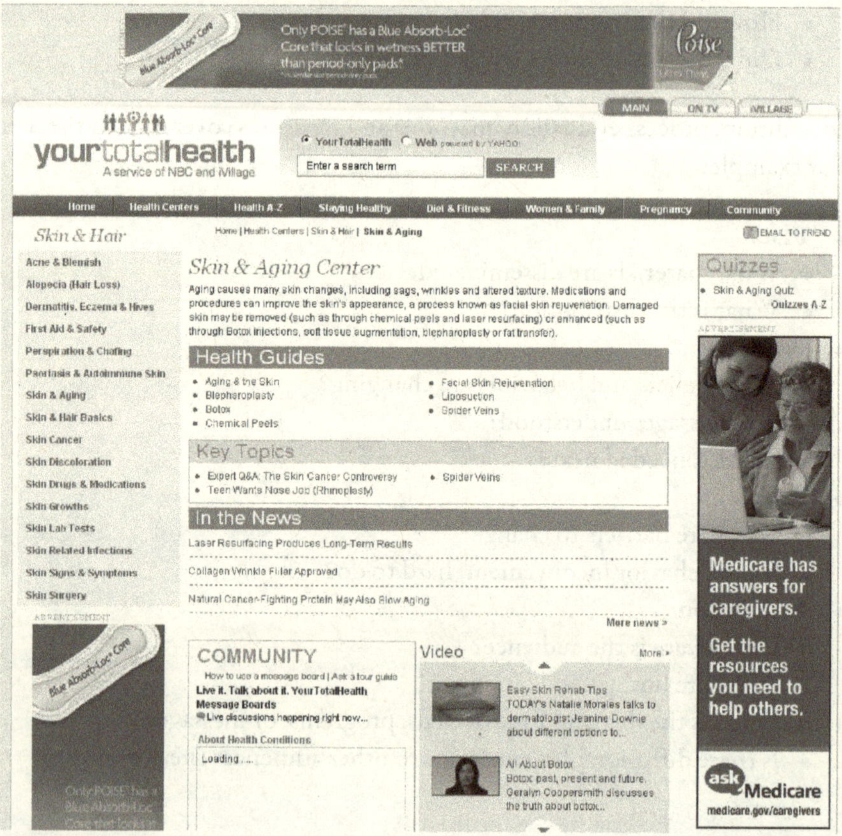

FIGURE 2-2 AskMedicare website screenshot.
Source: CMS website (https://www.cms.gov).

- E-newsletter: 8,300 subscribers
- Total media impressions (earned and social media):
  - More than 12.5 million impressions (including Jane Gross's *New York Times* blog)
  - TV: 2.3 million impressions, 13 stations
  - Radio: 415 broadcasts, 2.7 million impressions
- Widget
  - Total views: 6,458
- Partner engagement
  - Secured core partners
- Paid media update
  - Display banner ads: 2,963,477 impressions; 1,918 web page visits (display ads represent 82.6% of the total spent)

- Search engine marketing (SEM): 192,871 impressions; 2,306 web page visits represents 17.4% of the total spent)

Source: Introduction to Public Health Communication and Marketing course at George Washington University, Washington, D.C., October 4, 2008.

Outcome Evaluation

Outcome evaluation seeks to determine the link between a campaign and subsequent improvements in the welfare of the target population. Specifically, outcome evaluations aim to determine whether a campaign's 4P activities can be directly associated with improvements seen in the target population, such as achievement of specific communication (e.g., belief that physical activity is fun and health) or behavioral (e.g., increase daily physical activity) objectives (Evans, Davis, & Farrelly, 2008). They also aim to rule out alternative explanations, such as that such improvements in targeted attitudes, beliefs, intentions, and behaviors are not due to any external sources, such as local or national policies, other environmental influences, or secular trends in the population not associated with the campaign (e.g., ongoing reductions in smoking among youth in the context of an antismoking campaign).

There are several basic questions that campaign outcome evaluations seek to answer:

- Was the audience exposed to the message?
- How did the audience react to the message (was it believable, trusted, likable)?
- What attitudes and beliefs were formed by the target audience when exposed to the message?
- Do changes in attitudes/beliefs lead to the intended behavior change?

These questions take us back to process evaluation: To what extent was the campaign successful in exposing the audience to the message(s)? For outcome evaluation purposes, exposure (or dosage) data are important because they can be used to provide evidence that any reactions observed in the population, such as improved beliefs or behaviors, are *attributable* to the campaign and not other explanations. As we discuss in depth in further chapters, there are two main types of exposure measures (Hornik, 2002), shown here with a nonexhaustive list of examples:

1. Self-reported (aided and unaided, or confirmed recall)
   - If prompted, does respondent report message exposure (aided)?
   - If asked to provide a description of the message, does the respondent demonstrate exposure (confirmed recall)?
2. Environmental (population or market-level measures of exposure)
   - Nielsen media data on time/market audience size (gross rating points [GRPs] or total rating points (TRPs)
   - Social media metrics (e.g., Facebook likes, Instagram favorites, Twitter retweets)
   - Use of mobile phone apps, receipt of text messages, other forms of mobile device contact that are externally measurable

Final outcomes of interest in a campaign evaluation are self-reported or observed behaviors, such as smoking initiation, uptake (progression to established smoking; Choi et al., 2001), or cessation; time spent in moderate or vigorous physical activity; food choice and consumption; or condom use. Campaign outcome evaluations are interested in both *direct* effects of message exposure on behavior (i.e., Does exposure or dosage of exposure predict behavior change?) and *indirect (mediated)* effects (i.e., Does behavior change occur as a function of changes in my cognitive states, such as knowledge or beliefs?) (Figure 2-3).

As noted, impact evaluation is the final step in the research continuum. In social marketing, impact evaluation studies are rarely formally conducted. However, the purpose of assessing impact is to examine the long-term effects

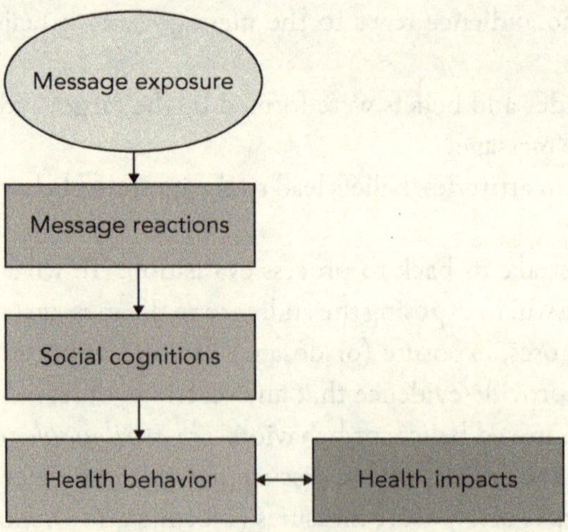

FIGURE 2-3 Basic model of social marketing effects on process of behavior change.

of campaigns beyond the time frame of their implementation on downstream public health outcomes (i.e., morbidity and mortality) from the disease conditions and other risk factors targeted by the social marketing effort.

For example, consider evidence from the *truth* campaign and its initial phase, starting in 2000 (call it *truth* version 1.0) (Farrelly et al., 2002). The campaign evaluation (described further in the next section) attributed over 300,000 fewer youth smokers to *truth* exposure among adolescents during the period from 2000 to 2002 (Farrelly et al., 2005). Assuming that smoking leads to approximately 7 lost life years (US Department of Health and Human Services, 2014), that equates to over 2.1 million life years lost in the United States. In addition, smokers would on average have much higher healthcare costs due to smoking-related illness (US Department of Health and Human Services, 2014). As a result, potentially billions of US dollars may have been saved by the *truth* campaign due to the downstream effects of reductions in youth smoking and new smokers attributable to the campaign. This type of example represents the data that may be available to attribute impact to social marketing campaigns when behavioral effects are well measured and there are known benefits and consequences of behavior change or the lack thereof.

Case Example: Initial Outcome Evaluation of the truth (Version 1.0) Campaign

The initial American Legacy Foundation (Legacy for Health; *truth* campaign [*truth* version 1.0]; details available at http://www.legacyforhealth.org/what-we-do/truth-r-youth-and-young-adult-tobacco-prevention) was a branded, national smoking prevention campaign designed to reach at-risk youth, ages 12 to 17, primarily through edgy television advertisements shown on youth-oriented channels/programs with an anti–tobacco industry theme (Farrelly et al., 2002, 2005). Young adults of college-going age, 18 to 24, composed an important secondary audience. The campaign initially launched in early 2000. Subsequent iterations of the campaign (versions 2.0, 3.0) continue to date. The following briefly describes the initial objectives, questions, and research activities undertaken by the *truth* 1.0 evaluation. The outcome evaluation was a long-term effort and included many facets, which we examine in depth further in the book.

Measure Exposure and Message Reactions. The first objective of the *truth* campaign was to increase youth exposure to *truth* messages and generate positive audience receptivity to those messages. Because *truth* was implemented with a fluid media schedule with new ads and "subcampaigns" (i.e., distinct messages that related to and supported the larger *truth* campaign messages) appearing regularly, a continuous media tracking survey of youth in the United States was needed to capture awareness of and reactions to the campaign and receptivity to its messages. At the time of the campaign's launch in 2000, telephone surveys could be administered quickly and relatively inexpensively while providing a nationally representative picture of youth awareness of the campaign. Because the *truth* campaign also targeted specific racial and ethnic groups, a telephone Legacy Media Tracking Survey (LMTS) was designed to provide estimates of campaign awareness and receptivity among 12- to 17-year-olds overall and separately among African American and Hispanic youth.

Awareness of the campaign was measured using a variety of metrics. Simple recall of *truth* would not be sufficient for identifying how many youth were exposed to specific messages. Thus, the LMTS included specific measures of confirmed awareness of each *truth* ad that was airing at any given time. These measures required respondents to identify specific features of the ads to confirm that they had actually seen them. The LMTS also included other, more general, measures, such as a construct that captured overall awareness of the *truth* campaign brand.

It was also important to assess how youth reacted to *truth* campaign messages. Did youth who saw campaign messages react to those messages favorably? To examine this, the *truth* campaign's evaluation plan called for measurement of a number of ad receptivity constructs, which captured the degree to which youth responded favorably or unfavorably to specific messages. These measures included whether an ad was "believable" or "gave good reasons not to smoke." The inclusion of these types of measures in the evaluation was based on the elaboration likelihood model (ELM), which asserts that attitudinal changes are a function of the level of cognitive elaboration and information-processing activity that occurs regarding a particular message (Petty & Cacioppo, 1986).

From a practical standpoint, continuous tracking of campaign awareness and receptivity to campaign messages provided real-time feedback to the campaign's media contractors, creative directors, and other stakeholders involved in designing and implementing *truth* ads. Specifically, continuous tracking provided the campaign's implementation team with useful information on whether the campaign was sufficiently reaching its youth audience and whether course corrections in message content were needed. The evaluation plan included strategies for sharing these data with the campaign's media contractors on a regular basis. Another, perhaps more important, function of these measures was to facilitate an examination of the relationship between exposure to the campaign and cognitive precursors to smoking. Therefore, the LMTS also included a wide range of items that measured specific knowledge, attitudes, and beliefs that were central to *truth*'s messages and believed to be predictors of the likelihood of smoking initiation. The novelty of the campaign's messages presented challenges for identifying these measures and necessitated an evaluation-planning process that was closely integrated with the campaign's creative development.

Assess Attitudinal Changes. Unlike many youth campaigns before it, the *truth* campaign was marketed as a brand, similar to other youth brands, to appeal to adolescents most at risk of smoking. At the time of the *truth* campaign's launch, the use of "branded" health messages that marketed the benefits of "buying into" a brand like *truth* was relatively new. Aside from several measures used in evaluations of the Florida *truth* campaign, there were few specific measures of knowledge, attitudes, and beliefs related to these sorts of messages. Thus, new measures had to be conceptualized that not only captured the essence of *truth* messages but also were associated with the likelihood of smoking initiation.

The initial wave of the LMTS was fielded in December 1999, just prior to the launch of the *truth* 1.0 campaign, to determine baseline levels of tobacco-related knowledge, attitudes, and beliefs. Before the baseline LMTS was fielded, campaign evaluators participated in intensive meetings with media contractor staff to learn about the specific content of *truth* messages and then develop measures of knowledge, attitudes, and beliefs that would be influenced by the specific message content. A second wave of the LMTS was conducted 10 months after the launch of the campaign. The first evaluation study published on these data showed that the campaign had made significant progress in achieving its first two goals. Awareness of the campaign was high, as approximately 75% of 12- to 17-year-olds in the United States reported being exposed to specific ads (Farrelly et al., 2002). There were also significant changes in knowledge, attitudes, and beliefs related to *truth* messages 10 months after the launch of the campaign, and these changes were statistically associated with exposure to the campaign (Farrelly et al., 2002).

Conclusions

Social marketing research is a distinct process with phases spanning the process of campaign design to have an impact on evaluation and steps in between. There are distinctive purposes, methods, and evidence at each stage of the research continuum. These include secondary research at the audience analysis stage, qualitative research at the formative research stage, mixed methods (qualitative and quantitative) at the formative and later stages, and a variety of research design and data collection methods to evaluate process (implementation), outcomes, and impacts of campaigns once they are launched and under way.

The remainder of this book explores the distinctive stages of research along the research continuum in depth. Each chapter that follows explores a specific stage of the continuum, distinctive research methods, and detailed case examples to illustrate the research at that point in the social marketing process.

Additional Resources: Web Based

- Making Health Communication Programs Work: http://www.cancer.gov/publications/health-communication/pink-book.pdf
- Theory at a Glance: A Guide for Health Promotion Practice: http://www.sneb.org/2014/Theory%20at%20a%20Glance.pdf
- Developing Health Communication Campaigns: http://www.nccmt.ca/registry/view/eng/75.html
- Oxford Bibliographies Online: Health Communication: http://www.oxfordbibliographies.com/

References

Abroms, L., & Maibach, E. (2008). The Effectiveness of Mass Communication to Change Public Behavior. *Annual Review of Public Health*, 29: 16.1–16.16.

Abroms, L.C., Padmanabhan, N., & Evans, W.D. (2012). Mobile Phones for Health Promotion. In *Interactive Health Communication Applications: Promising Strategies for Health Behavior Change*, S. Noar & N.G. Harrington (Eds.). New York: Routledge; 147–166.

Abroms, L.C., Padmanabhan, N., Philips, T., & Thaweethai, L. (2011). iPhone Apps for Smoking Cessation: A Content Analysis. *American Journal of Preventative Medicine*, 40: 279–285.

Adedze, P., Chapman-Novakofski, K., Witz, K., Orr, R., & Donovan, S. (2011). Knowledge, Attitudes, and Beliefs About Nutrition and Childhood Overweight Among WIC Participants. *Family and Community Health*, 34(4): 301–310. doi:10.1097/FCH.0b013e31822b53dd

Alcalay, R., & Bell, R.A. (2000). *Promoting Nutrition and Physical Activity Through Social Marketing: Current Practices and Recommendations*. Davis: Center for Advanced Studies in Nutrition and Social Marketing, University of California.

Boslaugh, S.E. (2005). Comparing Demographic, Health Status and Psychosocial Strategies of Audience Segmentation to Promote Physical Activity. *Health Education Research*, 20(4): 430–438. doi:10.1093/her/cyg138

Breton, E., Abroms, L.C., & Fuemmeler, B.F. (2010). Weight Loss iPhone Applications and Their Adherence to Best Practices For Weight Loss: A Content Analysis. Unpublished manuscript.

California Department of Public Health. (2001). *Examples of Formative Research*. Retrieved September 7, 2015, from https://www.cdph.ca.gov/programs/cpns/Pages/FormativeResearch.aspx

Centers for Disease Control and Prevention. (2013). *Youth Risk Behavior Surveillance System (YRBSS)*. http://www.cdc.gov/healthyyouth/yrbs/questionnaire_rationale.htm

Choi, W.S., Gilpin, E.A., Farkas, A.J., & Pierce, J.P. (2001). Determining the probability of future smoking among adolescents. *Addiction*, 2: 313–323.

Ciemens, E., Coon, P., & Sorli, C. (2010). An Analysis of Data Management Tools for Diabetes Self-Management: Can Smart Phone Technology Keep Up? *Journal of Diabetes Science and Technology*, 4: 958–960.

Cole-Lewis, H., & Kershaw, T. (2010). Text Messaging as a Tool for Behavior Change in Disease Prevention and Management. *Epidemiologic Reviews*, 32: 56–69.

County Health Rankings and Roadmaps. (2013). *2013 Georgia Data* [Data file]. Retrieved September 1, 2015, from http://www.countyhealthrankings.org/sites/default/files/state/downloads/2013%20County%20Health%20Ranking%20Georgia%20Data%20-%20v1_0.xls

Dutta-Bergman, M. (2003). Demographic and Psychographic Antecedents of Community Participation: Applying a Social Marketing Model. *Social Marketing Quarterly*, 9: 17–31.

Evans W.D. (2006). How Social Marketing Works in Health Care. *British Medical Journal*, 322: 1207–1210.

Evans, W.D. (2008). Social Marketing and Children's Media Use. *Future of Children*, 18(1): 181–204.

Evans, W.D., Blitstein, J., Vallone, D., Post, S., & Nilsen, W. (2015). Systematic Review of Health Branding: Growth of a Promising Practice. *Translational Behavioral Medicine*, 5(1): 24–36, doi:10.1007/s13142-014-0272-1

Evans, W.D., Davis, K.C., & Farrelly, M.C. (2008). Planning for a Media Evaluation. In *A Practical Guide to Program Evaluation Planning*, D. Holden & M. Zimmerman (Eds.). Thousand Oaks, CA: Sage.

Evans, W.D., Davis, K.C., Silber Ashley, O., Blitstein, J., Koo, H., & Zhang, Y. (2009). Efficacy of Abstinence Promotion Media Messages: Findings from an Online Randomized Trial. *Journal of Adolescent Health*, 45(4): 409–417.

Evans, W.D., Pattanayak, S.K., Young, S., Buszin, J., Rai, S., & Wallace, J. (2014). Social Marketing of Water and Sanitation: Systematic Review of Peer-Reviewed Literature. *Social Science and Medicine*. doi:10.1016/j.socscimed.2014.03.011

Evans, W.D., Uhrig, J., Davis, K., & McCormack, L. (2009). Efficacy Methods to Evaluate Health Communication and Marketing Campaigns. *Journal of Health Communication*, 14(3): 244–254.

Evans, W.D., Wasserman, J., Bertolotti, E., & Martino S. (2002). Branding Behavior: The Strategy Behind the truth® Campaign. *Social Marketing Quarterly*, 8(3): 17–29.

Farrelly, M.C., Davis, K.C., Haviland, M.L., Messeri, P., & Healton, C.G. (2005). Evidence of a Dose-Response Relationship Between "truth" Antismoking Ads and Youth Smoking. *American Journal of Public Health*, 95(3): 425–431.

Farrelly, M.C., Healton, C.G., Davis, K.C., Messeri, P., Hersey, J.C., & Haviland, M.L. (2002). Getting to the truth®: Evaluating National Tobacco Countermarketing Campaigns. *American Journal of Public Health*, 92: 901–907.

Fjeldsoe, B.S., Marshall, A.L., & Miller, Y.D. (2009). Behavior Change Interventions Delivered by Mobile Telephone Short-Message Service. *American Journal of Preventive Medicine*, 36: 165–173.

Flay, B.R. (1986). Efficacy and Effectiveness Trials (and Other Phases of Research) in the Development of health Promotion Programs. *Preventive Medicine*, 15: 451–474.

French, J., Blair-Stevens, C., McVey, D., & Merritt, R. (2010). *Social Marketing and Public Health*. Oxford, UK: Oxford University Press.

Gerend, M.A., Shepherd, J.E., & Monday, K.A. (2008). Behavioral Frequency Moderates the Effects of Message Framing on HPV Vaccine Acceptability. *Annals of Behavioral Medicine*, 35: 221–229.

Grilli, R., Ramsay, C.R. & Minozzi, S. (2002). Mass Media Interventions: Effects on Health Services Utilisation. *Cochrane Database of Systematic Reviews*, (1): CD00 0389.

Hornik, R.C. (1997). Public Health Education and Communication as Policy Instruments for Bringing About Changes in Behavior. In *Social Marketing*, M. Goldberg, M. Fishbein, & S. Middlestadt (Eds.). Mahwah, NJ: Erlbaum; 45–58.

Hornik, R.C. (Ed.). (2002). *Public Health Communication: Evidence for Behavior Change*. Mahwah, NJ: Erlbaum.

Hornik, R.C., & Kelly, B. (2007). Communication and Diet: An Overview of Experience and Principles. *Journal of Nutrition Education and Behavior*, 39(S2): S5–S12.

Kotler, P., & Lee, N. (2008). *Social Marketing: Influencing Behaviors for Good* (3rd ed.). Los Angeles: Sage.

Lim, M.S.C., Hocking, J.S., Hellard, M.E., & Aitken, C.K. (2008). SMS STI: A Review of the Uses of Mobile Phone Text Messaging in Sexual Health. *International Journal of STD and AIDS*, 19: 287–290.

Logan, A.G., McIsaac, W.J., Tisler, A., Irvine, M.J., Saunders, A., & Dunai, A. (2007). Mobile Phone-Based Remote Patient Monitoring System for Management of Hypertension in Diabetic Patients. *American Journal of Hypertension*, 20: 942–948.

Mays, D., Niaura, R.S., Evans, W.D., Hammond, D., Luta, G., & Tercyak, K.P. (2014). The Impact of Graphic Cigarette Warning Label Message Framing and Plain

Packaging on Motivation to Quit Among US Young Adult Smokers. *Tobacco Control*. doi:10.1136/tobaccocontrol-2013-051234

MCAH Community Health Assessment Survey—Module 3. California Maternal, Child and Adolescent Health Action (MCAH ACTION) Rural Caucus. (2003). Retrieved September 1, 2015, from https://www.cdph.ca.gov/programs/mcah/Documents/MO-MCAH-NeedAssessment-v6-10-15.pdf

McDermott, L., Stead, M., & Hastings, G. (2005). What Is and What Is Not Social Marketing. *Journal of Marketing Management*, 21: 545–553.

McKenzie-Mohr, D. (2011). *Fostering Sustainable Behavior: An Introduction to Community-Based Social Marketing*. Gabriola Island, BC: New Society.

Musher-Eizenman, D., & Holub, S. (2007). Comprehensive Feeding Practices Questionnaire: Validation of a New Measure of Parental Feeding Practices. *Journal of Pediatric Psychology*, 32(8): 960–972. doi:10.1093/jpepsy/jsm037

Noar, S.M., Benac, C., & Harris, M. (2007). Does Tailoring Matter? Meta-Analytic Review of Tailored Print Health Behavior Change Interventions. *Psychological Bulletin*, 113: 673–693.

Palmgreen, P., Stephenson, M.T., Everett, M.W., et al. (2002). Perceived message sensation value (PMSV) and the dimensions and validation of a PMSV scale. *Health Communication*, 14: 403–428.

Petty, R.E., & Cacioppo, J.T. (1986). *Communication and Persuasion: Central and Peripheral Routes to Attitude Change*. New York: Springer-Verlag.

Rao, A., Hou, P., Golnik, T., Flaherty, J., & Vu, S. (2010). Evolution of Data Management Tools for Managing Self-Monitoring of Blood Glucose Results: A Survey of iPhone Applications. *Journal of Diabetes Science and Technology*, 4: 949–957.

Reger, B., Wootan, M.G., & Booth-Butterfield, S. (1999). Using Mass Media to Promote Healthy Eating: A Community-Based Demonstration Project. *Preventive Medicine*, 29: 414–421.

Robinson, M.N., Tansil, K.A., Elder, R.W., Soler, R.E., Labre, M.P., Mercer, S.L., Eroglu, D., Baur, C., et al. (2014). Health Communication Campaigns That Include Mass Media and Health-Related Product Distribution: A Community Guide Systematic Review. *American Journal of Preventive Medicine*, 47(3): 360–371.

Rosenstock, I.M., Strecher, V.J., & Becker, M.H. (1988). Social Learning Theory and the Health Belief Model. *Health Education and Behavior*, 15(2): 175–183.

Saunders, R.P., Evans, M.H., & Joshi, P. (2005). Developing a Process-Evaluation Plan for Assessing Health Promotion Program Implementation: A How-to Guide. *Health Promotion Practice*, 6(2): 134–147.

Snyder, L.B., & Hamilton, M.A. (2002). Meta-Analysis of US Health Campaign Effects on Behavior: Emphasize Enforcement, Exposure, and New Information, and Beware the Secular Trend. In *Public Health Communication: Evidence for Behavior Change*, R. Hornik (Ed.). Hillsdale, NJ: Erlbaum; 357–383.

Stead, M., & Hastings, G. (1997). Advertising in The Social Marketing Mix: Getting the Balance Right. In *Social Marketing: Theoretical and Practical Perspectives*, M. E. Goldberg, M. Fishbein, & S. E. Middlestadt (Eds.). Mahwah, NJ: Erlbaum; 29–44.

Stetler, C.B., Legro, M.W., Wallace, C.M., Bowman, C., Guihan, M., Hagedorn, H., Kimmel, B., Sharp, N.D., & Smith, J. L. (2006). The Role of Formative Evaluation in Implementation Research and the QUERI Experience. *Journal of General Internal Medicine*, 21(Suppl 2): S1–S8. http://doi.org/10.1111/j.1525-1497.2006.00355.x

US Department of Health and Human Services. (2014). *The Health Consequences of Smoking—50 Years of Progress: A Report of the Surgeon General.* Atlanta, GA: US Department of Health and Human Services, Centers for Disease Control and Prevention, National Center for Chronic Disease Prevention and Health Promotion, Office on Smoking and Health.

Weiss, C.H. (1997). Theory-Based Evaluation: Past, Present, and Future. *New Directions for Evaluation*, 76: 41–55.

Whittaker, R., Borland, R., Bullen, C., Lin, R.B., McRobbie, H., & Rodgers, A. (2009). Mobile Phone-Based Interventions for Smoking Cessation. *Cochrane Database of Systematic Reviews*, 4: 1–22.

World Bank. (2012). *Africa Regional Dialogue on Financial Literacy and Capability: Final Report.* Washington, DC: World Bank.

3

Formative Research

W. Douglas Evans and Christina Nicols

Summary Points

- Formative research is the critical step in designing a social marketing campaign.
- It is a multistage process that in practice often ends up being condensed.
- Formative research is used to refine and settle on a theory-based campaign approach.
- This chapter offers practical guidance on when and how to apply specific formative research methods and case examples of their use in real-world campaign design.

THIS CHAPTER EXAMINES formative research and its role in the design, development, and testing of social marketing interventions. Social marketing applies commercial marketing principles and techniques to create programs that benefit society. Similarly, formative research in support of social marketing draws on principles and techniques of marketing research originally developed to sell products; however, these techniques have been adapted to influence behavior change to improve health and prevent injuries (Silk, Atkin, & Salmon, 2011). To understand how formative research is essential to social marketing interventions, we explore the following:

- where formative research fits in the research and evaluation continuum;
- its purposes and uses, including its role in evaluation;
- the phases of formative research, including exploratory research, concept testing, and pretesting;

- methods for conducting formative research; and
- how formative research is used to develop a theory-based social marketing strategy.

Overview of Formative Research

Marketing research conducted by commercial brands seeks to understand consumers' wants and needs for the primary purpose of selling products and services. The world's most successful brands constantly conduct research among consumers, including those who currently buy their products and those who do not (but *might someday*). A marketing research program to support a commercial brand may include the following components:

- in-depth exploration of consumers' wants and needs *on a regular basis*, particularly through product trials (e.g., taste tests, trial use of new technologies, etc.);
- ongoing competitive analysis, including constant surveillance of new products in development by competitors;
- monitoring of social trends and how trends may have an impact on product sales and development (e.g., social networking, mobile media use, interest in locally sourced foods, increased health consciousness, etc.); and
- tracking sales and revenue against marketing efforts to determine the most effective strategies and channels for outreach.

Ultimately, these research activities are conducted to achieve several objectives, all with an impact on "bottom-line" profitability of the company:

- increased market share;
- penetration of new markets; and
- increased sales and revenue outcomes.

A formative research program in support of *social marketing* may include similar components, but these research activities are directed toward different objectives and are usually conducted with smaller budgets and fewer resources. The overall purpose of formative research in support of social marketing is to understand how best to benefit the *audiences* rather than the marketers. The research processes are often the same—exploration of target audiences' wants and needs and their social environment—but the outcomes differ. The "sales" equivalent for social marketing is behavior change, which can be valued in monetary and nonmonetary terms. Monetary success factors in social marketing can include decreased healthcare costs to society, such as when increases in preventive care contribute to fewer visits to hospital emergency departments. Nonmonetary success factors can include improved quality of life among audiences, such as when reductions in overweight and obesity contribute to healthier, more active lifestyles. The outcomes of social marketing programs tend to be longer term, not tracked on a monthly or quarterly basis, as with commercial sales. Table 3-1 outlines the differences between commercial and social marketing in terms of the 4Ps—place, product, price, and promotion.

While commercial marketing focuses on products promoted through media and distributed predominantly through retail outlets, social marketing focuses on intangibles—usually desired behaviors such as healthy eating habits, having an annual mammogram, or wearing a helmet while cycling. Like commercial marketing, social marketing not only uses media to promote desired behaviors but also relies on influencers (e.g., friends, family, peers) and trusted intermediaries (e.g., teachers, clergy, physicians, pharmacists) to encourage adoption of desired behaviors. In social marketing, "place" is more than a retail outlet for selling products—it is where consumers live their lives (e.g., school, work, places of worship, community centers, parks) and where they may be most receptive to messages about healthier lifestyles and behaviors.

Table 3-1 Comparison of Commercial and Social Marketing Research by the 4Ps

Ps	Commercial	Social
Product	Mainly tangible, bought with money	Mainly intangible, not bought with money—but there are social marketing products (e.g., condoms, helmets for bicycling or motorcycling use; Robinson et al., 2014)
Price	Monetary price more relevant	Nonmonetary price more relevant
Place	Mainly distribute tangible products and services	Mainly distribute intangibles (e.g., ideas)
Promotion	More widespread, typically physical properties	Less widespread, typically abstract properties

Monetary price is important to commercial products, as consumers frequently compare prices to make a purchase decision. In social marketing, decision-making about "price" can be more complex, as price is typically nonmonetary. In social marketing, price is the cost consumers associate with adopting the desired behavior. For example, if the desired behavior is healthier eating habits, a nonmonetary price for this behavior is the time it takes to prepare a healthy meal. A nonmonetary price can also involve physical discomfort, as with having a mammogram or exercising regularly. Social marketers typically think of price as a barrier to the desired behavior that must be overcome if the intervention is to be successful. As with commercial marketing, consumers must decide if the "product"—the desired behavior—is worth the price they must pay in time, effort, or physical discomfort. The benefits consumers associate with the desired behavior must be sufficient inducement to overcome barriers or pay the price.

An essential purpose of formative research for social marketing is to establish whether consumers associate benefits with healthy behaviors and to determine how strongly they value those benefits. Because social marketing puts the needs of consumers first, social marketers must understand the interests, preferences, and behaviors of their audiences to develop successful interventions (Hastings, 2007).

Phases of Formative Research

The objectives of formative research in support of a social marketing intervention generally include the following:

- To identify one or more target audiences (segmentation) for campaign targeting
- To develop an understanding of the target audience's current practices, needs, wants, values, and competing behaviors
- To determine what bundle of benefits is most compelling and how it can best be made available
- To develop and test messages, materials, and promotional strategies (Siegel & Lotenberg, 2007)

The objectives outlined map directly to the three phases of formative research explored in this chapter: the exploratory phase, concept testing, and pretesting. The phases of formative research as they relate to the social marketing intervention and its evaluation are shown in Figure 3-1, which is repeated from

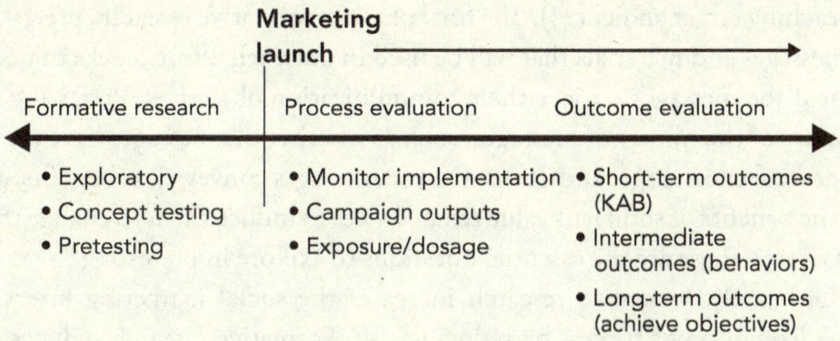

FIGURE 3-1 Formative research within the social marketing research framework. *Source: Evans,* W.D. (2015) A Social Marketing Research Paradigm. In *Social Marketing: Global Perspectives, Strategies, and Effects on Consumer Behavior,* W.D. Evans (Ed.). Hauppauge, NY: Nova Science; Chapter 1.

Chapter 1 to illustrate this stage of the research process. Formative research is conducted *before* the launch of the intervention, but elements of formative research contribute to the process and outcome evaluations that follow launch.

In the exploratory phase, the goal is to gain an understanding of our audiences by segmenting them according to factors that are meaningful to the social marketing intervention. Demographic factors, such as age, income, and education level, may be important; however, more meaningful (and useful) segments are sometimes defined by attitudes and lifestyle factors. Therefore, in the exploratory phase of research, it is important to understand the environmental context in which social marketing will occur. Ultimately, a social marketing intervention will request the audiences undertake a behavior change to improve their health, and we need to understand how appealing, realistic, and feasible that behavior change is, given the reality of daily life. A key part of this is to understand the barriers target audiences will face as they attempt to change their behavior. For example, if we are asking them to select healthier foods, including fresh produce, is cost a barrier? And, if cost is a barrier, what supports can we offer to help our audiences overcome the barrier?

Also essential to examine in the exploratory phase are the factors that may motivate target audiences to undertake behavior change. We know from social marketing research that audiences can overcome barriers when they perceive enough value in the benefits of the social marketing intervention. What is the *right* level of value, and what are the key motivators for behavior change? These are essential questions to answer in exploratory research.

The concept test phase seeks to determine what bundle of benefits is most compelling and how it can best be made available to audiences. This phase explores the ideal marketing mix (e.g., which channels will be most effective in reaching target audiences). The final phase of formative research, pretesting of messages and materials that will be used in outreach efforts, seeks to determine if the messages achieve their communication objectives. Pretesting is a measure of the *efficacy* of messages, such as whether the messages have the intended effect on target audiences. Do the messages convey clear benefits, and are the benefits of sufficient value to audiences to induce them to change their behaviors? These are the essential questions to explore in pretesting.

Ultimately, formative research increases the social marketing intervention's likelihood of success by reducing risk. Formative research reduces the risk of misunderstanding target audiences, including what motivates them, what they are willing to do to improve their health, and the likelihood that they can and may overcome barriers to achieve successful behavior change. Individual and structural barriers can easily undermine social marketing efforts. Individual barriers to healthy behaviors can include the following:

- Misperception of need/use
  - Example: A parent resists getting the flu vaccine for her child because she thinks the vaccine could cause the flu.
- Denial of personal applicability
  - Example: A parent cannot recognize that her child is overweight or obese.
- Unappealing change
  - Example: A patient newly diagnosed with diabetes resists regular glucose monitoring.
- Find messages boring
  - Example: A teenager with a new driver's license finds "the usual lecture" about no texting while driving to be boring.
- Lack of self- or outcome efficacy
  - Example: A smoker has tried to quit several times before and doubts he can succeed.

Not all barriers to behavior change rest with the individual. Structural barriers are also important to consider when developing a social marketing intervention. Structural barriers to healthy behaviors can include the following:

- Access and resources
  - Example: An overweight adult wants to eat fresh fruits and vegetables but has limited access to these in her neighborhood.
- Environmental barriers (e.g., media, community)

    - Example: A child wants to be more physically active but has no safe areas to play in the neighborhood.
- Policy barriers
    - Example: An employee without paid sick leave feels pressured to show up for work even though he will likely infect others with flu.

A key objective in formative research is to assess and prioritize the individual and structural barriers to behavior change. Including program elements to address barriers will increase the likelihood the social marketing intervention will succeed. Ultimately, health communication that uses formative research is more effective (Backer, Rogers, & Sopory, 1992).

Formative research can also help *demonstrate* success by contributing factors that will be used in process and outcome evaluations. For example, defining an audience is an essential part of formative research that is also essential to evaluation. To measure an effect within a target audience, social marketers must first have an accurate definition of the audience, including size and geographic dispersion. Similarly, baseline measures are often established in formative research to determine the extent of the challenge and the need for the intervention. These baseline measures provide an essential comparison for subsequent measures conducted midway through and after the intervention. Formative research enables social marketers to develop *measurable goals* for the intervention based on solid data and a realistic understanding of the audience; measurable goals, in turn, are essential for process and outcome evaluations because they provide the basis for measurement.

The sections that follow explore the three phases of formative research in greater detail and depth, beginning with the exploratory phase.

Exploratory Research

Social marketing interventions begin and end with audiences. Understanding a target audience is arguably the most important step in developing a successful intervention (Vega & Roland, 2005). Key questions to be answered in the exploratory phase of formative research include the following:

- Who is the audience?
- What is the size of the audience?
- Where does the audience live, work, and play?
- What do we know about the audience's relevant behaviors?
- How does social and physical environment matter?

- How can we best reach the audience?
- What attitudes and beliefs affect the target behavior?
- What are barriers or supports to the adoption of behavior?

Environmental Scanning (Also Called Situation Analysis)

Environmental scanning—the first step in the exploratory research phase—is a process for gaining an understanding of any individual, community, social, and behavior-related factors that can affect attitudes, behaviors, social norms, and policies about a health issue and its potential solutions. It is also called a "situation analysis," and it typically includes the following steps:

- Define and understand the health problem, based on epidemiology
- Identify key audiences and gain an understanding of their social, political, and other external influences
- Develop an audience profile and segmentation
- Research existing programs, initiatives, and resources
- Highlight unmet population needs
- Describe overall barriers to program implementation and proposed behavior change

An environmental scan should inform the social marketing strategy, and data gathered in the process should be considered within the framework of the 4Ps of marketing. Research into the audience's social, political, and other external influences will likely suggest which of the 4Ps may be most relevant and effective for the social marketing effort. For example, if the environmental scan reveals inconvenience and lack of access are key barriers to women having regular mammograms, the social marketer may emphasize a "place" strategy of bringing mobile mammogram vans to areas where they are most needed. All aspects of the environmental scan should be analyzed for opportunities and threats to the social marketing effort. For example, exploration of segments of the population most affected by the issue will likely yield opportunities, while a thorough analysis of barriers to behavior change will likely uncover threats to the success of the social marketing intervention. We can develop an overall social marketing strategy by considering how audience segments will likely respond to place, price, product, or promotion strategies.

These factors are typically explored and analyzed in five conceptual areas: economic, sociodemographic, social and environmental, competitive dynamics, and media and technology, outlined in the next sections.

Economic Areas

Consider the target audience's economic circumstances and the impact they may have on achieving behavior change. Examine these questions related to those in the target audience:

- Are they prosperous or struggling?
- Do they have the means for supporting the behavior change? (For example, can they afford smoking cessation products if they are trying to quit? Can they afford fresh produce if they are trying to have a healthier diet?)
- What are their economic aspirations, and how does the health issue have an impact on their likelihood of achieving their aspirations? (For example, could economic aspiration serve as a motivation for achieving the behavior change?)
- What do they fear or value, and could their fears or values influence their likely engagement in the social marketing effort?

Sociodemographic Areas

Consider key trends in the overall target market population:

- Is the population changing? (For example, are these individuals aging? Are they moving from urban to suburban areas? Are they retiring later?)
- What are the current social trends, and how could they have an impact on the social marketing intervention?
- What is the target audience's racial/ethnic, income, and age mix? Are there common cultural factors that could be leveraged for the intervention?
- What are the target audience's buying habits and needs, and have they changed over time? (For example, do their current buying habits create barriers to the behavior change?)

Social and Environmental Areas

Consider the audience's lifestyles and values:

- What aspects of the audience's lifestyle are relevant for the health issue? (For example, do those in the audience work full time or part time? How do they spend their nonwork time? What do they enjoy for entertainment?)

- What aspects of the audience's environment are relevant for the health issue? (For example, do they live in rural or urban areas? In what type of setting do they work—office or other?)
- What are the audience's current attitudes regarding the health issue and desired behavior change?
- Will the behavior change be easy or difficult to fit into the audience's existing lifestyle?
- Will the behavior change support or conflict with their values or religious views?

Competitive Dynamics Areas

Consider direct and indirect competitors to the desired behavior:

- Does the target audience currently engage in any behaviors that "compete" with the desired behavior? (For example, do these individuals have dietary habits that compete with healthy eating habits? Do they smoke or have a sedentary lifestyle?)
- Are there competitive products that are relevant to the health issue? (For example, does the target audience drink high-calorie beverages, such as sodas or soft drinks, instead of water and other less caloric beverages?)
- How are competitors reaching the target audience? (For example, do they use any 4P strategies?)

Media and Technology

Consider the target audience's media preferences and use of technology:

- What media may drive purchase decisions or health behaviors? (For example, does the audience rely on the Internet for news and other information? Where do these individuals go online? Do they rely on mobile apps? What are their trusted information sources? What other media do they use?)
- How are media use patterns changing over time? (For example, is the target audience moving or have they already moved to primarily mobile and social media use? Which channels are emerging as key resources?)
- Are there new forms of competition that could be relevant to the health issue, such as online retailers or mobile and social media advertising?

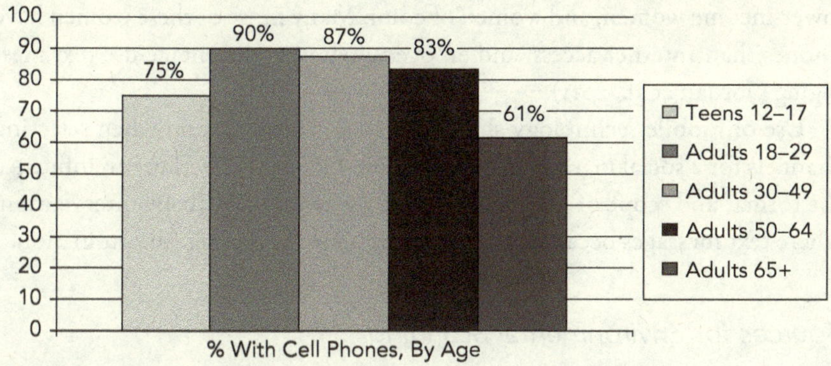

FIGURE 3-2 Use of cell phones by age group.
Source: Duggan, M. (2015). Mobile Messaging and Social Media—2015. Retrieved on September 2, 2015, from http://www.pewinternet.org/files/2015/08/Social-Media-Update-2015-FINAL2.pdf

Mobile media, including smartphones, tablets, and the various apps developed for them, represent a substantial opportunity for reaching target audiences today. Overall, recent data (which are updated constantly) indicated 85% of Americans have cell phones, representing 300 million untapped "behavior change devices" in the United States (Duggan, 2015). Penetration among young adults ages 18–29 is even higher, with 90% having cell phones (Duggan, 2015). Cell phone penetration in the United States is greater than for landlines, personal computers, and television. Figure 3-2 shows cell phone use by age group.

Among those with cell phones, 75% send and receive text messages. This percentage is even higher among Hispanic Americans, of whom 83% engage in text messaging (Duggan, 2015). Text messaging can be an effective means of delivering health messages to target audiences, as evidenced by the success of the *text4baby* mobile health (mHealth) program (Whittaker et al., 2012). This free mobile information service is provided by the Healthy Mothers Healthy Babies Coalition (HMHB). It provides pregnant women and new moms with motivation and information to help them care for their health and that of their baby. The service is available in English and Spanish to promote maternal and child health, especially among low-income moms. In addition to providing useful information and guidance for pregnant women and new moms, the text messages connect women to prenatal and infant care services and other resources in their local area. Text4baby is the largest mobile health initiative in the United States, reaching approximately 1,000,000 moms since its launch in 2010 (see https://text4baby.org/). Text messaging works as a channel for this intervention because cell phones are especially important in reaching the main target audience for text4Baby: young women, lower-income women, and women of color. Many more of these women have phones than Internet access, and an overwhelming percentage use text messaging (Jordan et al., 2011).

Use of mobile technology should be a key consideration when selecting channels for a social marketing intervention. Channel selection can influence the format and scope of messaging, as seen with the text4baby intervention, where text messages became the primary vehicle for message dissemination.

Sources for Environmental Scanning

Typical sources for environmental scanning data include large national health and lifestyle surveillance data sets, including those conducted by the US Centers for Disease Control and Prevention (CDC) and the US Census. Experimental data from research literature can also be a valuable source of insights about target audiences and previous interventions and can be searched through PubMed (http://www.ncbi.nlm.nih.gov/pubmed/). Commercial market data, particularly databases that outline media preferences among specific target audience segments, can also be useful in developing outreach and promotion strategy for the intervention. Examples of these sources are shown in Table 3.2.

Audience Segmentation

An essential component of environmental scanning is audience segmentation, which is dividing the audience into groups with similar characteristics and needs. Segmentation enables social marketers to develop tailored messages that are more likely to resonate and motivate audiences to make behavior changes to improve their health. Segmentation also enables a more targeted outreach effort—with media and other channels selected specifically for defined audience segments—to make communication more efficient and effective. This is particularly important in a time of limited funding for public health communication campaigns, when the demand for measurable results is greater than ever.

Social marketers conduct segmentation to accurately define audiences by one or more characteristics. Examples of characteristics that can provide the basis for segmentation include demographic attributes (e.g., age, income, education level, marital status); language; geographic dispersion; lifestyle attributes; core values; and attitudes regarding the health issue in question. A simple example of audience segmentation is shown in Table 3-3. The segmentation in this example is based on two characteristics: language (English vs. Spanish) and location (Texas vs. New York).

Table 3-2 Examples of Sources for Environmental Scanning Data

Sources for Environmental Scanning Data
Public Information Sources
National Health and Nutrition Examination Survey (NHANES)
National Health Interview Survey (NHIS)
Behavioral Risk Factor Surveillance Survey (BRFSS)
Youth Risk Behavior Surveillance Survey (YRBSS)
National Youth Tobacco Survey (NYTS)
Medical Expenditure Panel Survey (MEPS)
US Census
National Immunization Survey (NIS)
Nonprofit and Commercial Sources
Private foundations (e.g., Truth Initiative, Robert Wood Johnson Foundation, Kaiser Family Foundation, Commonwealth Fund)
Published experimental literature (from authors or sponsors, such as NIH and CDC) searched through PubMed
PRIZM: Segments US population into 62 lifestyles
Databases of media consumption: Mediamark/MRI, Simmons, Scarborough, Nielsen, comScore
Healthstyles: Health-related behavior data
Data on product or brand purchase

Even a simple segmentation like the one outlined in Table 3-3 can be useful for developing a social marketing intervention, as it can guide the format and tone of messages as well as channels selected for message dissemination. For example, while both primarily English-speaking and primarily Spanish-speaking Latinas may use the Internet to gain health information, Spanish-speaking Latinas may be more likely to use community resources due to factors such as cultural preference and familiarity (Edberg et al., 2010). Therefore, factors specific to an audience segment can suggest a particular 4P strategy, specific channels for disseminating messages, as well as the content and format of messages.

Another means of segmenting audiences can be seen in generational segmentation, such as the segmentation conducted by Thomson Reuters to determine how four adult generations use healthcare (MacCracken, 2009). Table 3-4 summarizes the differences in generations in terms of how adults

Table 3-3 Simple Audience Segmentation Example

English-speaking Latino women (Latinas) in Texas • Interview 9 women	English-speaking Latinas in New York • Interview 9 women
Spanish-speaking Latinas in Texas • Interview 9 women	Spanish-speaking Latinas in New York • Interview 9 women

relate to medical professionals, their expectations of quality in healthcare, and their own level of engagement in their care.

Segmenting by need is another approach that should be considered when segmenting audiences for social marketing interventions. Audiences who need the intervention most are usually priority audiences, and often in health issues, these segments represent vulnerable populations who may be disadvantaged in access to healthcare, health literacy, income, and education levels. Disadvantaged segments can be difficult to reach through traditional media (although the widespread use of mobile phones and social media is an important exception), as many are not media-rich consumers who spend a lot of time online, read consumer magazines, or watch cable television. Therefore, social marketers usually consider alternative channels for reaching disadvantaged audiences, including cell phones and text messages, community organizations such as the YMCA, government agencies and services such as the US Department of Agriculture's SNAP (Supplemental Nutrition Assistance Program) and WIC (Special Supplemental Nutrition Program for Women, Infants, and Children) programs, churches, and faith-based organizations.

Ultimately, effective segmentation combines data, knowledge, and experience. It can be based on consumer profiling data from secondary sources as outlined in Table 3-2 or on primary research through focus groups, interviews, and surveys. Social marketers can also learn from audience segmentations of previously conducted public health campaigns. Channel selection for outreach should always be a key consideration in audience segmentation, as it guides the tactical implementation of the social marketing intervention.

Effective segmentation demands decision-making, as a good segment should be tightly *defined* by a specific set of factors, whether they are demographic, attitudinal, need based, generational, or otherwise defined. Segments should also be *measurable*; for example, social marketers need to be able to estimate the size of the overall population the segment represents to be able to determine what percentage of that population they will likely reach through

Table 3-4 Example of Segmentation by Generational Characteristics

Greatest/Silent Generation (Adults Born Up to 1942): Physician Directs Me	Baby Boomers (1943–1960): Engage Me	Generation X (1961–1981): Educate Me	Millennials (Adults Born Since 1982): Connect With Me
Relationship With Medical Professionals			
• Rely on physician to provide medical care direction • Prepared to seek information from and defer to physician • Identify only physicians and nurses as health professionals	• Seek counsel from and bring information to the physician • Research physician recommendations • Identify only physicians and nurses as health professionals	• Define medical professionals broadly, including nurse practitioners, physician assistants, insurance companies, and pharmacies in addition to physicians and nurses	• Access healthcare system through primary care providers (PCPs), urgent care centers, and obstetricians/gynecologists (Ob/Gyns) • Low utilization of inpatient and outpatient services • Use and appreciate technology and a positive, personal relationship with physician
Expectations of Quality in Care			
• Rigid definition of good service; "the customer is always right" • Older adults are more satisfied and tend to stay with their PCP	• Value individual engagement in healthcare • Use third-party comparisons or ratings as a means of self-directing to specialists and providers	• Interested in being engaged and educated; actively seek information • More likely to switch physicians and hospitals based on most recent experience	• Value health information and seek information from multiple sources • More likely to switch physicians or hospitals based on most recent experience

Source: MacCracken, L. (2009). *Matching the Market: Using Generational Insights to Attract and Retain Consumers*. Thomson Reuters Healthcare. Retrieved on September 1, 2015, from http://www.healthcarestrategy.com/usermedia/TSHW-6185A_BRIEF_generational_0109.pdf

the intervention and motivate to change behavior. For the purposes of social marketing and health communications, effective segments need to be *reachable* through communication in an affordable way; that is, the segments need to be defined in a practical way that will facilitate outreach efforts. They also need to be *substantial* enough to warrant the effort. Perhaps most important, segments need to be *relevant* to an organization's mission in delivering better outcomes for public health.

The following case study provides an example of effective environmental scanning, describing an analysis that contributed to the strategy of the Heart Truth campaign (Long et al., 2011).

Case Study: Environmental Scan for the Heart Truth Campaign

Background

Through a literature review and secondary research, social marketers compiled several essential insights regarding women and heart disease:

- Heart disease is the **number 1 killer** of women in America.
- **One in four** women dies of heart disease.
- More women die from heart disease than from all forms of cancer combined.
- About **one-third** of women still underestimate their own personal risk of heart disease—they fail to make a connection between risk factors, such as high blood pressure and high cholesterol, and their personal risk.
- Having just **one risk factor doubles** the risk of developing heart disease; risk skyrockets with each added risk factor.
- Fully 80% of midlife women have one or more of the risk factors for heart disease.

Challenge

After reviewing the background data and developing the situation analysis, social marketers were able to determine the challenge that needed to be solved in the intervention:

- Despite their risks, women considered heart disease **a man's disease.**
- **Breast cancer** was their number one concern.

- You cannot convince a woman to address risk factors if **she does not think she is at risk.**

Objective

The challenge definition informed the primary objective of the intervention: change the perception of heart disease from a man's disease to the **number 1 killer of women** in the United States.

Segmentation Strategy

To narrow the target audience to make it manageable and effective for an intervention, social marketers considered which segment among women is most likely to change their perception of heart disease and thus be receptive to a social marketing effort (Long et al., 2011). In deciding on a core target audience, social marketers based their strategy on insights from several research questions:

- Which women would attend best to the message?
- Which women could influence others?
- Which women had not been reached?
- Which women would form a nucleus from which to build?

After consideration of attitudes and lifestyle factors, they determined middle-aged women (ages 40–60) are the key segment for whom increased risk is salient and realistic and for whom there are behavior changes available to address heart disease risks. Middle-aged women are also in a position to form a nucleus from which to build outreach efforts, as they influence daughters, nieces, and their own mothers.

Result

The analysis assisted social marketers in developing the Heart Truth campaign, outlined as follows in brief:

- **Launched:** September 2002 by the National Heart, Lung, and Blood Institute (NHLBI), National Institutes of Health (NIH)
- **Objective:** Increase awareness of heart disease as women's number 1 killer; motivate women to take action to reduce their risk
- **Audience:** Women ages 40–60

- **Overall approach:** Social marketing campaign incorporating a strong branding strategy
- **Implementation strategy**: Partnership development, media, community action; focus on women of color
- **Based on strong foundation of target audience research:** Leverage women's interest in their outward appearance to focus on what is inside (heart); deliver a strong wake-up call about personal risk; take a hard-hitting approach—a deliberate departure from campaign executions that existed at the time

Leveraging women's interest in fashion, the campaign created a national symbol—the **Red Dress**—that served as a highly visual reminder of women and heart disease. The Red Dress symbol became a central, driving force for the campaign, providing a unique platform through fashion industry partnerships, which yielded high-profile events and considerable media attention. The slogan, "Heart Disease Doesn't Care What You Wear—It's the #1 Killer of Women," strongly appealed to diverse women (Long et al., 2011).

As illustrated by the Heart Truth campaign example, environmental scanning and audience segmentation should effectively incorporate and support the 4Ps of marketing. The data should serve as the basis for planning social marketing efforts by identifying likely barriers to overcome, potential benefits to emphasize, and channels to leverage for outreach efforts.

The environmental scan should also provide guidance, particularly through the definition and understanding of the primary audience segment, for the next phase of exploratory research, the exploration of the audience's knowledge, attitudes, and beliefs (KAB) as they relate to the health issue.

Exploratory Research to Understand Audience Knowledge, Attitudes, and Beliefs

While environmental scanning is typically done through secondary research (i.e., review and analysis of previously conducted research), the second phase of exploratory research—the exploration of KAB—is typically done through primary research, which is original research conducted directly among target audiences. Primary research can be qualitative or quantitative in nature. This section of the chapter provides an overview of qualitative and quantitative research methods, followed by examples of how they may be used to explore KAB among audiences.

What Is Qualitative Research, and How Is It Used in Formative Research?

Qualitative research is used to understand and interpret social interactions. It can be an especially effective means of exploring KAB among audiences, as its aim is to gain a broad understanding of a process, situation, or group of people as it relates to a health issue or health behavior. The focus of the research is usually on participants' perceptions and experiences and the way they make sense of their lives. Common qualitative methods used in market research include focus group sessions and individual interviews. Compared to quantitative research, such as surveys, the samples for qualitative research are typically smaller and *not* randomly selected. In fact, the sample is often selected to fulfill a specific purpose, in that the social marketer screens participants for a particular set of characteristics, such as experience with or attitudes regarding a health behavior. While quantitative research is often intended to be generalizable to a larger population, qualitative research is less generalizable, providing in-depth insights that pertain to the participants screened for the research.

In focus groups and interviews to support social marketing interventions, a researcher asks a series of broad, open-ended questions to encourage participants to describe their attitudes and beliefs about a health issue or a health behavior, as well as their perceptions about the benefits of a health behavior and barriers to achieving it. In addition to asking broad, open-ended questions to elicit conversation, researchers often probe on specific topics of interest if these topics do not spontaneously occur in the course of the conversation. The following is a summary of commonly used qualitative methods:

- *In-depth interviews*: In-depth interviews are typically conducted one-on-one in person or by telephone. As the interview progresses, questions tend to evolve from broad and general to increasingly specific, usually with the interviewer probing on specific aspects of key research questions identified in advance. Interviews can vary in the degree of formality and structure, ranging from informal, unstructured interviews to formal interviews:
    - *Informal, unstructured interviews*: Open-ended answer format featuring broad questions; the conversation emerges spontaneously.
    - *Semistructured interviews:* The researcher has a basic line of questioning in advance but still relies on open-ended questions; the interview guide lists specific areas to probe.

- *Formal interviews:* These are completely structured, with uniform, close-ended questions that have preset response options.

- *Focus groups*: Focus groups are semistructured interviews conducted among small groups of participants. A trained moderator leads a discussion among 8 to 10 participants over the course of 1 to 2 hours. Focus groups are usually conducted in person in market research facilities that feature two-way mirrors. They can also be done online or by telephone. Recruitment is often done by the facility using a screener developed by the researcher. Participants are paid monetary incentives.

A key benefit of focus groups and in-depth interviews is that they can be conducted quickly and inexpensively. They provide valuable, spontaneous insights into participants' KAB regarding a health issue or behavior. Focus groups provide insights into *group interactions*, as they often stimulate a variety of views that would not arise in individual interviews. A group of individuals can more easily have a dynamic discussion exploring the pros and cons of an issue as well as various aspects of an experience than can a single individual. Individual interviews, on the other hand, can be particularly effective when a health topic involves sensitive issues that individuals may not feel comfortable discussing in a group. Individual interviews are also generally less expensive and more flexible than in-person focus groups, as they can be conducted by telephone at the participant's convenience.

A drawback to focus groups and in-depth interviews is that these methods do not always provide insights into how an individual's physical environment influences KAB or a broader view of the impact of social systems. To gain insight into the integration of KAB within social systems and the physical environment, researchers use observational and ethnographic methods. These methods are used less frequently in market research because they typically require a considerable amount of time for immersion into a natural setting (i.e., the target audience's community). The following is a summary of these methods:

- *Observation*: In naturalistic observation, the researcher collects data through observation *without interfering* with the ongoing behavior. It typically yields insights into the "what" of behavior, but because researchers do not interview audiences, it does not often explore underlying motivations (the "why").
- *Participant observation*: The researcher participates in ongoing activities and records observations. Participant observation extends beyond observation because the researcher participates in the action. The technique is

often used in anthropology and sociology. Often, the researcher actually takes on the role being studied, for example, working on a farm to observe and experience farm safety issues.

- *Ethnography*: This is a research approach using multiple methods, including observation, interviewing, mapping, and visual data collection through photographs or video. Conducted in a natural setting, the researcher takes the time needed to immerse him- or herself in the community to gain a broad understanding of the audience's physical environment, social processes, and systems and how these have an impact on KAB.

Qualitative research in general has several weaknesses to keep in mind. First, qualitative research is not an appropriate or effective means for arriving at statistical descriptions of large populations. It should not be used to predict attitudes and behaviors of a broader population. For example, attitudes and likely behaviors pertaining to smoking cessation discussed among focus group participants would *not* yield trustworthy estimates of attitudes and likely behaviors of the overall population of smokers. Nevertheless, qualitative research could provide important insights into attitudes and likely behaviors that could then be quantified through a survey to make predictions about the larger population.

Qualitative research is also subject to researcher bias, as observations and interpretations are subjective and personal. The researcher must strive for objectivity to prevent personal opinions and feelings from biasing the results and conclusions.

What Is Quantitative Research and How Is It Used in Formative Research?

Quantitative research is used to define and count variables (i.e., factors of interest) and assess relationships between variables, including the possibility that one variable is associated with or caused another to occur. In formative research, it can be used to predict audiences' likely health behaviors and reactions to messages and materials. In evaluation, quantitative research can be used to measure awareness, understanding, attitudes, or behaviors among audiences as a result of the social marketing intervention. Examples of variables that can be gathered, counted, and assessed in quantitative research include demographic factors, such as age, income, and education level; attitudes about a health behavior, issue, or message; values and beliefs; and self-reported experience.

Surveys, by either telephone or online, are the most commonly used method for data collection in quantitative market research. Quantitative studies are usually intended to yield generalizable findings that can be applied to a broader population beyond study participants. To achieve generalizability, researchers conduct the study among a representative sample of the audience of interest. The representative sample is known as a probability sample, in which all members of the population have an equal probability of being selected for the sample. The sample is selected at random and should be large enough to yield a low margin of error.

For surveys requiring a probability sample, the telephone method is typically used, with a random digit dial (RDD) approach to ensure all households have an approximately equal chance of being included in the sample. Because not all households have landlines anymore, market research firms have introduced a dual-frame approach, which includes 25% to 40% cell phones and 60% to 75% landline telephones in the sample. Telephone methodology tends to be more expensive than online, panel-based survey methodology. For studies that do not need to be generalizable to the US adult population, online methodology is often used because it is cost-effective and requires less time to field. Online surveys are usually conducted using opt-in panels, in which participants have agreed to take surveys to receive monetary or other incentives. Therefore, opt-in panels do not provide the random selection criterion needed for generalizability. (We explore online consumer panels in more depth in Chapter 5.) Omnibus surveys, in which clients buy questions on a multitopic survey that is conducted weekly or monthly, can be especially cost-effective.

Whether the survey is conducted online or by telephone, determining a sufficient sample size in part depends on the size of the population it is intended to represent. For example, market research firms typically use a randomly selected sample of 1,000 adults to represent the US adult population of approximately 230 million. This sample yields a fairly low margin of error of plus or minus 3.1%. The margin of error is the amount of sampling error in a survey's results, and it should be considered when interpreting survey results. For example, if a survey indicates 78% of women ages 18–29 and 75% of women ages 30–39 say they use social media to discuss and learn about nutrition, the 3-point difference in percentages falls within a plus or minus 3.1% margin of error. Without doing additional statistical tests for significance, the researcher determines the difference between the age groups is likely *not* significant, as the difference could be attributed to survey error. Therefore, when reporting these survey results, researchers would *not* claim that women ages 18–29 are more likely than women ages 30–39 are to use social media to discuss and learn about nutrition.

In contrast to questions in qualitative research, which are open-ended, a survey questionnaire typically features predominantly close-ended questions with set response options. Commonly used survey response options can be categorized as follows:

- *Categorical*: Categorical response options can be sorted into categories but cannot be measured. Bar charts and pie graphs are often used to graph categorical data. There are two types of categorical response options:
  - *Ordinal*: Ordinal response options can be ranked or have a rating scale attached but cannot be measured. Examples of ordinal response options include Likert-like scales in Table 3-5.
  - *Nominal*: Nominal response options can be assigned a code in the form of a number; the numbers are simply labels. They can be counted but not ordered, ranked, or measured. Nominal response options include yes/no and male/female. Additional examples are shown in Table 3-6.
- *Numerical*: Numerical responses can be measured and placed in ascending or descending order. Scatterplots and line graphs are often used to graph numerical data. There are two types of numerical responses:
  - *Discrete*: Discrete responses include values or observations and can be counted (e.g., 1, 2, 3, . . .) and are distinct and separate. Examples include the number of eggs in a basket or the number of fingers on a hand.
  - *Continuous*: Continuous responses are values or observations that may take on any value within a finite or infinite interval. Examples include height, weight, systolic blood pressure, age, or body mass index.

Likert-like scales are often used for questions intended to determine the level of agreement, satisfaction, relevance, importance, and other attitudinal factors. Likert-like scales typically range from 1 to 3, 4, 5, 7, or 10. For example, a 5-point Likert-like scale for the question, How important do you think it is for a woman to breastfeed her baby? could include

- Very important
- Important
- Somewhat important
- Somewhat unimportant
- Very unimportant

Other examples of commonly used Likert-like scales are shown in Table 3-5.

Table 3-5 Examples of Likert-Like Survey Scales

	Examples of Scales		Examples of Scales
Agreement	Strongly agree Agree Neither agree nor disagree Disagree Strongly disagree	**Concern**	Extremely concerned Moderately concerned Somewhat concerned Slightly concerned Not at all concerned
Satisfaction	Very satisfied Satisfied Neither satisfied nor dissatisfied Dissatisfied Very dissatisfied	**Priority**	Essential High priority Medium priority Low priority Not at all a priority
Importance	Very important Important Somewhat important Somewhat unimportant Very unimportant	**Problem**	Serious problem Moderate problem Minor problem Not at all a problem
Qualitative	Excellent Very good Good Fair Poor	**Opposition**	Strongly favor Somewhat favor Neutral Somewhat oppose Strongly oppose
Likelihood	Very likely Somewhat likely Neutral Somewhat unlikely Very unlikely	**Familiarity**	Extremely familiar Moderately familiar Somewhat familiar Slightly familiar Not at all familiar
Frequency	Always Often Sometimes Rarely Never	**Barrier**	Extreme barrier Moderate barrier Slight barrier Not at all a barrier

When qualitative and quantitative methods are used in formative research, conducting qualitative research first enables researchers to develop questions and nominal response options needed for follow-up in quantitative research. For example, Table 3-6 demonstrates how participant responses to open-ended questions in qualitative research can inform a set of nominal response options in a survey.

Table 3-6 Example of Developing Survey Response Options from Qualitative Research

Qualitative: Interviews	Quantitative: Survey
Question: What are some of the reasons why you don't breastfeed your baby?	*Question*: Which of the following are reasons why you don't breastfeed your baby? (Select all that apply)
Results from interviews: • Infant formula is just as good as breast milk. • I am not comfortable breastfeeding in public. • Others are not comfortable with me breastfeeding in public. • I do not have a place to pump milk or breastfeed at work.	• Infant formula is just as good as breast milk. • I am not comfortable breastfeeding in public. • Others are not comfortable with me breastfeeding in public. • I do not have a place to pump milk or breastfeed at work. • None of the above. • Other, please specify. *Results from survey*: • 59% indicated they are not comfortable breastfeeding in public. • 40% indicated others are not comfortable with me breastfeeding in public. • 29% indicated they do not have a place to pump milk or breastfeed at work. • 23% indicated Infant formula is just as good as breast milk.

After the survey has been fielded and data are collected, researchers assess and report survey results, most commonly using the following statistical methods:

- *Frequency*: A count of the number of responses associated with different values of *one variable*, for instance, the number of survey participants who select specific response options within a single survey question, typically expressed as a percentage.
  - For example, percentage of women who say they use social media to discuss and learn about nutrition
- *Cross-tabulation*: Cross-tabulation involves a table that shows *two or more variables* simultaneously, merging two or more frequency distributions into a single table; it is used to understand how one variable relates to another.
  - For example, cross-tabulation demonstrating how age relates to social media use.

- *Chi-square statistic*: The chi-square statistic is a commonly used test to determine statistical significance of associations between cross-tabulated variables, that is, a test used to determine if perceived differences among segments of survey participants are statistically significant rather than just occurring by chance.
  - For example, a chi-square test used to determine if the differences in the use of social media among different age groups of women are statistically significant

In addition to the methods outlined, social marketers often use *regression analysis* to predict how certain variables explored in the survey will have an impact on audiences' attitudes or behaviors related to the health issue. Regression analysis is a statistical procedure for analyzing associative relationships between a dependent variable and one or more independent variables. In the example previously discussed, the dependent variable is social media use. Independent variables that may or may not be associated with this dependent variable could include age, gender, household income, and education level. Researchers use regression analysis, for example, to predict whether a change in household income is associated with a change in social media use, if all other variables such as age, gender, and education level remain the same. Regression analysis can help social marketers determine which variables or combination of variables pertaining to a target audience can increase the likelihood that audience segments will engage in the desired health behavior.

Social marketers often use *cluster analysis* to group survey participants with similar characteristics into segments based on their responses to specific questions or sets of questions. The basis for forming the clusters varies depending on the needs of the social marketer. For example, social marketers may decide to base the clusters on survey participants' perceptions of the benefits associated with a desired health behavior. Figure 3-3 is a simple cluster segmentation demonstrating how survey participants can be grouped into clusters based on their perceptions of two variables associated with the benefit of a health behavior:

- *Perceived value of the benefit*: Survey participants indicate on a scale from 1 to 5 how important the benefit is to them. Examples of benefits associated with health behaviors include weight loss associated with increased physical activity, prevention of lung cancer associated with smoking cessation, or prevention of head injury associated with wearing a helmet when bicycling.
- *Belief benefit can be obtained through the health behavior:* Survey participants indicate on a scale from 1 to 5 how strongly they believe the health

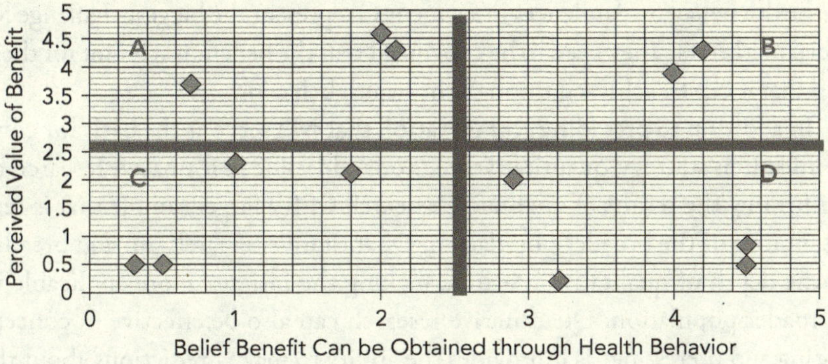

FIGURE 3-3 Example of cluster segmentation by perception of benefits.

behavior will actually yield the benefit, for example, how strongly they believe wearing a helmet when bicycling can prevent a head injury.

The cluster segmentation in Figure 3-3 shows four cluster segments in quadrants A, B, C, and D, defined as follows:

- Quadrant A: Participants value the benefit but do not believe the health behavior will yield the benefit.
- Quadrant B: Participants value the benefit, and they believe the health behavior will yield the benefit.
- Quadrant C: Participants do not value the benefit, and they do not believe the health behavior will yield the benefit.
- Quadrant D: Participants do not value the benefit, but they believe the health behavior will yield the benefit.

This type of cluster segmentation can help social marketers develop a theory-based strategy for the intervention. The segmentation in Figure 3-3, for example, would inform use of the theory of planned behavior by categorizing audience segments according to their attitudes toward the health behavior (Ajzen, 1985). The segmentation can also serve as the basis for tailoring messages and materials for audience segments. For example, segment B already values the benefit and recognizes the health behavior will likely yield the benefit. Therefore, audiences in segment B may not need messages to convince them that the health behavior is effective. Audiences in segment A, conversely, may need evidence to convince them that the health behavior is worth doing because it will likely yield the desired benefit. Audiences in segment D will need to be persuaded that the benefit is worth having, as they already believe it can be obtained through the health behavior. Audiences in segment C represent the biggest challenge for social marketers: They need to be convinced that the benefit is relevant for them and that it can be achieved through the health behavior.

In addition to providing segmentation that will serve as the basis for communications strategy, quantitative methods add value to formative research by confirming the results of qualitative research with a larger sample that is representative of the broader population. Quantitative research can add breadth to the depth of qualitative research, making the insights more applicable to a broader population. Quantitative research can also be effective in concept testing and pretesting, as it provides the ability to make predictions about the likely attitudes and behaviors of audience segments.

Concept Testing

Concept testing is the second phase of formative research, and it involves the initial testing of prototype messages and materials to determine if they resonate with audiences. It can be done through qualitative or quantitative methodologies; however, quantitative testing through a survey with a sufficient sample enables the social marketer to segment audiences based on their reactions to concepts. Social marketers can then predict which segments will be more or less receptive and likely to act on messages. This predictive insight can guide strategy for the social marketing intervention.

Concept testing aims to achieve two main objectives:

- determine which messages and concepts appeal to audiences and why; and
- determine which channels are likely to be effective in disseminating messages for the social marketing intervention.

Testing messages and concepts is a "best practice" in communication and social marketing research, and obtaining feedback from intended audiences during the development of messages and materials is crucial for the success of every communication effort. Messages, print ad concepts, visuals, and videos can all be effectively tested in surveys. In this approach, Likert-like scales are developed to assess audience attitudes regarding the following aspects of the message or concept:

- Clarity/comprehension
  - What is the main idea in this message or concept?
  - How well does the message or concept convey the main idea?
  - Is there anything in the message or concept that is unclear or confusing?

- Appeal
    - If you saw the message or concept, would it get your attention?
    - Do you like the message or concept?
- Personal relevance
    - Does the message or concept pertain to you?
    - Can you relate to the people in the concept?
- Credibility/believability
    - Is the message or concept believable?
    - Do you trust the source of the message or concept?
- Likelihood of acting on the message or concept
    - How likely are you to take the action recommended in the message or concept?

Concept testing can also be conducted effectively through qualitative methods, such as focus groups sessions or interviews. As an example of how qualitative methods can be useful, consider the process for developing video ads and public service announcements (PSAs). Videos are often developed first in storyboards that lay out plot and visual images on paper before filming. Creative teams often develop several concepts for videos, using storyboards to demonstrate the concepts for testing. Storyboards are too lengthy and cumbersome to test in a survey, but they are easily tested in focus groups. Through qualitative testing, the creative team can obtain valuable guidance on which concept resonates best with audiences before they expend budget, time, and creative energy in developing videos.

Also in concept testing, participants can indicate where and how they would like to see, hear, and learn about the messages and concepts to ensure their greatest level of receptivity. For example, in qualitative testing, participants can describe which media channels are effective in reaching them, whom they trust as intermediaries, and what sources they rely on for information. These insights are valuable in guiding outreach strategy and specific tactics through media. In quantitative testing, participants can easily indicate their channel and media preferences through questions with close-ended response options.

Pretesting

Pretesting is the final phase of formative research and involves assessing near-final offerings to make any necessary adjustments prior to the launch of the social marketing intervention. Pretesting explores many of the aspects explored in concept testing—clarity, appeal, personal relevance, believability, and likelihood of action—but what is being tested is close to final form.

Pretesting is a measure of the *efficacy* of messages; for example, do the messages have the intended effect on target audiences? Further in this book (Chapter 6), we discuss the distinctions between efficacy and effectiveness *evaluations* of messages and campaigns. But, for purposes of *design* and preparing for the launch of campaigns, pretesting research is done to confirm whether the draft messages, campaign materials, and 4P strategies are efficacious in a final phase of formative research. Do the messages convey clear benefits, and are the benefits of sufficient value to audiences to induce them to change their behaviors? Ultimately, pretesting is the social marketer's last chance before launch to determine if anything has been overlooked in messages or campaign strategy that might increase the likelihood for success.

Developing Theory-Based Strategy

An important function of formative research is to inform and guide the strategy for a social marketing intervention (Reigeluth, & Frick, 1999). Toward this end, insights from formative research are used to develop logic models based on behavioral theory, such as the next example drawn from the 2010 Census Integrated Communications Program Evaluation (CICPE), used to guide evaluation of the 2010 US Census national media campaign (Evans, Datta, & Yan, 2012), which is discussed in Chapters 6 and 8 of this volume.

Logic models such as Figure 3-4 serve several critical functions and are informed by careful pretesting research. The CICPE logic model was designed to ensure that all the factors that must be included in the subsequent evaluation of the Census 2010 media campaign plan were specified and that their potential influence is recognized. The logic model also supported selection of analytical methods appropriate for the structural model of the complex environment and the data that are gathered to represent all causal agents, outcomes of interest, and mediating factors, including those external to the campaign. In general, campaign logic models serve to

- represent the campaign's "theory of change";
- capture campaign goals and objectives;
- provide topic specificity (e.g., census participation);
- hypothesize main relationships among environment, behaviors, and health impacts; and
- identify measures that should reflect steps and relationships among environment, behaviors, and impact.

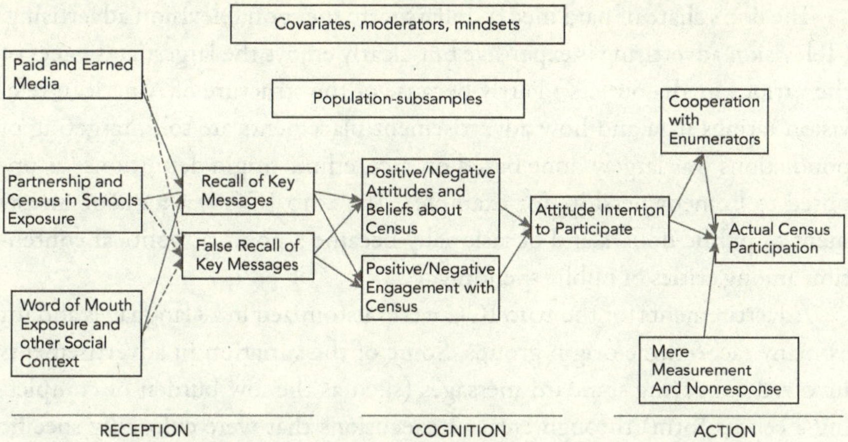

FIGURE 3-4 Census Integrated Communication Program Evaluation (CICPE) logic model.

The following case study highlights pretesting research conducted to develop the 2010 CICPE and logic model.

Case Study: Pretesting of the 2010 CICPE

Background

The US Census Bureau implemented the 2010 International Conference on Communications (ICC) to encourage participation in the 2010 Decennial Census, including coordinated delivery of targeted outreach to specific subpopulations. Components of the 2010 ICC included paid media advertising; an expansive grassroots partnership program that engaged organizations such as churches, civic groups, and local leaders; a Census in Schools program for students in elementary and secondary schools; and earned media, such as news and features coverage in traditional and digital media outlets. Outreach to households for the 2010 ICC began in late 2009, with peak paid media and partnership activities taking place from January through June 2010. The goals of the 2010 ICC were to increase mailback of the census form, improve cooperation with enumerators, and reduce differential undercounting (Bates et al., 2009). The 2010 ICC was indeed integrated, with a high degree of coordination in materials, images, and themes across the different components of the campaign. The campaign was also pervasive. The paid media campaign was one of the nation's most ubiquitous television advertising efforts in the early part of 2010—between January and June of 2010, census television advertising was ranked fourth behind that of McDonald's, Walmart, and Geico.

The lion's share of paid media dollars were spent on television advertising. (Television advertising is expensive but clearly enjoys the largest audiences of the various media outlets.) Partly because of the structure of American television ratings data and how advertisement placements are sold, targeting of populations was largely done based on race/ethnic origin definitions (as opposed to homeownership, for example). The 2010 ICC was a major investment of public dollars and occasionally became a point of political contention among critics of public spending.

Advertisements for the 2010 ICC were customized in 28 languages and for as many race/ethnic origin groups. Some of the variation in advertisements involved conveying standard messages (such as the low burden of completing a census form) through creative executions that were culturally specific (including through dress, music, and even style of rice cooker). Others involved messages tailored to the particular concerns of the target group, for example, fears of contact with government agencies among Muslim Americans. Target ads almost exclusively used non-English languages common to each target group (except for non-Hispanic blacks). As a result, many native-born or long-term immigrants who may not have frequented in-language media outlets received only the nontargeted general population messages that ran in the mainstream English language media.

Pretest Methods

The US Census Bureau conducted multiple waves of pretesting research. Based on results from a survey in 2008 to better understand Americans' perceptions of, knowledge of, and attitudes toward the decennial census, initial ad concepts were designed by the media firm DraftFCB. Analyses of the data from this survey informed development of themes for the 2010 media campaign and the mapping of themes to population subgroups (Bates et al., 2009). Extensive focus groups along with quantitative surveys of the same focus group participants were conducted to understand their reactions to specific ads. These mixed methods were used to iteratively test preliminary versions of census ads to refine themes and creative material, especially for small subgroups who were not well represented in the 2008 survey.

Results

As part of the research and development planning efforts for the 2010 Census, the US Census Bureau conducted several activities to assess potential barriers to participation and reasons why people may be motivated to respond to the census and to better understand methods of communication that work for different target audiences. Barriers were explored through the mixed-method focus groups and surveys. This work helped provide input into the creative ad material developed by DraftFCB and their partner agencies for the campaign. These creative executions were tested with the relevant audiences, in all 28 of the linguistic and cultural subgroups targeted by the campaign. DraftFCB conducted copy testing sessions in January through February 2009. Due to more creative developments and revisions to the initial draft ads, DraftFCB conducted additional copy testing sessions through the summer of 2009. A total of 37 mixed-method, focus group, and survey sessions were conducted in 10 cities around the United States to pretest ads at various stages of copy testing and preproduction. Focus group and survey results were used to make revisions, reiterations, and final creative development of campaign ads. A good example of one such ad that emerged as an effective campaign execution may be viewed online (http://adsoftheworld.com/media/tv/2010_census_campaign_roads).

Use of mixed methods and multiple iterations of testing can reveal barriers and opportunities to refine ads during pretesting. The Census 2010 media campaign, one of the largest and best-funded public service campaigns conducted in the United States, is a good example of the use of effective pretesting research methods.

Conclusion

This chapter examined each step in the formative research phase of the social marketing research continuum. While in practice many campaigns do not execute each of these discrete steps through separate research projects, some attention to each step is important to a well-designed social marketing effort. Formative research is also the point in the social marketing process at which researchers and campaign developers often have the most contact. It represents a critical phase when creative efforts can be informed by data, and campaign theory can be integrated with planned implementation efforts and plans for future process and outcome evaluation. The integration of these elements is discussed in Chapters 5 and 6 of this volume.

Additional Resources: Literature

- Arulmani, G., & Abdulla, A. (2007). Capturing the Ripples: Addressing the Sustainability of the Impact of Social Marketing. *Social Marketing Quarterly*, 13(4): 84–107. doi:10.1080/15245000701678438

- Higgins, D., O'Reilly, K., Tashima, N., Crain, C., Beeker, C., Goldbaum, G., & Guenther-Grey, C. (1996). Using Formative Research to Lay the Foundation for Community Level HIV Prevention Efforts: An Example From the AIDS Community Demonstration Projects. *Public Health Reports (Washington, D.C.: 1974)*, 111(Suppl): 128–135.
- Jones, S.C., Waters, L., Holland, O., Bevins, J., & Iverson, D. (2010). Developing Pandemic Communication Strategies: Preparation Without Panic. *Journal of Business Research*, 63: 126–132.
- Reigeluth, C.M., & Frick, T.W. (1999). Formative Research: A Methodology for Creating and Improving Design Theories. In *Instructional-Design Theories and Models, Volume II: A New Paradigm of Instructional Theory*, C.M. Reigeluth (Ed.). Mahwah, NJ: Erlbaum; 633–651.
- Vega, M.Y., & Roland, E.L. (2005). Social Marketing Techniques for Public Health Communication: A Review of Syphilis Awareness Campaigns in 8 US Cities. *Sexually Transmitted Diseases*, 32: S30–S36.

References

Ajzen, I. (1985). From intentions to actions: A theory of planned behavior, In J. Kuhl and J. Beckmann (Eds.), *Action-control: From cognition to behavior*, Heidelberg, Germany: Springer, 11–39.

Backer, T.E., Rogers, E.M., & Sopory, P. (1992). *Designing Health Communication Campaigns: What Works?* Thousand Oaks, CA: Sage. doi:http://dx.doi.org/10.4135/9781483325521

Bates, N., Conrey, F., Zuwallack, R., Billia, D., Harris, V., Jacobsen, L., & White, T. (2009). Messaging to America: Results From the Census Barriers, Attitudes and Motivators Survey (CBAMS). *Proceedings of the 2009 American Statistical Association*, Survey Research Methods Section, 5807–5821.

Duggan, M. (2015). *Mobile Messaging and Social Media—2015*. Retrieved on September 2, 2015, from http://www.pewinternet.org/files/2015/08/Social-Media-Update-2015-FINAL2.pdf

Edberg, M., Cleary, S., Klevens, J., Collins, E., Leiva, R., Bazurto, M., Rivera, I., Taylor, A., Montero, L., & Calderon, M. (2010). The SAFER Latinos Project: Addressing a Community Ecology Underlying Latino Youth Violence. *Journal of Primary Prevention*, 31: 247–257.

Evans, W.D., Datta, R., & Yan, T. (2012). *Paid Media and Hard-to-Reach Populations: Lessons From the 2010 Census*. New York: Russell Sage.

Hastings, G. (2007). *Social Marketing: Or, Why Should the Devil Have All the Best Tunes*. London: Butterworth-Heineman.

Jordan, E.T., Ray, E.M., Johnson, P., & Evans, W.D. (2011). Early Results: Text4baby Program Reaches the Intended Audience. *Nursing for Women's Health*, 15(3): 206–212.

Long, T., Taubenheim, A.M., McDonough, S., Austin, P., Wayman, J., & Temple, S. (2011). Delivering *The Heart Truth*® to Women Through Community Education. *Social Marketing Quarterly*, 17(4): 24–40. doi:10.1080/15245004.2011.620682

MacCracken, L. (2009). *Matching the Market: Using Generational Insights to Attract and Retain Consumers*. Thomson Reuters Healthcare. Retrieved on September 1, 2015, from http://www.healthcarestrategy.com/usermedia/TSHW-6185A_BRIEF_generational_0109.pdf

Reigeluth, C.M., & Frick, T.W. (1999). Formative Research: A Methodology for Creating and Improving Design Theories. In *Instructional-Design Theories and Models, Volume II: A New Paradigm of Instructional Theory*, C.M. Reigeluth (Ed.). Mahwah, NJ: Erlbaum; 633–651.

Robinson, M.N., Tansil, K.A., Elder, R.W., Soler, R.E., Labre, M.P., Mercer, S.L., Eroglu, D., Baur, C., Lyon-Daniel, K., Fridinger, F., et al. (2014). Health Communication Campaigns That Include Mass Media and Health-Related Product Distribution: A Community Guide Systematic Review. *American Journal of Preventive Medicine*, 47(3): 360–371.

Siegel, M., & Lotenberg, L.D. (2007). *Marketing Public Health: Strategies to Promote Social Change* (2nd ed.). New York: Jones and Bartlett.

Silk, K.J., Atkin, C.K., & Salmon, C.T. (2011). Developing Effective Media Campaigns for Health Promotion. In *The Routledge Handbook of Health Communication*, T.L. Thompson, R. Parrott, & J.F. Nussbaum (Eds.). New York: Routledge; 203–219.

Vega, M.Y., & Roland, E.L. (2005). Social Marketing Techniques for Public Health Communication: A Review of Syphilis Awareness Campaigns in 8 US Cities. *Sexually Transmitted Diseases*, 32: S30–S36.

Whittaker, R., Matoff-Stepp, S., Meehan, J., Kendrick, J., Jordan E, Stange, P., Cash, A., Meyer, P., Baitty J, Johnson, P., Ratzan, S., Rhee, K. (2012). Text4baby: Development and Implementation of a National Text Messaging Health Information Service. *American Journal of Public Health*, 102: 2207–2213. doi:10.2105/AJPH.2012.300736.

4

Brand Research

W. Douglas Evans and Steven Chapman

Summary Points

- Social marketing brands add value to the relationships between health products and behaviors and consumers.
- Social marketing brand research has two main purposes: (1) identify determinants of brand choice and (2) evaluate outcomes of consumer behavior.
- Brand research is growing in global social marketing, and its goal should be a standardized set of methods and evidence.
- More research is needed on how public health brands work, how they determine consumer choice, and what effects they have on behavior.

What's a brand? A singular idea or concept that you own inside the mind of the prospect.

—AL RIES

Brand value is very much like an onion. It has layers and a core. The core is the user who will stick with you until the very end.

—EDWIN ARTZT

Introduction and Background

Brands build relationships between consumers and products, services, or lifestyles by providing beneficial exchanges and adding value to their objects. They can be measured through associations that consumers hold for products and services. Through brand promotion, these associations can become established and lead to a long-term relationship, or brand loyalty, between the product or service and consumer. These relationships are the building blocks of marketing and explain much of the success commercial marketers have enjoyed in building the global economy at least since the Industrial Revolution (Evans & Hastings, 2008).

Similarly, "behavioral brands" are the relationships that individuals form with behaviors and lifestyles that embody multiple health behaviors, and these can be measured by the associations they form with health behaviors and lifestyles (Evans, Price, & Blahut, 2005; Evans, 2013). In the health sector in particular, the concept of behavioral branding has become a major component of social marketing campaigns to change a wide range of behaviors, from HIV prevention to tobacco use prevention and physical activity promotion (Evans et al., 2014). Brands in both the commercial and noncommercial sectors can also apply to organizations and upstream factors that promote organizational impact and well-being. Health branding—building positive associations with healthy behaviors and lifestyle choices—is the primary strategy by which commercial marketing is applied in social marketing (Evans, 2013).

The purpose of brands and branding is to organize and frame choices (Keller, 2000): to buy a product, to use a service, or to live a physically active lifestyle or use condoms. Brands use symbols and imagery to organize our potential choices and frame the benefits a particular product, service, or behavior has to offer. We must always keep in mind that, for the most part, public health programs are voluntary in nature, meaning that prospective customers are free to accept or reject the products or services offered to them. As social marketers, success therefore typically hinges on the ability to design products and services that members of our intended target audience—that is, our prospective customers—will see value in and embrace. Branding is increasingly a central strategy in the process of creating value for health consumers.

This chapter focuses on brand research in social marketing and its place in the toolkit of methods available to researchers. While brand research is not explicitly identified as a point on the research continuum introduced in Chapter 1, it represents a crosscutting methodology and domain of inquiry. Brand research can occur at the formative stage in the design of branded campaigns and at the campaign implementation stage when the effectiveness of the brand in creating customer associations and changing behavior is being evaluated (Evans et al., 2014; Schultz & Schultz, 2005).

Brand research serves two functions and occupies two places on the social marketing research continuum. First, it is about measuring and evaluating *determinants of brand choice.* Consumers choose to use a category of branded product or behavior (e.g., condoms as a *category* of product) and individual branded *products* within a category (e.g., Love Plus condoms in Romania) due to market factors such as price, availability and to the brand associations they form with the category or individual product. Brand research is concerned with identifying and analyzing those determinants of brand choice and informing brand managers to improve brand positioning and execution. Thus, it represents a kind of formative research.

Second, brand research is concerned with evaluating the outcomes of brand choice. Consumers who use the category of condoms, or individual condom products, will with some probability have different health outcomes than those who do not. What effect do brand choices and utilization of brands (categories or individual products) have on individual-level communication outcomes targeted by campaigns (e.g., specific beliefs targeted by messages) and behavioral outcomes (e.g., the call to action embodied in the campaign) (Hornik, 2002)? Brand research, in its evaluation function, is concerned with this question. In particular, it is concerned with the role of brand associations as *mediators* of communication and behavioral outcomes. This chapter explores brand research and its place in social marketing research and evaluation.

Peeling the Brand Onion

Brands and the role of brand research can be explained using the concept of the brand onion (Calder, 2005; Chapman et al., 2013). Brand development can be largely explained in terms of three basic nested concepts: positioning, personality, and execution.

Figure 4-1 illustrates the brand onion concept.

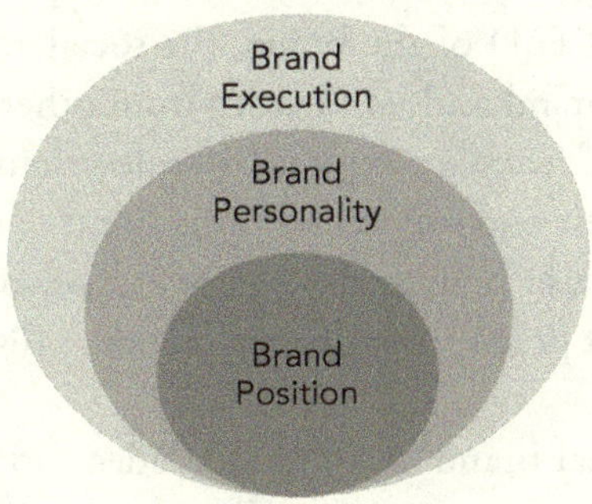

FIGURE 4-1 Brand onion.

Brand Positioning

Brand positioning summarizes what the marketer wants consumers to know and feel about a product, service, or (in social marketing) a behavior (Tybout & Sternthal, 2005). A brand's position is what it stands for, the essence of its reputation. Echoing Walter Landor's famous quotation—"Products are created in the factory. Brands are made in the mind."—the positioning of a brand positioning represents its life in the minds and hearts of the target audience. Positioning serves as a shortcut for consumer decision-making and helps to determine product or behavioral choice.

Brand positioning is often summarized in a "positioning statement." Positioning statements have three basic components:

1. Statement of the target audience
2. Description of the frame of reference (of choices in which the brand exists)
3. Point of differentiation (PoD, or benefits) of the brand from competitors, including both social (emotional) and functional benefits

Positioning statements can be framed in terms of the following model or template: For (target), (brand) is the (frame of reference) that (PoD). Consider this example from Population Services International's (PSI's) water treatment social marketing program (Chapman et al., 2013): "Certeza is the simplest water treatment method that leaves your water tasting pleasant and makes it easier to be a good mother."

Brand Personality

What if a brand were to suddenly come alive? What would he or she say and do? How would he or she say and do it? These are the questions to be answered in determining a brand's personality. Brand personality is the expression of the emotional PoD of the brand, the social and emotional features that distinguish the brand and its identity from others. It can be expressed in adjectives like "fun," "sexy," or "serious," like describing a person. These features can shape the tone and sometimes the content of brand promotion and marketing. They can also be measured as brand personality traits in brand research and represent predictors of brand choice as discussed further in this chapter.

Consider a fictional brand of condoms called Good Times. The brand personality is young, upbeat, and friendly. How might that personality be

FIGURE 4-2 Fictional Good Times brand logo depicts condom brand personality.

expressed in packaging, media, promotional messages, and other features of the personality? Figure 4-2 is a fictional logo.

Or, consider a real brand, Marlboro cigarettes. Marlboro has one of the most clearly defined brand personalities in marketing history. The Marlboro man is a rugged individual, a man's man, self-confident, able to get the job done, the strong silent type. Marlboro cigarettes personify these traits and thereby gain identity and credibility with target audience members who value them. To quote Philip Morris marketing consultants Bruce Eckman, Inc. (1992), Marlboro is "all-American; hardworking/trustworthy; rugged individual, man's man (experienced, sure of self, confident, in charge, self-sufficient, down to earth, cool/calm, get the job done); admire his strength." Whatever we may think of the health risks of cigarettes, that reputation is the basis for associations Marlboro consumers may form with the brand. Figure 4-3 says it all.

Brand Execution

The only strategy the consumer experiences is execution.
—A.G. LAFLEY, *P&G chief executive officer*

Brand execution is how the brand is implemented in the real world. It is the images, colors, symbols, logo, tag lines, shapes, type fonts, language, touch/feel,

FIGURE 4-3 Marlboro brand personality.

sound/music, scent, and any other physical manifestations of the brand position and personality used to represent the brand and market it to consumers. It is what the consumer experiences when coming in contact with the brand in the real world and what shapes brand associations. Thus, like personality, it can be measured and evaluated: How did consumers experience the brand execution, and what were their reactions?

Or, consider symbols. Without even describing a brand in words or more complex images, symbols can represent a brand and convey meaning. The Nike "swoosh" symbol, the iconic Coca-Cola curved bottle, and similar images require no explanation—they represent the brand without any accompanying description.

But, widely recognized brands did not become well known simply through good strategy, by strategic positioning and personality planning. Strong execution, high levels of consumer exposure (i.e., dosage of the marketing efforts), and consistent implementation of a 4P (place, price, product, and promotion) strategy of implementation over time produce those results. Thus, execution is a critical element in creating brand equity. Measuring and evaluating brands requires assessing implementation (process evaluation), brand equity, and outcomes of exposure to the brand execution.

Brand Equity

The personality traits that a brand projects through specific executions are the measurable features of its underlying brand positioning. These features represent the building blocks for brand research. We can develop measures of how consumers respond to a brand and how they drive consumer choice and evaluate their effects on consumer behavior. The overarching construct that has been used to capture these measurable brand characteristics is "brand equity" (Evans & Hastings, 2008; Keller, 2000; Aaker, 1996).

Brand equity is what the brand stands for in the hearts and minds of consumers, and as a metric, it captures their identification with and intentions to purchase, use, and engage with the brand. It is a primary driver influencing product choice, especially for public health commodities with little product attribute (e.g., look, feel, convenience, utility) differentiation (e.g., condoms or bed nets). Given that most purchase decisions are made within the market context of various brand choices (e.g., a luxury brand of condoms, inexpensive, or perhaps free), purchase analysis requires reliable measures of existing brand equity, in terms of both use and perceived characteristics. In social marketing, especially in the developing world, many brands have existed for years and thus have established brand equity, whether or not that equity has been actively managed or measured (Evans, Longfield, et al., 2012). Effective brand development and management requires rigorous research into brand equity and its relevance and appeal to target audiences.

In addition to its role in the consumer purchase decision, the need to measure brand equity is magnified by the changing epidemiology of some diseases, in particular for HIV and the role condoms play in prevention efforts. For example, in Zimbabwe, the Protector Plus (P+) brand of condoms was originally marketed during a period of high HIV prevalence and incidence of new cases prior to 2000 (Evans et al., 2011). However, from 2001 to 2009 HIV prevalence among 15- to 49-year-olds declined from 26% to approximately 14% (Zimbabwean Ministry of Health, 2009). Behavior change and condom use may in part explain this decline (Gregson et al., 2010). Furthermore, the country's currency was revalued and pegged to the US dollar in late 2009, raising the effective price of condoms and changing the total market for the socially marketed product (Pollard, 2014).

As a result of these major changes in the marketplace of condoms and for HIV-related behaviors, the question arose how perceptions of P+ may have changed, how its brand equity was evolving, and what effect this may have on future condom use and purchase of the socially marketed brand. This represented an important situation in which understanding brand equity was critical and led to PSI (http://www.psi.org/) commissioning a study to evaluate P+ brand equity and its relationship to pricing and condom use outcomes (Evans et al., 2011). This is not unlike the situation many commercial brands face in an evolving marketplace, with new competition and lifestyle preferences driving consumer decision-making (think of the declining market share and threat from Pepsi that led Coca-Cola to introduce the ill-fated New Coke in the 1980s) (Schindler, 1992).

Consider the situation with most socially marketed condom brands in the developing world. When most of these brands were launched, they were positioned to appeal to youth given that group's perceived high-risk profile. However, the original audience members have now aged, and recent evidence suggests that older cohorts are now most at risk given concurrent partner behaviors (Evans, Longfield, et al., 2012). In response, marketers may be tempted to reposition existing brands to this older audience (in many cases, the same individuals in their original target segment). However, this cannot be done with precision without a clear understanding of existing brand equity and audience segmentation data.

For example, in the Zimbabwe example, the changing market environment led to a study to investigate the current brand equity in P+ and other in-market condom brands, differences in brand equity between P+ and other in-market brands between specific audience segments, and whether higher brand equity in P+ and other in-market brands was associated with willingness to pay higher prices for condoms overall or for specific brands. Answers to these questions would help PSI identify opportunities both to improve P+ brand equity by addressing specific audience segments and brand attributes and to evaluate the effects of the changing market environment and marketing efforts on condom use outcomes. Study results would also inform decisions about how to grow the total condom market in Zimbabwe by establishing appropriate prices for socially marketed products that would permit commercial brands to enter the market in the future (Ndiaye & Evans, 2014; Pollard, 2014).

Similarly, marketers may wish to alter a brand's equity based on a new benefit (e.g., shifting a condom brand's primary benefit from HIV prevention to contraception) or based on an increased price for cost recovery. However, these shifts may compromise a brand's existing equity. Brand equity is based in part on a price point and the metric "price premium" (or "willingness to pay"). The marketer needs to understand a brand's equity among purchasers to effectively manage and promote the brand.

Branding Products Versus Categories

What Is It to Brand a Category?

Most often, when we think of branding we think of individual products, services, organizations, behaviors, and the like. Individual *things* are branded. Brands represent individual products or other things in the minds of consumers. We think of Coca-Cola, Fritos, Nike, BMW, iPod, Virgin Atlantic, the Centers for Disease Control and Prevention's (CDC's) VERB: It's What You Do, South Africa's loveLife, and so on. But, at the same time, brands and branding can be thought of in terms of *groups* or *categories* of things. After all, brands are like reputations, and reputations can apply to categories of products, services, organizations, behaviors, people, and other things as well as to individual members of the category (Boundless, 2015).

Consider the example of condom use behavior. Condom use is the overarching category that includes use of any individual condom, such as commercial (e.g., Durex branded condoms), socially marketed (e.g., Trust condoms in Kenya), and free brands. Condom use can be branded as a means to increase the behavior among a target audience, say teenagers and young adults, and positioned, given a personality, and promoted through specific executions.

For example, condom use could be positioned as follows: "For socially active young people, using condoms is the best way to have fun and be safe and makes you more popular with the opposite sex." The behavior of using condoms can be personified as "hip," "in the know," "edgy," or other socially desirable traits for young people. Executions can show young people with these traits choosing to use condoms, attracting more of the opposite sex, and having more fun.

Branding a category means branding a *type* of product, service, or behavior. If categories can be branded in this sense, then individual behaviors within categories can be branded as well.

Concept of Branding Health Behaviors and Lifestyles

The concept of brand equity has been widely studied in marketing and advertising research and can be generally defined as a set of attributes and associations that an individual or potential consumer has regarding a product, service, or, as in the case of the *truth* campaign, a lifestyle. High brand equity is traditionally associated with increased brand loyalty (Aaker, 1996). That is, consumers will continue to purchase the same brand regardless of available alternatives. In the case of the *truth* brand, we are proposing that individuals make a commitment to a certain lifestyle (i.e., not smoking). This application of brand equity to a lifestyle is less common than the application to a product.

Case Study of a Lifestyle Brand: The Gasy Band Cool Brand in Madagascar

Situation

In Madagascar, PSI socially markets condoms and represents a large share of the total market (estimated > 80% in 2009) (Evans, Longfield, et al., 2012). As in Zimbabwe, the socially marketed brand there is also called Protector Plus, and its positioning is that "Protector Plus is the condom that makes sexually active men feel confident and strong."

To complement P+ and create a social environment in which condom use in general would be perceived as normal and socially desirable, PSI also created a lifestyle brand to promote condoms as a desirable choice overall among the target audience of young, sexually active men. The Gasy Band Cool (GBC) brand was created to promote condom use behavior (i.e., the act of using a condom during sexual intercourse) as a normal, standard part of a young man's sexual lifestyle (Evans, Longfield, et al., 2012).

Strategy

The strategy behind the brand was to associate GBC with "extreme" (or X-treme) sports such as windsurfing, sky diving, BMX biking, surfing, and skateboarding to draw a parallel with sexual risk taking. To the uninitiated outsider, X-treme athletes might look like they are reckless and risk takers. In reality, though, they are highly skilled athletes who take every precaution to minimize their risk so that they will not be injured. Their craving for excitement and adventure might be more than the average man's, but they are always in control. For example:

- A video spot that is distributed to bars in hot zones could feature an X-treme sport. Imagine 10 minutes of fast-paced video clips that show X-treme athletes sky diving or downhill motorbiking. The music is fast, young, and hip. The editing is equally fast and has high sensation value (e.g., as would be seen on music video channels).
- This is followed by 5 minutes of "debriefing" by a presenter host during which we learn how the stunts might have seemed outrageous and dangerous but were actually well controlled. For example, we learn the following:
  - The helmet worn by an X-treme athlete is described, as is how it can withstand impact.
  - The skydiver has three ripcords—two backups.
  - The downhill motorbiker knows how to fall to escape being run over by the motorbike.
- Then, the final 5 minutes of the video make the analogy to sexual risk-taking. A person who follows the GBC brand knows how to minimize risk so he can live the fun and exciting lifestyle he craves.

Eventually, after an extended period of time in campaign execution, this brand can be expanded to local events that have an X-treme sport feel to them, such as auto racing, motor biking, and so on. It is critical, though, that the event be one where *all the necessary safety precautions are taken* (e.g., helmets worn, seatbelts used, etc.). GBC's role at the event is to ensure safety:

- for example, logo placement on the helmet, paying to ensure that mechanics inspect the vehicles; and
- distribution of condoms and STI vouchers with risk reduction messages.

Because it is more difficult to ensure that such events stay "on strategy," sponsorships can be added over time to continue to build the brand after some brand equity has been built between the brand and target group. GBC can be cobranded with X-treme athletes and other organizations associated with them to continue to build a relationship with the audience.

Case Study of the Adelante Brand for Latino and Immigrant Adolescents

The *Adelante* (or "forward" in Spanish) program uses a modified asset-based positive youth development (PYD) approach that seeks to build various assets and community supports for youth and families as a prevention mechanism (Edberg et al., 2010). Recognizing the social-ecological nature of health (L.W. Green & Mercer, 2002), Adelante is innovative and community driven and addresses multiple contributing factors for substance abuse and co-occurring health issues (including interpersonal and family violence and sexual risk behaviors) in the suburban Langley Park, Maryland, community in the United States.

A key community engagement strategy of the Adelante program is to build awareness of and promote Adelante's identity. Development of program identity, or the Adelante brand identity, extends to digital media, including an interactive website and Facebook page, Adelante gear and promotional materials, mobile phone–based promotion (e.g., text messaging to engage youth and parents), and video-based narrative stories depicting the lives of youth in the Langley Park community.

The Adelante program also uses an innovative, participatory approach to youth-led brand identity development and execution (Evans, Blitstein, et al., 2014). Adelante youth participants have been engaged in all aspects of brand identity development, and their participation in the creation of logos and gear and development of the website and digital media episodes have been key components of the Adelante intervention itself. The development of the brand identity, as well as the development of other Adelante intervention components, is guided by the Adelante PYD model. The brand identity is intended to engage youth in the intervention, as well as embody ideals laid out by the PYD model's constructs.

As part of the engagement strategy, and to design the Adelante brand itself, investigators conducted formative research to develop the Adelante brand identity in two phases (Evans et al., 2015). First, investigators tested the brand positioning and personality—what Adelante stands for and how it would best be represented in program activities and promotions to Latino teens—through focus groups with youth. This included initial positioning and personality concepts developed by the investigators. Based on those focus groups, the concepts were revised to create a final brand-positioning statement, a logo, and style concepts and identified the need for a *consumer archetype*, or individual(s) who embody and personify what the brand stands for (Calder, 2005). This is a widely used approach in marketing, as illustrated by the kinds of actors, celebrities, and other pitch people used in advertising. In the case of Adelante, these would be youth archetypes who embody the aspirations of young people living in Langley Park and the struggles they face in reaching these aspirations.

In the second phase, investigators conducted additional focus groups to design and test two potential youth archetypes, the physical manifestation of Adelante and its personality. These were identified as *Victor*, a boy almost 17 years old, and his girlfriend *Erika*, a 15-year-old girl, both attending high school in Langley Park. The focus groups were used to identify, describe, and create detailed backgrounds for these characters, develop the characters around them (friends, family, and others), and sketch out initial plots for subsequent narrative storylines.

After this research, a small group of Langley Park youth were identified who were already involved with the Adelante program. These youth worked with program staff to design and film initial executions of the Victor and Erika story to bring the Adelante brand personality to life and diffuse the story of Adelante through adolescent social networks in the community (Andrade et al., 2015).

Brand Research and the Brand Onion

Brand research can and should occur at each level of the brand onion. First, formative research, such as in the Adelante example, helps to identify what audiences value and how they think about a product, behavior, or category to establish positioning. Social marketers need *audience insight* to build a solid brand-positioning statement and develop subsequent strategy. Audience insight can also identify what kinds of personality traits might best convey the brand positioning and establish the value of the brand in the minds of consumers. In this way, we can segment consumers and identify determinants of consumer brand choice. Consider the PSI example of the Certeza water treatment product again. Figure 4-4 illustrates how audience insight is used and how brand research can be applied.

Second, research on the effectiveness of a brand can identify whether its personality is perceived as intended. Brand personality is projected through imagery, logos, colors, shapes, and other features used in brand execution. It

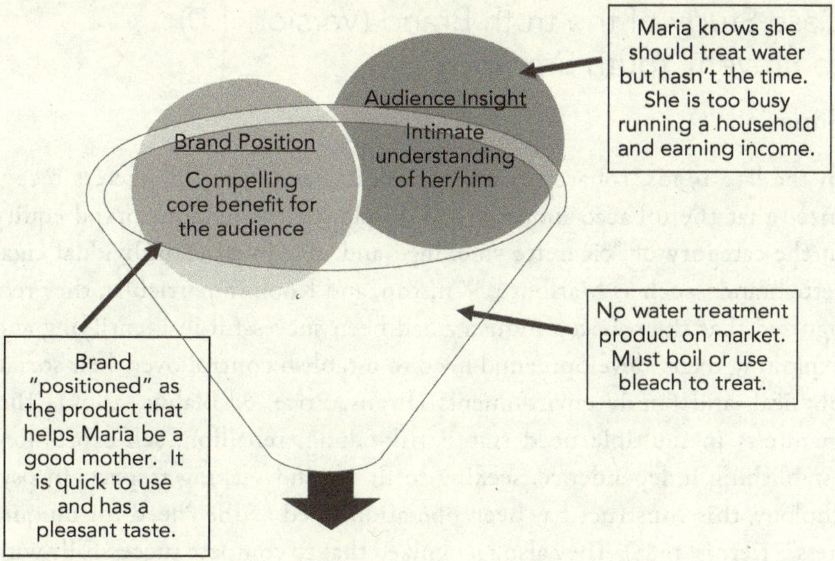

FIGURE 4-4 Certeza audience insight and brand-positioning research.
Source: PSI (http://www.psi.org/).

can be measured through brand associations—personality traits such as being fun, serious, sexy, or cool—and through social norms, attitudes, and behaviors the target audience associates with the brand. To the extent that these associations represent social or functional benefits for the target audiences, they will be more likely to engage in the target behavior (e.g., purchasing a particular brand of condoms or using condoms in general). Brand research can measure these associations and the extent to which they are associated with engaging in target behaviors.

Third, researchers can evaluate the effectiveness of brand executions in changing targeted consumer knowledge, attitudes, beliefs, and behaviors. Brand executions are the advertising and promotion designed to project the intended personality, establish the brand's position, and build equity with the audience. As noted, the consumer only experiences the brand execution, not the strategy behind it. So, to the extent consumers are (1) aware of brand executions (i.e., are actually exposed and capable of recalling exposure to executions) and (2) react positively to those executions, we expect that they will form the desired associations and build brand equity.

The following brief case study of *truth* campaign development and evaluation helps to capture the rationale behind research on the effectiveness of brand executions.

Case Study of the truth Brand (Version 1.0) to Prevent Youth Smoking

Situation

In the late 1990s, tobacco control advocates and social marketers recognized that the tobacco industry had developed tremendous brand equity in the category of "cigarette smoking" and in numerous individual cigarette brands, such as Marlboro, Winston, and Kool. In particular, they recognized that the tobacco industry had been successful in identifying and exploiting teens' developmental need to establish control over their social, physical, and family environments (Evans, Price, & Blahut, 2005). This manifests in multiple need states: risk-taking, rebellion, self-expression, establishing independence, seeking to fit in, and seeking respect. In psychology, this construct has been operationalized as the "need for uniqueness" (Kernis, 1983). They also recognized that to compete successfully with tobacco industry marketing, tobacco control social marketing would need to develop brands that could outdo tobacco brands. They recognized the following specifically:

- Teens identify with brands that fulfill one or more of these "need states."
- Tobacco brands in particular fulfill and connect at almost every need state.
- For example, the Marlboro man "is rugged," "is independent," "plays by his own rules," and is a "man's man."
- Tobacco brand promotion depicts an idealized image of smoking as satisfying needs and making an individual more in control, independent, and rebellious.

In essence, tobacco brands were positioned as having positive, desirable characteristics of empowering youth and fulfilling their need states. To take this dominant brand position away from tobacco, social marketers needed to outcompete them and needed to replace the position filled by cigarettes with something that did exactly the same thing tobacco brands do: fulfill these need states and provide control.

The American Legacy Foundation (Legacy) *truth* campaign did exactly that. The *truth* campaign created a brand that teens could identify with that had all the attributes (rebellion, risk, self-expression, independence, fitting in, respect) of brands they flocked to and felt as powerful as Big Tobacco brands. It did this by depicting youth engaging the *truth* movement against tobacco and realizing the same or better benefits that cigarettes offered (Allen et al.,

2010). Depicted graphically, *truth* "outflanked" tobacco brands along the lines in Figure 4-5. Understanding the relative positioning of truth and its competition from the industry was a key question to be answered by the *truth* campaign evaluation (Farrelly et al., 2005).

Brand Research Methods

Research on Determinants of Brand Choice

This chapter focuses on brand research on consumer choice. Consumers determine and drive the value of a brand (Evans & Hastings, 2008). On a personal level, the consumer forms "social images" of the brand based on the consumer's reception of the message, forming associations between his or her self-image and the brand's projected imagery. As a result, the consumer exposed to marketing efforts in support of the brand develops a level of equity, or value in his or her relationship with the brand. They become co-owners of the brand. What are the dimensions of ownership? This is the focus of brand research and evaluation.

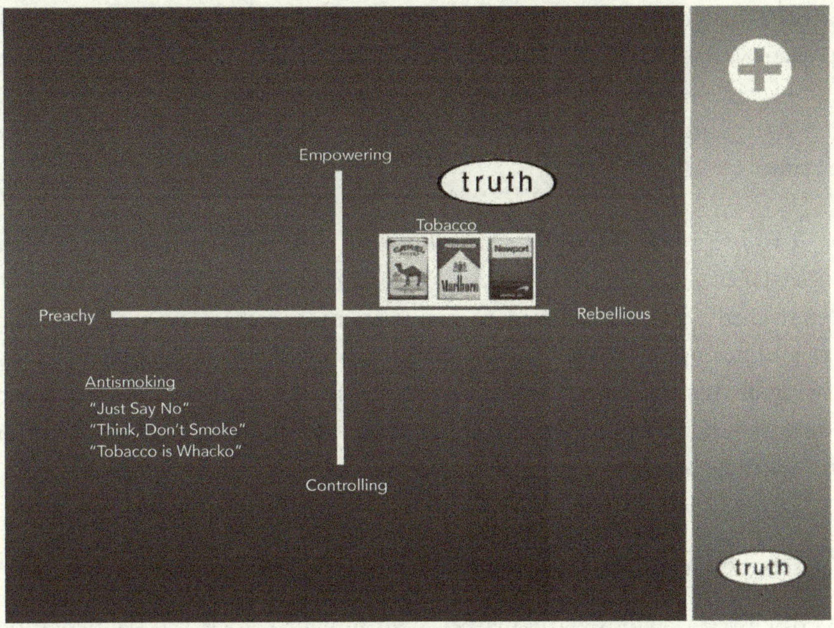

FIGURE 4-5 Truth repositions tobacco control versus tobacco brands.
Source: Evans, W.D., & Hastings, G. (Eds.). (2008). *Public Health Branding: Applying Marketing for Social Change*. London: Oxford University Press.

The Consumer Purchase Cycle

Branded product and category purchase and use can be divided into five stages—the consumer purchase cycle. This categorization scheme forms a basis for proposed analyses and has been used for research implemented previously by socially marketed brands (Evans, 2013). The purchase cycle suggests a linear progression in depth of brand affinity and purchase. Marketers need to understand the barriers to this progression, particularly because there will be a common objective to have as many in the defined target audience reach the "loyal" stage of the cycle. Brand equity and related behavioral determinants can be used to construct these categories and measure the distribution of a target audience by category.

Stages in the consumer purchase cycle may be summarized as follows:

1. Awareness: There are three levels of awareness to be considered: top-of-mind (first brand mentioned), unaided (all brands mentioned), and prompted (all brands aware when prompted).
2. Trial: This is defined as those in a population who have "ever purchased" a product at any point in memory (e.g., defined as past year).
3. Penetration: This is defined as those in a population who have purchased and used a brand or product in the recent past (e.g., defined as past 30 days).
4. Repeat: This indicates those who have purchased and used a brand at least twice in the recent past (e.g., defined as past 30 days).
5. Loyal: This indicates those who purchase a particular brand "most of the time" or "all of the time."

Two basic types of tables can be developed using the consumer purchase cycle stages: (1) segmentation based on brand equity and related behavioral determinants (which are used to construct the purchase cycle stages); and (2) monitoring of stages, and movement between stages, over time. The following discussion and tables illustrate purchase cycle analyses based on brand equity and behavioral determinants segmentation and how it can be used for monitoring purposes.

Segmentation and Monitoring Analyses

As discussed previously, the market environment is a critical segmentation factor. Socially marketed brands' equity, and other brands' equity, is a function of the market environment. Brand management is in part governed by the level and type of competition (public sector vs. commercial) in a total market approach (TMA) to social marketing in a developing economy (Pollard, 2014). Brand managers in a highly competitive market with a mix of socially marketed, public (free), and commercial condom brands (e.g., Favorite in PSI-Romania) face very different marketing challenges from those in markets dominated by socially marketed products (e.g., Number One in PSI-Laos) (Ndiaye & Evans, 2014; Pollard, 2014). As shown in Exhibit 4-1

Exhibit 4-1 Illustrative Segmentation Table Shell: Behavioral Opportunity, Ability, and Motivation Determinants by Total Market Categories

Brand Equity and OAM Determinants	Categories (% Agreement by Item/Scale)		
	Socially Marketed	Public (Free)	Commercial
Brand awareness			
Awareness of each brand in category			
Aided brand promotion awareness			
Aided awareness of specific brand advertisements in target market			
Unaided (confirmed) brand promotion awareness			
Unaided (confirmed) awareness of brand advertisements in target market			
Reactions to brand promotion			
Receptivity to promotional messages			
Brand equity for each brand in category			
Price premium			
Satisfaction/loyalty			
Perceived quality			

Leadership/popularity			
Perceived value			
Brand personality			
Organizational associations			
Brand awareness			
Market share			
Market price			
Market barriers/supports			
Brand costs more than I would expect			
Would be willing to pay more for brand			
Perceived value for price of brand			
Behavioral intentions			
Brand purchase intent			
Category use intent (e.g., of condoms in general)			
Self-reported likelihood of purchase within 30 days			
Self-reported likelihood of category use within 30 days			
Likelihood of promoting brand use to others			
Likelihood of promoting category use to others			
Social cognitive mediators			
Self-efficacy to use category			
Outcome efficacy that category will be effective			
Descriptive norms for category use (perceived frequency of use by peers)			

Subjective norms for category use (perceived acceptability of use by peers)			
Behavior			
Use of category in last 30 days			
Brands purchased in last 30 days			
Brands used in last 30 days			
Brand purchase prior to last 30 days (never, more than 1 year ago, 6 months to 1 year, 3 to 6 months, 1 to 3 months)			
Social environment			
Perceived popularity of category (use by peers)			
Perceived popularity of brands (use by peers)			
Perceived availability of category			
Perceived availability of brands			
Number of opportunities to use category in past year			
Number of times category used in past year			

Note: This table or a similar format could be used to present between-group statistical comparisons (e.g., crosstabs) across columns or multivariable analyses.

(a sample table shell without data), one type of segmentation analysis would be to examine brand equity (among socially marketed and other in-market brands) and other opportunity, ability, and motivation (OAM) determinants between total market categories.

Another segmentation analysis would be to compare socially marketed and other brands head to head. This analysis would be based on brand equity and OAM determinant measures, such as those outlined in Exhibit 4-2. Analysis would compare socially marketed and other brands in-market to

Exhibit 4-2 Sample Segmentation Table Shell: Socially Marketed Brand Equity and Determinants Versus Competitors

Statistically Significant Determinants (From Exhibit 5-7)[a]	Socially Marketed[b]	Public (Free)	Commercial
Leadership/popularity			
Brand personality			
Likelihood of promoting brand use to others			
Self-reported likelihood of purchase within 30 days			
Descriptive norms for category			
Self-efficacy to use category			
Outcome efficacy that category will be effective			
Perceived popularity of category			

[a]Demographics such as ability to pay may be used as covariates.

[b]Cells would be a statistic-capturing relationship between determinant and brand purchase/use, such as regression coefficient (R^2).

identify statistically significant differences by outcome (comparisons done analytically based on self-reported responses regarding each individual brand, not direct comparisons between brands by respondents). For example, as illustrated in Exhibit 4-2, differences can be compared between purchase of brands in-market by determinants.

Socially marketed, subsidized products such as condoms aimed at a particular socioeconomic segment of the total market—those who have enough income to buy condoms but not enough to buy commercially marketed condoms at retail prices. In a TMA, social marketing seeks to avoid "crowding out" (i.e., taking market share away from) commercial brands. Thus, it fills a critical niche, but one that must be actively managed. In market environments with multiple competitors, such as in Central America (Evans, Rivas, et al., 2012), this is a complex endeavor that requires enhanced brand equity and related data. Exhibit 4-3 illustrates a potential segmentation analysis comparing socially marketed versus other brand purchase/use by income level. It seeks to answer the question whether a socially marketed brand competes effectively within—and not beyond—its mandated market space.

Exhibit 4-3 Sample Segmentation Table Shell Comparing Brand Purchase by Socioeconomic Status Target Audience

Brand Purchase Behavior	Ability to Pay for Category		
	Too Poor to Buy Condoms	Enough Income to Buy Subsidized	Enough Income to Buy Commercial
Socially marketed brand purchase			
Commercial brand X purchase			
Free brand Y use			

Note: This table allows marketer to examine possible encroachment on commercial market and movement over time between free, subsidized, and commercial markets by socioeconomic status target audience.

The purchase segmentation may be analyzed based on OAM determinants specific to purchasers' shopping habits (where they shop, planned vs. stimulus purchase, who buys) and brand equity asset categories (see Exhibit 4-1) for specific brand purchase behavior.

Research on the Effectiveness of Brands in Changing Behavior

There are five overarching questions to be answered in evaluating the effectiveness of branding efforts:

- Was the audience exposed to the message, and what was the dosage of exposure?
- What were the audience message reactions (message perceived as credible, likable?)
- What associations were formed by the target audience with the brand?
- Is exposure/dosage associated with positive brand associations?
- Are reactions and associations related to the intended behavior change?

Brand Equity as an Outcome

Purchase cycle stages can also be used to design monitoring analyses. Exhibit 4-4 illustrates how a socially marketed brand such as PSI's Trust or Legacy's *truth* could be monitored over time.

Exhibit 4-4 Sample Table Shell: Social Marketing Brand Monitoring by Purchase Cycle Stage

Purchase Cycle Stage	Brand Monitoring by Year (% Respondents in Category)				
	2015	2016	2017	2018	2019
1. Awareness					
2. Trial					
3. Penetration					
4. Repeat					
5. Loyal					

Another application of purchase cycle stages would be to compare socially marketed and other brands at a point in time in a TMA within a country setting. Exhibit 4-5 provides an example for PSI-Romania, a highly competitive and dynamic marketplace.

Market Environment

In the sample measures and tables of the exhibits, we assume market dynamics in which market share is divided to some extent between socially marketed and other brands—a market in which there is a level of true competition. But, it is important to recognize multiple market environment scenarios in a total market (public and private brands included). In a TMA, the need for

Exhibit 4-5 Sample Table Shell: Brand Comparison of All Brands Within 2009 Romania Total Market

Purchase Cycle Stage	2009 Romania Brand Comparison (% Respondents in Category)			
	Favorite	Public (Free)	Commercial Brand 1	Commercial Brand 2
1. Awareness				
2. Trial				
3. Penetration				
4. Repeat				
5. Loyal				

Note: Assumes point-in-time data comparing brands by consumer purchase category.

and uses of brand management, brand measurement, and research efforts will differ depending on market environment (Pollard, 2014). Generally speaking, there are three types of scenarios, with variations within and between them (Evans, Longfield, et al., 2012):

- Scenario 1: There is total or near-total market share for socially marketed brands (the socially marketed brand *is* the market).
- Scenario 2: Socially marketed brands have a high percentage of public market share, with some commercial market competition (e.g., PSI's *Trust* in Kenya, which has an emerging commercial sector).
- Scenario 3: Socially marketed brands are among many competitors in a market (e.g., PSI's Favorite in Romania).[1]

The marketers' need for brand equity data differs to some extent depending on which of these scenarios, or their variants, faced. For example, in scenario 1, the social marketer needs regular brand equity data not to compete head to head but to keep the brand fresh, relevant, and appealing to the market and to expand the total number of category consumers (Evans, Longfield, et al., 2012). The goals are (1) maintenance and (2) expanding the total market size over time. Also, market conditions may change, and periodic monitoring of societal changes, behavioral epidemiology, introduction of new products, and other factors may be needed. Monitoring analyses such as those illustrated in Exhibits 4-4 and 4-5 would be most valuable.

In scenario 2, the range of competition may be limited, but the issue arises whether socially marketed brands are hitting their intended target within the total market. In this case, active brand management to compete head to head on brand equity associations (e.g., creating and maintaining a more appealing brand personality or building popularity or loyalty) are essential. Segmentation analysis such as that illustrated in Exhibit 4-1 would be informative, as would continuous monitoring.

1. It is also possible that socially marketed brands can themselves compete within a category. For example, in 2015, tobacco control in the United States has three distinct prevention brands: *truth* (Legacy), The Real Cost (US Food and Drug Administration), and Tips From Former Smokers (CDC). These tobacco use prevention brands are designed to achieve the same purpose, but they operate and hypothetically compete within the category of prevention social marketing. The research question of interest is whether this competition is synergistic, leading to less overall tobacco use, or whether the brands compete for market "share of mind." Stated another way, is higher brand equity in one of these brands correlated with higher or lower brand equity in the others?

In scenario 3, socially marketed brands may be trying to gain market share but still need to avoid encroaching on commercial brands. In this case, active brand management is even more challenging, so more frequent head-to-head brand equity comparisons may be needed. Also, to avoid encroachment on an audience intended for public or commercial brands, analyses such as in Exhibit 4-5 may be important.

Finally, the scenario in which social marketing brands compete within a category, such as substance use prevention or tobacco control, raises new challenges. The most recent version of Legacy's famous and highly successful *truth* campaign (*truth* 3.0 or Finish It; https://www.thetruth.com/) operates in a vastly altered tobacco control and tobacco industry marketplace. There were three major antismoking campaigns funded and currently operating in 2015 in the United States: Legacy's Finish It, the CDC's Tips From Former Smokers (http://www.cdc.gov/tobacco/campaign/tips/), and the Food and Drug Administration's The Real Cost (http://therealcost.betobaccofree.hhs.gov/). This represents competition within the *category* of tobacco control brands that needs to be accounted for in future research. Finally, the tobacco industry continues to sponsor its own alleged tobacco control campaigns, which have been shown to be ineffective or to encourage youth smoking (Wakefield et al., 2006). This kind of dynamic marketplace calls for brand equity research and monitoring of brand equity relative to purchase cycle stage, as suggested in Exhibit 4-5.

Measurement and Analysis Objectives

Recent brand equity studies (Evans, Holtz, & Snider, 2014) have led to standardized metrics for use across social marketing brand research. They reflect the items and scales described in Exhibit 4.5 and will be based on previously validated measures (Evans et al., 2008). These metrics will need to be customized to the content of specific brands, but the standardized metrics will serve as a reliable template for this process in each case.

Based on the enhanced brand equity and OAM determinants measures and illustrative output tables described previously, social marketers will have the opportunity to conduct more extensive analyses of product purchase and category use behaviors and their determinants. Exhibits 4-6 and 4-7 illustrate the types of outputs that can be expected for segmentation and monitoring purposes.

In addition, there are a number of specific topics and analytical objectives that can be achieved through a brand research program. Researchers will be able to answer the following types of analysis questions, and for each question, we can envision a potential analysis table:

Exhibit 4-6 Sample Table Shell: Brand Awareness of Romanian Condom Brands

Measures of Brand Awareness and Reactions	2009 Romania Brand Comparison (% Agreement With Left-Hand Column Items by Brand)			
	Favorite	Public (Free)	Commercial Brand 1	Commercial Brand 2
Brand awareness				
Awareness of each brand in category				
Aided brand promotion awareness				
Aided awareness of specific brand advertisements in target market				
Unaided (confirmed) brand promotion awareness				
Unaided (confirmed) awareness of brand advertisements in target market				

- What is the target audience's awareness of *social marketing* and other free and commercial brands?
- What are audience reactions to socially marketed and other in-market brands?
- What is the target audience brand equity in socially marketed and other brands (head-to-head comparisons on brand associations) (Exhibit 4-8)?

Brand Execution Research: Case Study on Vive Condoms From PSI–Pan American Social Marketing Organization

Background

The overall purpose of this study was to conduct brand equity research to assist in development of the new Pan American Social Marketing Organization (PASMO; http://www.asociacionpasmo.org/) Vive brand condoms and to

Exhibit 4-7 Sample Table Shell: Brand Reactions to Romanian Condom Brands

Measures of Brand Awareness and Reactions	2009 Romania Brand Comparison (% Agreement With Left Hand Column Items by Brand)			
	Favorite	Public (Free)	Commercial Brand 1	Commercial Brand 2
Reactions to brand promotion (repeat items below for multiple messages)				
Credibility of promotion				
Likability of promotion				
Promotion gave good reasons to purchase brand				
Promotion made me want to tell my friends to purchase brand				
Receptivity to promotional messages (repeat items below for multiple messages)				
Agreement with main theme or point of message				
Agreement with main attitude or belief promoted by message				

establish a baseline of brand equity between Vive brand lines and in comparison to other in-market brands (Evans, Rivas, et al., 2012). Specific objectives were to

1. Develop and test brand equity measures specific to PASMO brands;
2. Design and implement a conjoint experiment to compare brand equity dimensions between existing and new planned Vive and other in-market brands; and
3. Identify relationships between price points and brand equity characteristics (personality, etc.) between brands in the planned midtier and low tier (between Vive lines and across all in-market brands).

Exhibit 4-8 Sample Table Shell: Brand Equity Scale Scores for Kenya Condom Brands

	Categories (% Agreement by Item and Overall Scale)		
Brand Equity Scale	Trust	Public (Free)	Commercial
Brand equity scale score (and for individual constructs below)			
Price premium			
Satisfaction/loyalty			
Perceived quality			
Leadership/popularity			
Perceived value			
Brand personality			
Organizational associations			
Brand awareness			
Market share			
Market price			

This study addressed the following research questions:

1. What is the current brand equity of existing Vive line brands?
2. How does their brand equity compare to other in-market brands?
3. How do Vive brands' price points compare, and do they cluster into a low tier and midtier as planned?
4. How do Vive brands' price points compare to other in-market brands?

Strategy

Evans, Rivas, et al. (2012) designed an experiment to compare brand equity dimensions between pairs of brands. Brand equity scales will be adapted based on the PSI brand equity concept paper and draft brand equity scales. Scale items will be customized to specifics of Vive brands and local country context. It is anticipated the study will be conducted in Guatemala.

Tables 4-1 and 4-2 provide the study design and conjoint comparisons between low-tier brands. The total resulting sample size is 600 in this example.

Table 4-1 Illustrative Study Design and Conjoint Comparisons: Low-Tier Brands (Sample Size Within Each Cell; XX Indicates No Comparison, Same Brand[a])

Brands	Amore	Escudo	Original
Amore	XX	100	100
Escudo	100	XX	100
Original	100	100	XX

[a] Sample size was powered to detect 15% difference in brand equity in each conjoint comparison (Evans, Rivas, et al., 2012).

Table 4-2 provides the same comparisons for midtier brands, with a resulting sample size of 600. The total across both tiers would be 1,200. We anticipate stratifying this sample by the population target segments for Vive brands (archetypal consumers are named "Ramon" for the low-tier line and "Jose Carlos" for midtier). Thus, the sample for low-tier brand comparisons (cells) would represent the Ramon population segment and midtier comparisons the Jose Carlos segment. The comparisons represent planned conjoint analyses comparing in-market brand attributes (P.E. Green & Srinivasan, 1990).

The sample was recruited with assistance of a professional market research facility in the PASMO countries in Central America. To be eligible for the study, participants had to (1) be male and 18 to 49 years of age; (2) have used one of a predetermined list of socially marketed or commercially marketed condoms available in Guatemala in the past 3 months (brands listed in Table 4-1); (3) be present at the time of the interview and complete the informed consent;

Table 4-2 Illustrative Study Design and Conjoint Comparisons: Midtier Brands

Brands	Mass[a]	Durex
Mas	XX	300
Durex	300	XX

[a]Mas contains several subbrands (Sensitive, Rings, Retalante), and we stratified the sample for each of these subbrands and compared to the main commercial brand, Durex (100 for each subbrand in the Mas-Durex comparison).

and (4) be sexually active. Individuals not eligible to participate were those who did not meet the inclusion criteria. This study was reviewed and approved for human subjects' protection by the PSI Research Ethics Board.

Researchers randomly sampled from a list-based sample (i.e., list of eligible population segments available from the facility), recruit participants, and randomly assign those who agree to participate in the study to cells in the design. Data collection was completed using digital tablets and administered by a trained interviewer at the participants' home or a central location. The facility was responsible for delivering a complete, clean dataset to the research team.

Briefly, in the low-tier group, consumers had high brand equity in the Vive Amor line of condoms. Their brand equity compared favorably to that of competitor Escudo brands. However, Escudo had loyal users who perceived high value in their brand and were willing to pay more for it. The brand appeared to be the "premium" condom line in the low-tier category.

Users of multiple condoms—individuals who primarily use one line of condoms but sometimes use another line, such as with different kinds of partners (e.g., with a sex worker rather than a regular partner)—represented potential switchers between primary brand used. Overall, Escudo users were more likely to use another brand with a sex worker and occasional partners, and Amor users were more likely to use another brand with their regular partners than the comparison brands. Given that Escudo was also more expensive, it may be perceived as more of a "premium" or "elite" brand that is reserved for regular partners.

Overall in the midtier, Vive Colors was perceived as a highly popular brand by its consumers and was competitive with Durex Tropical, whose users were highly loyal. Vive Mas Fuerte users perceived high quality and value but did not perceive brand personality. They were also young, which may present opportunities to change their perceptions because consumer habits were not established.

One hypothesis raised by the research team was that low-tier condom brands may benefit from association with midtier condoms and their perceived higher premium status. The clear example of this potential phenomenon is the Escudo low-tier line and its potential association with the midtier Scudo Oro Retardante line. The Escudo brand generally had high premium perceptions, and users expressed willingness to pay more for it, as noted previously. This may be due to close association of product name, logo, packaging, and promotion with its midtier cousin. If true, this would represent a strategic opportunity for Vive lines to emulate this strategy by associating low-tier lines more closely with premium properties of midtier brands.

Results of the PASMO brand equity study were used in development of future brand marketing strategies in Central America (Evans, Rivas, et al., 2012). Immediate results were the relaunching of the Vive lines and changes to product offerings and pricing in line with the brand equity study findings.

Future of Social Marketing Brand Research

While there are important differences between social marketing and commercial marketing in terms of values and objectives, as discussed elsewhere (Kotler & Lee, 2008), there are important similarities. One area where the fields converge, and may be becoming more alike over time, is in the need to understand brands within categories and competition between socially marketed brands (e.g., the new situation in tobacco control) as well as competition between those brands and commercial counterparts (e.g., PSI brands competing with commercial condoms).

There is also a need to manage socially marketed brands more actively and to understand the total market in which they operate (Pollard, 2014), as well as changes in the marketplace over time and need for segmentation and monitoring research (Evans, 2013). These trends call for more research and utilization of research by brand managers (or, as some now call them, "brand advocates").

Results of brand research enable brand managers and social marketers to address larger strategic questions, such as, What are the implications of brand equity outcomes for revising audience segmentation and brand evolution? The situations in which market research will be conducted, and marketers will utilize results, will vary; this needs to be considered in deciding how to respond. For example, the market environment and dynamics discussed previously will need to be considered. However, there are some simple rules of thumb that can be used to make decisions based on results of the kinds of analyses described in this chapter.

1. *Maximize brand awareness:* For socially marketed brands and any category branding that we do, the manager should always seek very high brand awareness of over 90% among the target audience, and a continuing goal should be to maintain awareness over time.
2. *Cost-effective ad budgets:* For aided brand awareness, a manager should compile data on cost to achieve varying thresholds of awareness (50%, 60%, 70%, 80%, and more) and then conclude what is a cost-effective campaign in terms of reach and frequency. Results should be used for maintaining brand awareness and future promotional ad spending.

3. *Brand equity goals:* Managers should have specific brand positioning goals in terms of brand equity measures (e.g., loyalty, personality). Managers should always aim to achieve or exceed positioning goals based on brand equity scale scores.
4. *Subsidized brand preference:* Managers should always aim to maximize the gap between brand equity scale scores for PSI subsidized brands and free products.
5. *Brand repositioning cues:* If brand awareness is high and brand equity goals are achieved but purchase is low (lack of correlation), then consider repositioning the brand. Conduct pretesting of the repositioned brand.
6. *Category branding cues:* If brand awareness is high and brand equity goals are achieved but product use is low (not purchase, but use), then brand advertising funds may be productively invested in category branding (e.g., condom benefits, not product) to promote use.
7. *Crowding out:* If commercial market share is decreasing and brand equity scale scores exceed those of the commercial brands, then crowding out is occurring, and the manager should develop an action plan to mitigate the effect.

Additional Resources: Web Based

- For reviews and case studies of current commercial branding, see http://timcalkins.com/
- For more on branding perspectives on social marketing, see http://www.acrwebsite.org/search/view-conference-proceedings.aspx?Id=7887
- For more on brand equity measurement and analysis, see http://www.marketingresearch.org/issues-policies/best-practice/brand-equity-models-and-measurement
- For more on brand equity survey items and data collection, see https://aytm.com/blog/research-junction/brand-equity-basics-3/

References

Aaker, D. (1996). *Building Strong Brands.* New York: Simon & Schuster.

Allen, J., Vallone, D., Vargyas, E., & Healton, C.G. (2010). *The truth® Campaign: Using Countermarketing to Reduce Youth Smoking.* New York: Jones and Bartlett.

Andrade, E., Evans, W.D., Edberg, M., Cubana, I., & Cleary, S. (2015). Victor and Erika Webisodes for the Adelante Brand: An Innovative Audience Engagement Strategy for Prevention. *Journal of Health Communication*, 20(12): 1465–1472. doi:10.1080/10810730.2015.1018648

Boundless. (2015, July 21). Brand Categories. Boundless Business. Retrieved August 7, 2015, from https://www.boundless.com/business/textbooks/boundless-business-textbook/product-and-pricing-strategies-15/product-packaging-and-branding-99/brand-categories-464-5565/99/brand-categories-464-5565/

Bruce Eckman, Inc. Tobacco Document # 2045060177. Cited in: Ling, P., & Glantz, S.A. (2002). Why and How the Tobacco Industry Sells Cigarettes to Young Adults: Evidence From Industry Documents. *American Journal of Public Health*; 92(6): 908–916.

Calder, B.J. (2005). Designing Brands. In *Kellogg on Branding*, A. Tybout & T. Calkins (Eds.). Hoboken, NJ: Wiley, 27–39. Chapter 2.

Chapman, S., Ayers, J., LeTouze, O., & Renard, B. (2013). Branding and Social Marketing. In *Psychology of Branding*, W.D. Evans (Ed.). Hauppage, NY: Nova Science, 171–190. Chapter 10.

Edberg, M., Cleary, S., Andrade, E., & Leiva, R. (2010). SAFER Latinos: A Community Partnership to Address Contributing Factors for Latino Youth Violence. *Progress in Community Health Partnerships*, 4(3): 221–233.

Evans, W.D. (Ed.). (2013). *Psychology of Branding.* Hauppauge, NY: Nova Science.

Evans, W.D., Andrade, E., Villaba, R., Cubana, I., & Edberg, M. (2016). Turning the Corner: Design and Testing of the Adelante Health Promotion Brand for Latino Youth. *Social Marketing Quarterly*, 22(1): 19–33. doi:10.1177/1524500415614838

Evans, WD., Blitstein, J., Hersey, J., Renaud, J., & Yaroch, A. (2008). Systematic Review of Public Health Branding Research. *Journal of Health Communication*, 13(8): 351–360.

Evans, W.D., Blitstein, J., Vallone, D., Post, S., & Nilsen, W. (2014). Systematic Review of Health Branding: Growth of a Promising Practice. *Translational Behavioral Medicine.* DOI: 10.1007/s13142-014-0272-1.

Evans, W.D., & Hastings, G. (Eds.). (2008). *Public Health Branding: Applying Marketing for Social Change.* London: Oxford University Press.

Evans, W.D., Holtz, K., & Snider, J. (2014). Effects of the Above the Influence Brand on Adolescent Drug Use Prevention Beliefs. *Journal of Health Communication*, 19(6): 721–737. doi:10.1080/10810730.2013.837559

Evans, W.D., Longfield, K., Shekhar, N., Rabemanatsoa, A., Snider, J., & Reerink, I. (2012). Social Marketing and Condom Promotion in Madagascar: A Case Study in Brand Equity Research. In *Handbook of Global Health Communication*, R. Obregon & S. Waisboard (Eds.). New York: Wiley.

Evans, W.D., Price, S., & Blahut, S. (2005) Evaluating the truth® Brand. *Journal of Health Communication*, 10(2): 181–192.

Evans, W.D., Rivas, J., Andrade, B., Longfield, K., Lungo, S., Sinder, J., & Wallace, J. (2012). HIV Prevention Through Condom Brand Social Marketing: Case Study of Brand Equity Research in Central America. In *2011 International Communication Association Theme Book*, S. Jones (Ed.). New York: Hampton Press; Chapter 13.

Evans, W.D., Taruberekera, N., Longfield, K., & Snider, J. (2011). Brand Equity and Willingness to Pay for Condoms in Zimbabwe. *BMC Reproductive Health*, 8: 29. doi:10.1186/1742-4755-8-29

Farrelly, M.C., Davis, K.C., Haviland, M.L., Messeri, P., & Healton, C.G. (2005). Evidence of a Dose-Response Relationship Between "truth" Antismoking Ads and Youth Smoking. *American Journal of Public Health*, 95(3): 425–431.

Green, L.W., & Mercer, S.L. (2002). PRECEDE-PROCEED Model. In *Encyclopedia of Public Health*, L. Breslow, B.D. Goldstein, L.W. Green, D.W. Keck, J.M. Last, & J.M. McGinnis (Eds.). Retrieved August 31, 2015, from http://www.encyclopedia.com/doc/1G2-3404000675.html

Green, P.E., & Srinivasan V. (1990). Conjoint Analysis in Marketing: New Developments With Implications for Research and Practice. *Journal of Marketing*, 54: 3–19.

Gregson, S., Gonese, E., Hallett, T.B., et al. (2010). Evidence from a comprehensive epidemiological review. *International Journal of Epidemiology*, doi:10.1093/ije/dyq055 [Epub 20 April 2010].

Hornik, R. (2002). *Public Health Communication: Evidence for Behavior Change*. Mahwah, NJ: Erlbaum.

Keller, K.L. (2000, January–February). The Brand Report Card. *Harvard Business Review on Marketing*.

Kernis, M.H. (1983). Need for Uniqueness, Self-Schemas, and Thought as Moderators of the False-Consensus Effect. *Journal of Experimental Social Psychology*, 20(4): 350–362.

Kotler, P., & Lee, N. (2008). *Social Marketing: Influencing Behaviors for Good* (3rd ed.). Los Angeles: Sage Publications.

Ndiaye, K., & Evans, W.D. (2014). Growth of the Total Market Approach in Developing Countries. *Cases in Public Health Communication & Marketing*, 8(Suppl 1): S1–S3.

Pollard, R. (2014). Total Market Approaches to the Social Marketing of Health Services and Commodities in Low-Income Countries. *Cases in Public Health Communication & Marketing*, 8(Suppl 1): S4–S18.

Schindler, R.M. (1992, December). The Real Lesson of New Coke: The Value of Focus Groups for Predicting the Effects of Social Influence. *Marketing Research*, 22–27.

Schultz, D., & Schultz, H. (2005). Measuring Brand Value. In *Kellogg on Branding*, A. Tybout & T. Calkins (Eds.). Hoboken, NJ: Wiley.

Tybout, A., & Sternthal, B. (2005). Brand Positioning. In *Kellogg on Branding*, A. Tybout & T. Calkins (Eds.). New York: Wiley.

Wakefield, M., Terry-McElrath, Y., Emery, S., Saffer, H., Chaloupka, F.J., Szczypka, G., Flay, B., O'Malley, P.M., & Johnston, L.D. (2006). Effect of Televised, Tobacco Company–Funded Smoking Prevention Advertising on Youth Smoking-Related Beliefs, Intentions, and Behavior. *American Journal of Public Health*, 96(12): 2154–2160. http://doi.org/10.2105/AJPH.2005.083352

Zimbabwe Ministry of Health and Child Welfare. Zimbabwe National HIV and AIDS Estimates 2009. Harare: Zimbabwe Ministry of Health and Child Welfare.

5

Efficacy and Message Testing Methods for Social Marketing Research

W. Douglas Evans

Summary Points

- Social marketing outcomes research has historically focused on effectiveness studies and ignored efficacy research.
- Efficacy research is important because it answers questions about message properties and intensity and provides context for future effectiveness studies.
- Social marketing efficacy research is growing due to new technologies and can learn from commercial marketing research methods.
- In an increasingly competitive marketing environment, with multiple messages, channels, and stimuli, more social marketing efficacy research is needed.

Introduction

Consider the case of a busy researcher who conducts formative research and evaluations of social marketing campaigns on a wide variety of subjects, including health and social change programs. The researcher, Angelika, works closely with program staff and campaign designers to gain insight into audiences and evaluate whether campaigns are effective in promoting behaviors that benefit those audiences. Why should this social marketing researcher use efficacy research methods?

One question that may face Angelika and her colleagues is whether a campaign strategy, such as specific messages promoting the use of condoms among a high-risk audience, may have been developed based on formative research, such as in-depth interviews and focus groups that the researcher and the team conducted. But, before the campaign team promotes these messages in a campaign, places ads using the messages in different locations and media channels, and applies price and product strategies using the messages, the question arises: Do these messages produce any measurable effects under controlled conditions? In other words, the researcher may want confirmation that the message design is efficacious before going to the effort and expense of implementing the message in a campaign and evaluating effectiveness. This chapter explores methods for conducting this stage of social marketing research, which represents the step between formative research and program evaluation discussed in the research continuum concept introduced in Chapter 1.

Background

As discussed in previous chapters and elsewhere, social marketing campaigns are effective in changing health behavior (Snyder & Hamilton, 2002; Snyder & LaCroix, 2013; Evans, 2006). Evaluating the effectiveness of social marketing efforts is common, but relatively few rigorous efficacy studies have been conducted on behavior change programs that use social marketing. This chapter investigates the potential for enhanced efficacy research as part of a broad social marketing research agenda.

An efficacy study is designed to evaluate the effects of an intervention under optimum conditions, whereas an effectiveness study evaluates the effects of an intervention under real-world conditions (Flay, 1986). In medical research, efficacy studies are regarded as necessary in the development of a new drug, treatment, or technology (Flay, 1986). As a result, when medical researchers conduct an effectiveness study, it is only after the intervention has been shown to be efficacious.

In contrast, in social marketing evaluations, effectiveness studies are often conducted without previously determining whether the campaign messages are truly efficacious (Evans, Uhrig, et al., 2009). Rather, the messages are tested using qualitative, formative research methods, implemented in the campaign, and then evaluated as part of an effectiveness study without experimentally demonstrating that the messages are efficacious. Without first determining the efficacy of the campaign messages, results of effectiveness studies can be more difficult to interpret (Flay, 1986). For example, if a campaign produces negative or null results, is the reason because the campaign was implemented in an ineffective way or because the campaign messages were not efficacious from the beginning? If efficacy was not established prior to the effectiveness study, this question cannot be answered.

Efficacy studies permit researchers to assess response to social marketing strategies within each of the 4Ps (place, price, product, and promotion) of marketing under controlled conditions. While much of the following discussion addresses message efficacy testing (promotion P), pricing, product, and placement strategies can equally be tested using experimental methods prior to campaign implementation. Key design features of efficacy studies include the ability to randomly assign participants to treatment and control conditions and the researcher having control over treatment condition participants' exposure to campaign messages (see Table 5-1). These features lead to high internal validity, facilitating much stronger causal inferences than typically possible in effectiveness studies. On the other hand, efficacy studies typically have lower external validity than do effectiveness studies. Also, they do not allow researchers to make conclusions about the effectiveness of the campaign messages under real-world conditions or enable us to achieve population-based

Table 5-1 Key Design Features and Benefits of Efficacy Versus Effectiveness Studies

Feature	Efficacy Study	Effectiveness Study
Randomize participants	Yes	No
Manipulate intervention: Messages (promotion), channels (placement), price, product	Yes	No
Measure campaign exposure	No	Yes
Longitudinal tracking	Yes	Yes, with limitations
Internal validity	Higher	Lower
Measure dose-response	Yes	Yes, with limitations
External validity	Lower	Higher
Cost	Lower	Higher

Source: Adapted from Evans, W.D., Uhrig, J., Davis, K., & McCormack, L. (2009). Efficacy Methods to Evaluate Health Communication and Marketing Campaigns. *Journal of Health Communication*, 14(3): 244–254.

estimates of actual awareness of or exposure to campaign messages that are possible with effectiveness studies.

Effectiveness studies are typically conducted in the field as a campaign is running: They are linked to the launch of the campaign, when a baseline data collection would be taken with follow-ups to measure implementation and outcomes, as shown in the research continuum model in Chapter 1 of this volume. As a result, effectiveness designs often do not allow for randomization of participants into treatment and control conditions or the use of other experimental methods, such as case-control, or enable the researcher to manipulate participants' exposure to campaign messages. These design features lead to lower internal validity and more difficulty in attributing causal links to the campaign. However, effectiveness designs do provide for higher external validity, the ability to derive conclusions about the effectiveness of the campaign messages under real-world conditions, and the ability to determine estimates of campaign awareness and exposure.

What We Can Learn From Commercial Marketing Research

Marketing researchers in the commercial sector have long used both quantitative and qualitative methods for "copy testing" or "pretesting" to improve the efficacy of advertising. Copy testing is a form of customized research that predicts in-market performance of an ad before it airs; it analyzes audience levels of attention, brand linkage, motivation, entertainment, and communication, as well as breaks down the ad's flow of attention and flow of emotion. Pretesting is also used on ads still in rough (ripomatic or animatic) form (Young, 2005).

Commercial marketing researchers use a variety of methods to test copy, including focus groups, in-depth interviews, and other projective tests. The last include personality tests designed to let a person respond to ambiguous stimuli to reveal hidden emotions, such as how they feel about an offered product or service (Cordón, 2005). But, commercial marketing researchers also make extensive use of experimental methods to test consumer reactions to new and redesigned products and services. Experiments are conducted in controlled environments, such as a market research facility or online setting, to try to control spurious factors (e.g., environmental noise), then they manipulate at least one of the variables in the product or service, such as packaging, color, brand logo placement, and so on. Examples of such experiments include purchase laboratories and test markets.

Case Study of a Commercial Purchase Laboratory Experiment

Consider the following example drawn from the Ofcom (English telecommunications regulator) on consumer behavior related to telephone call pricing (Ofcom, 2010). This example is a controlled laboratory experiment that is framed. That is, participants in the experiment are university students, and they interact in a controlled environment in which the only features that vary in the experiment are the different ways call cost information is revealed to participants: a mobile phone environment and a landline environment. Participants know they are making phone calls, but they do not actually use a handset; instead, they interact with computer screens, electing to make calls or searching for price information given the different information setups. Ofcom requested that four different methods of providing price information to consumers were tested in the experiment. The four price revelation methods were:

- precall announcements with the exact price of the call announced to the caller;
- precall announcements with the maximum price the call may cost announced;
- price information on the monthly bill in form of a list detailing all call charges for all telephone numbers such that, in principle, consumers have easy access to all relevant price information; and
- telephone short codes such that consumers can learn the costs of different calls easily at greatly reduced costs.

The performances of these interventions in terms of consumer welfare were compared using two different environments, landline and mobile phone environments. This is because when using a mobile phone it is more difficult for consumers to search and find price information, and price dispersion is much bigger, creating greater risks. In addition to the interventions, Ofcom wanted to learn about consumer behavior given the current systems to provide access to price information. Specifically, do consumers:

- Actively seek price information?
- Make different decisions depending on whether they know the cost of a call?
- Learn from bill shock, that is, from seeing high-cost telephone calls on their telephone bill?

Based on this experiment, Ofcom concluded that precall announcements with the exact price of the call and the possibility to opt out were the best-performing option in both the landline and mobile phone environments (Ofcom, 2010). Consumers learned prices effectively and then typically switched announcements off.

The Need for Efficacy Message Testing Research

In social marketing research, qualitative methods have predominated for formative research and pretesting. There are likely a few major reasons for this. First, social marketing campaigns typically run on shorter timelines than major product and service brand campaigns. Major commercial marketers such as Coke, McDonald's, and Nike essentially run campaigns continuously, making modifications and launching new messages and promotions through the product development cycle (Evans & Hastings, 2008). This puts a premium on rigorous copy testing and offers numerous opportunities.

Second, social marketing budgets are inevitably much smaller than those of commercial marketers. Historically, quantitative copy testing would have been prohibitively expensive for most campaigns, requiring sizable samples to be recruited and shown messages in some kind of controlled setting such as a market research facility. Repeat contacts to measure results of copy testing on behavior over time would increase costs.

Third, the value of quantitative copy testing to commercial marketers, and the importance of this area of research, had not been entirely clear to the public health and social marketing communities because of the proprietary nature of the data. While marketing journals include many experimental studies, the true value of copy testing for marketing decision-making seldom reached the literature. Commercial enterprises conduct market research for their own internal purposes and generally do not publish it as it may contain trade secrets or confidential information used in marketing decision-making.

This situation changed to some extent beginning in the 1990s with the discovery of tobacco industry documents in the Master Settlement Agreement in the United States and continued in the 2000s with numerous other disclosures of industry marketing practices and research base in the pharmaceutical, food, and other industries (Evans & McCormack, 2008; Steinman et al., 2006; Schlosser, 2012). The importance of quantitative marketing research, including copy testing experiments, has become more salient in light of these developments. At the same time, the rise of widespread Internet use and the development of online consumer panels greatly reduced costs of conducting such research, opening the door to use of quantitative copy testing methods by social marketers. The following sections explore methods and case studies for applying these experimental consumer research methods in the health and social sectors.

Efficacy Methods and Metrics

Much of the outcomes research in social marketing, especially mass media, utilizes effectiveness designs conducted in real time in the media markets or communities in which messages are delivered. For example, the national evaluation of American Legacy Foundation's *truth*® campaign was based on a quasi-experimental design in which campaign exposure was measured both from environmental measures (gross rating points, or GRPs, derived from designated market areas, or DMAs) and self-reported "confirmed awareness" of campaign ads. Based on a nationally representative sample of students aged 12–18, this study found that smoking prevalence declined from 25.3% to 18.0%, and that the *truth* campaign was associated with approximately 22% of that decline (Farrelly et al., 2005).

In substance abuse, the Office of National Drug Control Policy (ONDCP) has developed a large-scale, multichannel, antidrug campaign delivered nationwide though print, radio, television, and Internet sources. The ONDCP evaluation (Hornik & Yanovitsky, 2003) was also based on a repeated cross-sectional, quasi-experimental design that collected data from a nationally representative sample of adults and youth in DMAs across the United States.

In physical activity, the VERB: It's What You Do campaign used a media-tracking methodology, the VERB Continuous Tracking Survey (VCTS), to monitor the performance of the VERB brand and advertising (Huhman, Price, & Potter, 2008). To evaluate campaign outcomes, cohorts of tweens and parents were interviewed annually via a telephone survey (Youth Media Campaign Longitudinal Survey). Starting at baseline in 2002, the cohort was reinterviewed in 2004, and a third, cross-sectional sample was surveyed in 2006. Each cohort consisted of a nationally representative sample of tweens to enable generalizability to the nation as a whole. Propensity scoring was used to control for confounding influences. The outcomes were analyzed for dose-response effects (i.e., whether higher levels of awareness led to stronger effects) and overall awareness of VERB among all tweens in the United States (Potter et al., 2008).

These represent large, well-funded campaigns with strong outcome evaluations in place. But, suppose our social marketing researcher, Angelika, were leading a research team collaborating with the designers of any of these campaigns. After completion of formative research, the question may arise: Are our strategies for campaign messaging and implementation likely to be effective when delivered in the real world? With substantial investments in advertising and promotion, placement, pricing (making healthy behavioral choices easier), and product (the behaviors themselves) development, should not Angelika investigate these strategies in a controlled, relatively low-cost environment first, as a commercial marketer would?

In other instances, large-scale effectiveness evaluations are impractical or impossible, limiting opportunities to advance the state of social marketing research and the knowledge base on effective campaign strategies, messages, and channels. In the case of paid media campaigns, the reasons for such limitations include limited funds, and thus limited reach, to generate sufficient levels of exposure to detect campaign effects using population survey methodologies. There may also be logistical constraints, such as campaign implementation timelines that preclude collection of precampaign survey data.

In the case of unpaid media, or public service announcements (PSAs), there are additional limitations in that campaign exposure in any given DMA is typically low. For example, television PSAs typically air at times when audiences are small (e.g., late at night or on midweek afternoons). Thus, relatively few individuals in a given DMA receive the message during a set period of time, and it is therefore difficult to detect campaign effects, resulting in low statistical power.

There is limited published research on the reliability and validity of health marketing measures and methods tested in a controlled environment (i.e., laboratory-type setting), testing of health messages, and development of refined messages and materials in controlled settings—so-called forced exposure tests. Much of this research comes from the commercial product literature and is often proprietary and not published.

There are reasons why commercial firms devote substantial resources to efficacy research on advertising campaigns before a single media spot is purchased. The high cost of implementing the campaign, let alone the cost of designing the product to be advertised, necessitates anticipating as many factors that might come into play as possible and conducting research to determine how, if at all, they will affect sales. While few companies release data that indicate they wasted money on poor advertising, examples of failed attempts are easy to find. Ford's marketing of the Nova automobile (meaning "no va" or "no go" in Spanish) is a classic example of failure to conduct adequate research. Public health, because it often has far less to spend on social marketing campaigns, must be just as careful in its investigations.

Efficacy Message Testing Measures

Social marketing researchers often choose to use shorter-term measures of responses to public health campaigns that are predictive of longer-term behavioral changes, particularly those linked to well-established and time-tested behavior change theory (e.g., the theory of planned behavior; Fishbein & Ajzen, 2010). These include recall and recognition of messages, appraisals of ad appeal, ad processing, perceived efficacy, attitudinal correlates of campaign-targeted behaviors, behavioral intentions, and behavior change (Southwell et al., 2002; Niederdeppe et al., 2007; Donohew, Lorch, & Palmgreen, 1998). These measures underlie a social process of diffusion that occurs as individuals are exposed to health marketing messages and gain new information, process the information, form attitudes and intentions related to the information, and finally implement new behaviors promoted in the message (McGuire, 1981).

In addition, short-term, immediate ad reactions borrowed from commercial advertising (e.g., likability, credibility) have been employed as outcome measures (e.g., Dillard & Peck, 2001; Biener et al., 2004). These measures are limited, however, in that they are not tied to theory-driven models of persuasion and have not been adequately validated as reliable predictors of downstream behavioral precursors (at least in social marketing contexts).

Table 5-2 illustrates typical measures used in social marketing efficacy and effectiveness evaluation designs. Social marketing efficacy and effectiveness studies use similar measures in terms of message reactions, moderators, and mediators of behavior change. Major differences between the two design approaches arise in that efficacy studies assume, and control the conditions of, exposure to messages. Audience members are shown messages (e.g., antismoking advertisements) in a defined protocol as part of the experiment. In effectiveness studies, exposure must be measured, either through self-reported recall and recognition or through environmental measures such as GRPs or total rating points (TRPs) that capture media market estimates of population exposure to a message (Evans, Blitstein, & Hersey, 2008).

As in other fields of health research, social marketing efficacy studies typically have higher internal validity and lower external validity, while effectiveness studies have the reverse characteristics. The main differences in validity stem from the researcher's ability to (1) control the conditions of message

Table 5-2 Measures of Efficacy and Effectiveness Used in Social Marketing Studies

Measures	Efficacy	Effectiveness
Recall and recognition	Yes	Yes, but requires self-reported exposure
Reactions to message targeting, tailoring, and specific ad executions	Yes	Yes
Behavioral precursors (e.g., attitudes, beliefs, intentions) compared across exposed and unexposed populations	Yes	Possible, but often not done
Behavior change compared across exposed and unexposed populations	Yes	Possible, but rarely done
Paid media campaign implementation (e.g., GRPs, TRPs)	No	Yes
Unpaid media campaign implementation (e.g., self-report)	No	Possible, but rarely done
Moderators of behavior change	Yes	Yes
Mediators and other constructs from communication and behavior change theory	Yes	Yes, with limitations

Source: Evans, W.D., Uhrig, J., Davis, K., & McCormack, L. (2009). Efficacy Methods to Evaluate Health Communication and Marketing Campaigns. *Journal of Health Communication*, 14(3): 244–254.

exposure and (2) measure exposure under the conditions in which audiences are likely to encounter messages when a campaign is implemented.

The ultimate goal of social marketing campaigns is to promote positive changes in health behaviors. Theories of behavior change, such as the integrated model of behavior change (Fishbein & Yzer, 2003), predict that changes in behavior in the context of social marketing campaigns occur through a process whereby individuals are first exposed to a health message; react to the message; form attitudes, beliefs, and intentions around that message; and finally act on the information provided in the message by changing behavior. Unfortunately, research on message effectiveness that employs audience response methodologies says little about the effects of exposure to social marketing messages on campaign-targeted behaviors.

For example, experimental studies with well-controlled treatment conditions offer no evidence on whether exposure to smoking cessation ads generates an increase in quit attempts among current smokers due to their focus on immediate cognitive outcomes. This gap in the current body of research is due largely to the absence of follow-up components in studies that use audience response methodologies with experimental treatment and control conditions. This gap is particularly glaring in light of the fact that follow-up components have long been commonplace in commercial advertising research, on which social marketing seeks to build (Evans & Hastings, 2008; Terry-McElrath et al., 2005).

Case Studies of Efficacy Message Testing Research

We have just discussed the basic methods for efficacy research and the purposes and motivations social and health researchers may have to use these methods. As in the commercial sector, efficacy methods can be used in the social and health sectors to test messages, product offerings (where these may be behaviors), and campaign strategies prior to implementation. This can provide valuable evidence that can guide future campaign decisions and provide information for use by others in the field. It solves many problems in obtaining experimental data present in real-world effectiveness evaluations.

Now, let us discuss several case examples of such research and how it can be conducted. The evolution and increasing sophistication of consumer research platforms is a major development in the field. The availability of online consumer research options and associated reductions in cost of these methods has enabled social and health researchers to utilize previously difficult and prohibitively expensive efficacy testing options.

Consumer research panels have existed for decades and have long been widely used in commercial market research. For example, the DDB Needham Lifestyle, the largest consumer survey in the United States, with a sampling frame of over 500,000 panelists (enrolled members who regularly complete surveys), and has existed since 1975. The Lifestyle survey is conducted annually and consists of about 300–400 questions that tap into constructs such as perceived personality traits; media habits (TV, radio, newspapers, and magazines); shopping habits; political beliefs in general; religiosity; civic involvement; sensation-seeking scales; general life satisfaction; demographics, including family structure; and several other lifestyle type questions (Putnam, 2001).

Another example is the Healthstyles Survey (http://www.cdc.gov/healthcommunication/toolstemplates/entertainmented/healthstylessurvey.html), which draws a subsample from the annual Needham Lifestyle sampling frame, and conducts additional Lifestyle surveys for underrepresented (minority) populations, along with health-relevant data from the entire sample, and then merges the two data sets. Healthstyles supplements Lifestyle information with data on health-promoting and disease-preventing behaviors, risk behaviors, and health-related lifestyle factors, including smoking, nutrition, physical activity, injuries, and reproductive health behaviors. The estimated sample each year is 3,000. The sample is weighted on seven demographic variables to be representative of the US population (Centers for Disease Control and Prevention [CDC], 2014).

Other examples include the AC Nielsen media and consumer survey, polling by organizations such as Harris and Gallup, and most recently, online consumer panels (Evans, Uhrig, et al., 2009). The rest of this section focuses on the development of consumer panels and their implications for social marketing efficacy research.

Online Consumer Panels and Efficacy Research

The shift from mail and telephone-based consumer research, such as Lifestyle and polling operations, has been swift and stark. Historically, consumer research surveys were less frequent, due to technology constraints, and tracked a somewhat limited range of topics, including product purchase, lifestyle, and media use. More recent online surveys are more frequent and collect similar data but have expanded to cover a range of new and social media use and social and health behaviors. They also include more customized sampling and segmentation of samples due to the opportunities afforded by the Internet to capture extensive panelist data and quickly targeted populations with specific data collection instruments. For example, large consumer panels such as e-Rewards have millions of panelists in the United States and can target surveys based on specific consumer behaviors (e.g., purchase of a specific make of car in the past year), health behaviors (e.g., self-reported asthma patients), and life stage combined with other sociodemographic factors (e.g., parents under 45 years of age with at least two young children living in major metropolitan areas). The ability to target samples in this way creates many new opportunities for social marketing research, especially quantitative copy testing and efficacy studies.

The literature on social marketing suggests opportunities to build the knowledge base through more targeted and effective use of efficacy study designs. Opportunities for efficacy research are greater now with the advent of new media marketing research tools, such as Web-based panels. Two major examples that often host academic and public sector–oriented studies are Knowledge Networks (http://www.gfk.com/products-a-z/knowledgepanelr-north-america/), which offers a probability-based sample, and Harris Interactive (http://www.harrisinteractive.com), which offers access to a large sample of individuals who have "opted in" to their panel. There are also numerous panels, such as e-Rewards (http://www.erewards.com) and Mysurvey (https://www.mysurvey.com), that to date have been used primarily for commercial market research purposes. Most available panels make efforts to maintain samples that closely resemble the US population, and many are developing specialized panels, such as healthcare provider panels or Latino panels. A key feature of conducting an efficacy study online is the ability to expose participants to multimedia interventions via their personal computers. Each of these panels provides opportunities to show multimedia to respondents and to select a sample based on specific target audience characteristics. These features facilitate multifactorial designs (e.g., exposure × time) to test the efficacy of messages and specific advertising executions. At the same time, there are trade-offs in choosing an online efficacy approach, such as lower external validity (e.g., multimedia not experienced in a natural setting) but significant design advantages.

Case Study of the Parents Speak Up National Campaign

The Parents Speak Up National Campaign (PSUNC) ran in the US from 2007–2012 and was designed to promote parent-child communication about sexual activity, as a means to delay sexual debut among adolescents. PSUNC was a US national multimedia campaign that has as its major theme the message that parents should talk "early and often" to their preadolescent and adolescent children aged 10–14 years about delaying the onset of sexual activity. Its purpose was to increase parent-child communication as a proximal behavioral outcome leading to delayed onset of sexual activity. The strategy of aiming messages promoting parent-child communication at this target audience has been used on a smaller scale in school- and community-based interventions, but never on a national scale in a mass communication campaign. The campaign was publicly released in June 2007.

Paid and unpaid advertisements were used by PSUNC and were designed for a general audience of parents and targeted versions of the general ads were used for African American, Hispanic, and Native American audiences. The unpaid ad campaign launched in summer 2007, with a spot called

"Talk to Me" that featured preadolescent children encouraging their parents to talk to them about sex and waiting to become sexually active. In the winter and spring of 2008, the campaign continued with a second spot called "Muffinhead," which sought to allay parents' fears about talking to their child, and this spot aired as a paid ad on cable channels nationwide. The campaign also utilized outdoor advertising (billboards), bus media, posters, Web banners, and media kits.

PSUNC Efficacy Study Using Knowledge Networks

As campaign plans for the PSUNC developed, it became clear that a rigorous effectiveness evaluation would be difficult. This is because the campaign initially relied on unpaid ads (and only later adopted paid advertising), which tend to have very low reach and to generate low audience awareness during the limited period of time available for evaluation. Such campaigns can have high reach and a major impact over long periods of time (as illustrated by widespread recognition of campaigns and characters such as Smokey the Bear or McGruff the Crime Dog after many years), but evaluations conducted in a limited period, or without a very large sample size, would not likely detect appreciable levels of awareness or behavioral effects.

In response, evaluators adopted an efficacy study design to evaluate under controlled conditions the PSUNC and its messages (Figure 5-1). This represented the best possible opportunity to maximize the quality of the design and answer key evaluation questions. The approach entailed selecting a random sample of parents and collecting baseline data on their knowledge, attitudes, beliefs, intentions, and behaviors related to parent-child communication about abstinence and the PSUNC's central message to delay the onset of sexual activity. This study represents an "efficacy" methodology in that parents would be divided into treatment and control conditions where parents in the treatment conditions would be exposed to the campaign spots (TV, radio, print, as appropriate) through delivery over the Internet on a home computer, a form of "forced exposure" within the confines of the experiment Thus, their exposure would occur under controlled conditions, without the distractions and variability of potential exposure in the real world.

The resulting PSUNC evaluation study was a randomized controlled trial (RCT) of parents of children aged 10 to 14, the campaign's target audience. Mothers and fathers drawn from the Knowledge Networks panel were randomly assigned to control, treatment (exposure to a core set of PSUNC messages), and treatment plus booster (core plus additional PSUNC messages)

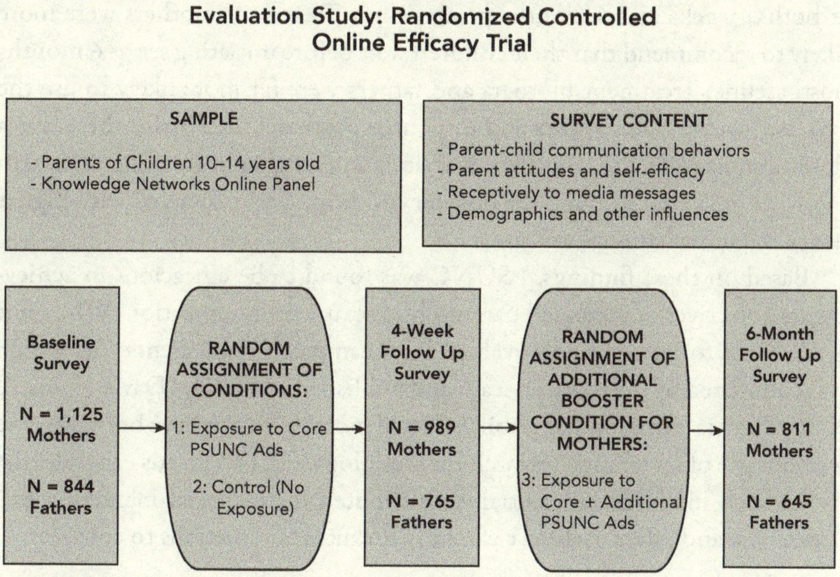

FIGURE 5-1 PSUNC study design.
Source: Evans, W.D., Davis, K.C., Silber-Ashley, O., Blitstein, J., Koo, H., & Zhang, Y. (2009). Efficacy of Abstinence Promotion Media Messages: Findings From an Online Randomized Trial. *Journal of Adolescent Health*, 45(4):409–417.

conditions and surveyed at baseline (prior to message exposure) and at four follow-up time points: 4 weeks, 6 months, 12 months, and 18 months after baseline. Table 5-3 summarizes the study sample.

Evans, Uhrig, et al. (2009) reported preliminary results based on the first three waves of survey data from a five-wave, randomized controlled trial to test the efficacy of PSUNC messages in changing parent's sexual communication behaviors. This study found that treatment fathers were more likely than control fathers to initiate conversations about sex at 4 weeks postbaseline and were more likely to recommend that their children wait before initiating sex

Table 5-3 PSUNC Study Design Summary (Sample Sizes in Each Cell)

	Baseline		4-Week Follow-Up		6-Month Follow-Up	
Study condition	Mothers	Fathers	Mothers	Fathers	Mothers	Fathers
Control	349	340	326	321	270	280
Core treatment	776	504	663	444	266	365
Booster Treatment	—	—	—	—	275	—

at both 4 weeks and 6 months postbaseline. Treatment mothers were more likely to recommend that their children wait before initiating sex at 6 months postbaseline. Treatment mothers and fathers were far more likely to use the PSUNC website at 4 weeks and 6 months postbaseline. Finally, there was a dose-response effect for mothers' website use: A higher dose of the campaign messages delivered through the booster condition was associated with higher use of the informational website.

Based on these findings, PSUNC was found to be efficacious in achieving its objectives of increased parent-child sexual communication. While not a substitute for effectiveness evaluation of campaign implementation, which was conducted by the research team and published separately (Davis, Evans, & Kamyab, 2012), this level of published evidence would not have been possible without use of an efficacy research methodology. Clearly, in this example, the use of such methods substantially contributed to the social marketing evidence base and offers useful a case study for future evaluations to consider.

Case Study: Testing Messages on Adherence to Preventive Health Services Guidelines

With the enhanced role of US Preventive Services Task Force (USPSTF; http://www.uspreventiveservicestaskforce.org/) recommendations in healthcare reform and insurance benefit design following the US Affordable Care Act (ACA, often called "Obamacare"), it is essential that patients understand how these evidence-based guidelines are developed. It is also important that patients and providers be able to communicate effectively about USPSTF recommendations. This is especially critical when, in recommending *against* some services, the guidelines create confusion and uncertainty regarding personal behavioral choices. Uncertainty regarding the recommendations and the process that created them is related to both over- and underuse of preventive services. Thus, patient-centered, informed preventive care requires an understanding of the purpose, process, and results of evidence-based guidelines and how to interpret and use them for personal care decisions.

The overall purpose of this message testing study was to develop and pilot test communication frames/messages for patients regarding the USPSTF process and recommendations through a novel, Internet-based experiment with adults. The study was divided into two parts: (1) general testing of the USPSTF and its process for creating guidelines and (2) experimenting to test specific preventive services recommendations. The part 1 objective was to determine what keywords and concepts affect positive and negative reactions and promote understanding of USPSTF guidelines in the general US adult population. For part 2, the objective was to test which message frames about specific guidelines best encourage people to follow them in their own health care.

Study part 1: Researchers recruited a sample of approximately 2,400 respondents currently enrolled on the GfK (formerly Knowledge Networks, now GfK Knowledge Panel) platform. The study objective was to recruit equal numbers of men and women and include only noninstitutionalized adults living in the United States who were 21 years of age and older. This included an oversample of people age 40–74 years of age to provide an adequate sample for part 2 of the study. Informed consent, based on a protocol approved by the George Washington University institutional review board protocol, was conducted through the GfK website prior to data collection.

After consent, all individuals in the sample were invited to complete an approximately 10-minute questionnaire that presented two definitional statements (on preventive care and guidelines) and then a series of nine statements that described the USPSTF guidelines and their purposes, uses, and potential role in the respondent's healthcare. For the two definitions, the respondent was asked to use a Web-based highlighter tool with their mouse to identify words and phrases in each definition that (1) made them more in agreement that guidelines should be followed in making patient healthcare decisions, (2) made them less in agreement that guidelines should be followed, or (3) they found confusing.

The nine statements were based on findings from a previous study that was part of the overall project (Lantz et al., 2015). The order of the statement was randomly assigned. After each statement, respondents were asked a set of questions regarding (1) importance of USPSTF; (2) positive/negative feelings; (3) trust in USPSTF and its recommendations; (4) relevance to self or family; (5) how likely they were to consider USPSTF guidelines; and (6) how likely they were to follow USPSTF guidelines when making decisions about preventive services.

Study part 2: Immediately after completing the part 1 questionnaire, during the same GfK online session, participants were randomly assigned to one of six message testing experimental conditions for specific guidelines: The Papanicolaou (Pap) test and PSA preventive screenings. Following recent research on differences in response to gain- and loss-framed messages, we developed messages based on content about the individual benefits/consequences of following/not following the specific guidelines.

Within each condition, participants then completed an approximately 15-minute survey in which they reviewed a series of approximately four specific vignettes about their own life situation and then within the vignette a message framed in terms of gain, loss, or a balance of gain and loss as a result of following or not following the specific guideline, either Pap test or PSA. The vignettes were randomly assigned to each participant and then messages were presented in a randomly assigned sequence. The questionnaire included the same word/phrase highlighting exercise as in part 1. It also included questions about knowledge, attitudes, and beliefs about the individual's own health, healthcare, and self-efficacy (Are they able to follow the guidelines?) and outcome expectations (whether they would be better off) related following the specific guideline in that study condition. Finally, for each message frame presented, respondents were asked if they would actually follow the guideline in deciding about their own healthcare given the vignette presented. Table 5-4 depicts the 2 × 3 study design and shows the total sample sizes by condition.

Eight weeks after the baseline assessment, participants were invited to log in to the GfK survey web page again and complete a follow-up survey. The follow-up contained the same questions and again randomly presented the sequence of vignettes/message frames. The survey included additional questions asking whether the respondent had searched online, or through other sources, for additional information about the USPSTF, for information about specific guidelines, and whether they had taken other actions, such as speaking to their doctor about USPSTF or specific guidelines, conditioned on whether the respondent had the opportunity to do so.

Overall, the study confirmed previous findings (Lantz et al., 2015) indicating low levels of knowledge and understanding of guidelines in the general public. Lower knowledge and understanding were associated with lower intentions to follow guidelines in clinical care. The study also found that gain-framed messages were most highly associated with intention to follow prostate cancer screening guidelines in men and HPV (human papilloma virus) guidelines in women (Evans et al., 2015).

Mixed-effect regression models revealed that higher receptivity to messages was associated with greater intentions to seek cancer information and to speak to a doctor about PSA screening and the Pap test (Evans et al., 2015). The loss frame condition was associated with a higher intention to speak to friends and family about PSA screening and Pap. Finally, researchers found that perceived importance and personal understanding of guidelines predicted intentions to seek more information about them.

Table 5-4 Message Testing Design

Message Frame	Guidelines Tested (Sample Sizes per Condition)			
	Pap Test (Pretest)	PSA (Pretest)	Pap Test (Posttest)	PSA (Posttest)
Gain	319	417	243	334
Loss	368	393	259	311
Both (balancing gain and loss)	413	411	287	296

Overall, this efficacy study was significant in that it identified messages that appear promising to increase knowledge and understanding about the USPSTF and the importance of following guidelines. While more research is needed, this study helps to build the evidence base on how best to inform and engage consumers and how best to promote informed decision-making about preventive services.

Brand Efficacy Testing

Commercial marketers routinely conduct experimental studies in the process of developing, testing, and marketing product and service brands. In turn, social marketers have recently begun to expand work in experimental studies. One example of experimental efficacy research is in the area of brands and comparison of socially marketed product brands. Large global health organizations and donor agencies have a particular interest in increasing sales of socially marketed condoms, bed nets, and similar health promotion and prevention products (Willey et al., 2012). But, little is known about consumer preferences and the determinants of specific product brand and category (groups of branded products) choice.

There are several types of efficacy research on socially marketed products that can contribute to knowledge in the field. First, there is experimental research on consumer perceptions of brand positioning and personality (Evans, 2013). As discussed in Chapter 4 of this volume, brands represent value in the minds of consumers and stand for specific qualities. How do consumers perceive them? Do socially marketed brands occupy the space social marketers intend? Efficacy experiments can shed light on these questions.

Second, like commercial brands, socially marketed brands are in competition with other products and the category with other, often less healthy, behaviors (e.g., consistent condom use vs. unprotected sex). Conjoint studies that compare socially marketed brands with other brands such as those sold by commercial marketers and those given away freely by governments, within a marketplace, can be extremely valuable. Such studies can also examine perceptions of the subject brands compared between users and nonusers (or former users) of the product can shed light on the determinants of socially marketed product choice within a total market (Evans et al., 2011).

Finally, studies comparing prices between socially marketed brands and commercial brands are important and can be examined in efficacy experiments. Willingness and ability to pay are crucial variables, and they interact with perceptions of brand personality and positioning (Evans, 2013). Consumer behavior is driven by perceived brand value at a price point, but to date little has been reported in the social marketing research literature on this subject. Efficacy studies, such as those designed according to the guidelines given next, can investigate these topics.

Future of Social Marketing Efficacy Research

Social marketing efficacy study designs have a number of advantages over effectiveness designs. In particular, they offer researchers

- an important opportunity to answer research questions about message reactions, dose-response relationships, and causal effects of message exposure not easily, or as rigorously, answered by effectiveness studies;
- solutions to problems in terms of comparison conditions and experimental design facing effectiveness studies; and
- an opportunity to optimize exposure to messages independent of the timing or logistics of campaign implementation.

In addition, online efficacy studies based on existing panels are significantly cheaper than field-based studies that rely on telephone surveys. This is because (1) recruitment is easier and (2) surveys are self-administered and thus do not require telephone or in-person interviewers. Some campaigns are only piloted in select communities and have severely restricted advertising budgets and restricted evaluation budgets to match. Efficacy studies may be an economical evaluation tool compared to field-based studies.

Given the advantages of efficacy studies, and the opportunities to use this methodology afforded by modern technology, the research agenda in this area should be further developed. Many of the critical research questions typically asked in social marketing evaluations can be answered with rigorous efficacy studies conducted under controlled conditions. In particular, efficacy studies can determine how messages affect audiences' health knowledge, attitudes, beliefs, intentions, and behaviors.

An efficacy study may be chosen as the preferred evaluation design for a few different reasons. First, an efficacy study may be conducted to ensure that campaign messages are efficacious prior to a health communication or marketing campaign's implementation. As a result, only messages shown to be efficacious would be used in a subsequent campaign and tested later using a field-based or effectiveness design. Second, an efficacy study may be an option to evaluate messages when a campaign is already been implemented. As in the PSUNC example, sometimes a field-based effectiveness study is not feasible for any number of reasons (e.g., timing, funding, anticipated low campaign exposure). Finally, an efficacy study may be used in combination with other methods as part of a multifaceted campaign evaluation. In this last scenario, results from different data collection methods can be triangulated (i.e., multiple data sources can be used to reach a conclusion) to create a more comprehensive picture of the effectiveness of a campaign (Rossi & Freeman, 1993).

In short, the advantages of efficacy designs in social marketing research and the gaps in the evidence base on message effectiveness described previously suggest the need to develop a targeted research agenda. Such an agenda would build on the work described in this chapter and have the following broad characteristics:

- Develop techniques to maximize external validity of efficacy studies while maintaining already high internal validity (e.g., study and develop methods to maximize the reality of laboratory-type message exposures to simulate real-world encounters)
- Conduct mode studies (e.g., Are results from efficacy studies conducted online, or through technologies such as handheld devices, systematically different from those conducted in other settings or by other modes such as mailing respondents DVDs containing video, radio, or print campaign messages and doing phone/mail surveys?)
- Examine the effects of different marketing strategies (e.g., repetition, use of celebrities, embedding messages in other content such as entertainment

programming) and message strategies (e.g., individually based vs. normative behavioral messages) across different health topics

- Conduct comparative studies (including potentially meta-analyses) of health and behavioral outcomes observed in social marketing efficacy versus effectiveness studies (e.g., a forced exposure study of a nutrition promotion campaign compared to an effectiveness trial of such a campaign)

This chapter suggests the importance of efficacy research in social marketing because of the dearth of evidence and major outstanding research questions it is poised to answer. With a rapidly evolving media environment, there are new and expanding opportunities to deliver health messages to audiences that interact with and cocreate social marketing content in novel ways (Lefebvre, 2007). As a result, efficacy research is needed to understand message effectiveness in the world of new media technologies.

ADDITIONAL RESOURCES

- For more on message framing and online experiments:
  - O'Keefe, D.J., & Jensen, J.D. (2007). The Relative Persuasiveness of Gain-Framed Loss-Framed Messages for Encouraging Disease Prevention Behaviors: A Meta-Analytic Review. *Journal of Health Communication: International Perspectives*, 12(7): 623–644.
  - Evans, W.D., Davis, K.C., Umanzor, C., Patel, K., & Khan, M. (2011). Evaluation of Sexual Communication Messages. *BMC Reproductive Health,* 8(15). doi:10.1186/1742-4755-8-15
- For more on risk and emergency response message testing, see http://www.firstresponder.gov/TechnologyDocuments/Comprehensive%20Testing%20of%20Imminent%20Threat%20Public%20Messages%20for%20Mobile%20Devices.pdf
- For more on commercial message testing research, see https://aytm.com/blog/research-junction/consumer-testing/

References

Biener, L., Ji, M., Gilpin, E., & Albers, A.B. (2004). The Impact of Emotional Tone, Message and Broadcast Parameters in Youth Anti-smoking Advertisements. *Journal of Health Communication*, 9: 259–274.

Centers for Disease Control and Prevention. (2014). HealthStyles Survey—Public Beliefs and Attitudes About Breastfeeding: 2014. Retrieved on September 8, 2015, from http://www.cdc.gov/breastfeeding/data/healthstyles_survey/survey_2014.htm

Cordón, L. A. (2005). *Popular Psychology: An Encyclopedia*. Westport, CT: Greenwood.

Davis, K.C., Evans, W.D., & Kamyab, K. (2012). Effectiveness of a National Media Campaign to Promote Parent-Child Communication About Sex. *Health Education and Behavior*, 40(1): 97–106. doi:10.1177/1090198112440009

Dillard, J.P., & Peck, E. (2001). Persuasion and the Structure of Affect: Dual Systems and Discrete Emotions as Complementary Models. *Human Communication Research*, 27: 38–68.

Donohew, L., Lorch, E.P., & Palmgreen, P. (1998). Applications of a Theoretic Model of Information Exposure to Health Interventions. *Human Communication Research*, 24: 454–468.

Evans, W.D. (2006). How Social Marketing Works in Health Care. *British Medical Journal*, 322: 1207–1210.

Evans, W.D. (Ed.). (2013). *Psychology of Branding*. Hauppauge, NY: Nova Science.

Evans, W.D., Blitstein, J., & Hersey, J.C. (2008). Evaluation of Public Health Brands: Design, Measurement, and Analysis. In *Public Health Branding: Applying Marketing for Social Change*, W.D. Evans & G. Hastings (Eds). Oxford, UK: Oxford University Press; 43–71.

Evans, W.D., Davis, K.C., Silber-Ashley, O., Blitstein, J., Koo, H., & Zhang, Y. (2009). Efficacy of Abstinence Promotion Media Messages: Findings From an Online Randomized Trial. *Journal of Adolescent Health*, 45(4): 409–417.

Evans, W.D., & Hastings, G. (2008). Future Directions for Public Health Branding. In *Public Health Branding: Applying Marketing for Social Change*, W.D. Evans and G. Hastings (Eds.). London: Oxford University Press, Chapter 1.

Evans, W.D., Lantz, P., Mead, K.H., & Alvarez, C.P. (2015). Efficacy of Messages to Promote Adherence to Preventive Services Guidelines: Online Randomized Trial. *Social Science & Medicine: Population Health*. DOI: 10.1016/j.ssmph.2015.11.003.

Evans, W.D., Longfield, K., Shekhar, N., Rabemanatsoa, A., Snider, J., & Reerink, I. (2011). Social Marketing and Condom Promotion in Madagascar: A Case Study in Brand Equity Research. In *Handbook of Global Health Communication*, R. Obregon & S. Waisboard (Eds.). Thousand Oaks, CA: Sage.

Evans, W.D., & McCormack, L. (2008). Applying Social Marketing in Health Care: Communicating Evidence to Change Consumer Behavior. *Medical Decision Making*, 28: 781–792. doi:10.1177/0272989X08318464

Evans, W.D., Uhrig, J., Davis, K., & McCormack, L. (2009). Efficacy Methods to Evaluate Health Communication and Marketing Campaigns. *Journal of Health Communication*, 14(3): 244–254.

Farrelly, M.C., Davis, K.C., Haviland, M.L., Messeri, P., & Healton, C.G. (2005). Evidence of a Dose-Response Relationship Between "truth' Antismoking Ads and Youth Smoking. *American Journal of Public Health*, 95(3): 425–431.

Fishbein, M., & Ajzen, I. (2010). *Predicting and Changing Behavior: The Reasoned Action Approach*. New York: Psychology Press.

Fishbein, M., & Yzer, M.C. (2003). Using theory to design effective health behavior interventions. *Communication Theory*, 13: 164–183.

Flay, B.R. (1986). Efficacy and Effectiveness Trials (and Other Phases of Research) in the Development of Health Promotion Programs. *Preventive Medicine*, 15: 451–474.

Hornik, R., & Yanovitsky, I. (2003). Using Theory to Design Evaluations of Communication Campaigns: The Case of the National Youth Anti-Drug Message Campaign. *Communication Theory*, 13(2): 204–224.

Huhman, M., Price, S., & Potter, L. (2008). Branding Play for Children: VERB™ It's What You Do. In *Public Health Branding: Applying Marketing for Social Change*, W.D. Evans & G. Hastings (Eds.). London: Oxford University Press, Chapter 6.

Lantz, P., Evans, W.D., Mead, K.H., Alvarez, C.P., & Stewart, L. (2016). Knowledge and Attitudes Regarding Guidelines for Clinical Preventive Services: Results From a National Survey. *Milbank Quarterly*. In press.

Lefebvre, R.C. (2007). The New Technology: The Consumer as Participant Rather Than Target Audience. *Social Marketing Quarterly*, 13(3): 31–42.

McGuire, W. (2013). Theoretical Foundations of Campaigns. In *Public Communication Campaigns*, R. Rice & W. Paisley (Eds.), 4th Ed. Chapter 9. Thousand Oaks, CA: Sage.

Niederdeppe, J., Davis, K.C., Farrelly, M.C., & Yarsevich, J. (2007). Stylistic Features, Need for Sensation, and Confirmed Recall of National Smoking Prevention Advertisements. *Journal of Communication*, 57:272–292.

Ofcom. (2010). *Using Experiments in Consumer Research*. London: London Economics.

Potter, L.D., Judkins, D.R., Piesse, A., Nolin, M.J., & Huhman, M. (2008). Methodology of the Outcome Evaluation of the VERB Campaign. *American Journal of Preventive Medicine*, 34(6 Suppl): S230–S240. doi:10.1016/j.amepre.2008.03.007

Putnam, R.D. (2001). *Bowling Alone*. New York: Simon & Schuster.

Rossi P., & Freeman, R. (1993). *Evaluation: A Systematic Approach*. Thousand Oaks, CA: Sage.

Schlosser, E. (2012). *Fast Food Nation: The Dark Side of the All-American Meal*. Boston: Houghton Mifflin Harcourt.

Snyder, L.B., & Hamilton, M.A. (2002). Meta-analysis of US Health Campaign Effects on Behavior: Emphasize Enforcement, Exposure, and New Information, and Beware the Secular Trend. In *Public Health Communication: Evidence for Behavior Change*, R. Hornik (Ed.). Hillsdale, NJ: Erlbaum; 357–383.

Snyder, L.B., & LaCroix, J.M. (2013). How Effective Are Mediated Health Campaigns? A Synthesis of Meta-analyses. In *Public Communication Campaigns*, 4th Ed., R. Rice & C. Atkin (Eds.). Thousand Oaks, CA: Sage; 113–129.

Southwell, B.G., Barmada, C.H., Hornik, R.C., & Maklan, D.M. (2002). Can We Measure Exposure? Evidence From a National Campaign. *Journal of Health Communication*, 7: 445–453.

Steinman, M.A., Bero, L.A., Chren, M.-M., & Landerfeld, C.S. (2006). Narrative Review: The Promotion of Gabapentin: An Analysis of Internal Industry Documents. *Annals of Internal Medicine*, 145: 284–293.

Terry-McElrath, Y., Wakefield, M., Ruel, E., Balch, G.I., Emery, S., Szczypka, G., Clegg-Smith, K., & Flay, B. (2005). The Effect of Antismoking Advertisement Executional Characteristics on Youth Comprehension, Appraisal, Recall, and Engagement. *Journal of Health Communication*, 10(2): 127–143. doi:10.1080/10810730590915100

Willey, B.A., Paintain, L.S., Mangham, L., Car, J., & Schellenberg, J.A. (2012). Strategies for Delivering Insecticide-Treated Nets at Scale for Malaria Control: A Systematic Review. *Bulletin of the World Health Organization*, 90: 672–684E. doi:10.2471/BLT.11.094771

Young, C.E. (2005). *The Advertising Handbook*. Seattle, WA: Ideas in Flight.

6

Monitoring and Evaluation Research

TOOLS AND EVIDENCE FOR UNDERSTANDING SOCIAL MARKETING PERFORMANCE DURING AND AFTER IMPLEMENTATION

W. Douglas Evans

Summary Points

- Social marketing monitoring and evaluation aims to determine the effectiveness of campaigns in achieving their communication and behavioral outcome objectives.
- They seek to answer two questions: (1) "**Did** the campaign achieve its objectives?" (2) If so, "**How** did it achieve them?"
- Monitoring and evaluation studies are both concerned with process and outcome evaluation, and impact of campaigns can be inferred from process and outcome.
- Digital technologies, including the Internet and mobile phones, are increasingly part of the monitoring and evaluation toolkit.

Introduction and Background

This chapter explores the methodology of monitoring and evaluation (M&E) research as it is specifically applied in social marketing. M&E research represents the right-hand side of the social marketing research continuum conceptual framework introduced in Chapter 1. As such, it can be divided into process and outcome evaluation methods (Valente, 2002). Process evaluation helps to assess whether (1) the target audience has been exposed to a campaign's messages (e.g., did adolescents hear the *truth*® campaign tobacco use prevention message?) and (2) the target audience reacts favorably to the messages in real-world circumstances (e.g., how did adolescents react to *truth* messages when they heard them?). Outcome evaluation helps to determine the effects of messages on health behavior and determinants of behavior such as health knowledge, attitudes, and beliefs (e.g., were adolescents who heard *truth* messages less likely to try smoking or become an established smoker?).

Social marketing evaluations often capture process and outcome data simultaneously to offer the immediate formative feedback that can enhance the campaign effort (Evans, Blitstein, & Hersey, 2008). At the same time, immediate reactions to media messages and outcomes are correlated; thus, process and outcome evaluation efforts need to work hand in hand. Further in this chapter, we examine how two campaigns illustrate the methods by which evaluations assess four key process and outcome dimensions of effectiveness:

- exposure and recall;
- message reactions and receptivity;
- behavioral determinants (knowledge, attitudes, beliefs); and
- behavioral outcomes.

As noted in Chapter 2, for purposes of this book, we treat "outcomes" as the primary endpoints of M&E research. Achievement of communication and ultimately behavioral objectives is what social marketing campaigns are designed to do. However, for public health purposes, the long-term objective is to achieve *health impact*: to reduce morbidity or mortality of disease conditions such as diabetes, cancer, or HIV/AIDS. But, in this chapter, we restrict discussion mainly to evaluating social marketing implementation outcomes, primarily behavior change.

By contrast, *impact* evaluation is concerned with effects of social marketing implementation on health indicators, including morbidity and mortality prevalence and incidence (Valente, 2002; Rossi & Freeman, 1993). We can in some cases infer impact from the results of campaign evaluations. For example, in the case of the early *truth* campaign evaluation, exposure to the campaign was shown to have accounted for over 300,000 fewer youth smokers from the period 2000–2002 (Farrelly et al., 2005). Given the known, long-term health effects of smoking over a lifetime, which result in an average of about 7 years' premature death, we can infer that over 2.1 million life years were saved by the campaign (i.e., reduced mortality), along with countless reductions in smoking-related illnesses (i.e., reduced morbidity), as well as tremendous reductions in expected healthcare costs (Evans, Davis, & Farrelly, 2008).

What Questions Are Social Marketing M&E Studies Trying to Answer?

There are five overarching questions that social marketing M&E studies seek to answer. Each of these questions is related, and they represent the steps or connections in a campaign's conceptual model or theory of change, as discussed in Chapter 2.

- Was the audience exposed to the message and with what dosage?
- How did the audience react to and receive the messages (e.g., were they perceived as credible, likable)?
- What associations were formed by the target audience with the campaign messages?
- Does the audience acquire the knowledge, attitudes, beliefs targeted by the campaign (i.e., were the *communication objectives* of the campaign achieved)?
- Does the audience adopt and maintain the targeted behaviors (i.e., were the *behavioral objectives* of the campaign achieved)?

The M&E studies are not developed in a vacuum; they are designed in relation to a campaign's inputs, outputs, and outcomes. The evaluation should be *sensitive* to the campaign in terms of its design, measures, and data collection, all of which should be in sync with campaign plans and objectives (Evans, Davis, & Farrelly, 2008). A well-designed campaign will have a clearly articulated theory of change, a model that specifies how campaign activities will lead to achievement of specific communication and behavioral objectives. The evaluation in turn will be designed to measure and assess both whether those objectives have been achieved attributable to the campaign and how they were achieved or by what mechanisms (Evans, Davis, & Farrelly, 2008; Valente, 2002).

In designing an evaluation to be sensitive to a campaign's objectives, evaluators typically follow a *logic model* or structured set of relationships between constructs to be affected by campaign activities (Valente, 2002; Chapman et al., 2013). In this way, social marketing M&E studies are *theory based* in that they are designed to test hypothesized relationships between constructs represented in the campaign (Evans, Davis, & Farrelly, 2008; Guba & Lincoln, 1994).

Well-designed social marketing M&E studies have a clearly articulated theoretical basis and are designed and implemented with the aim of testing and confirming or disconfirming their underlying hypotheses.

Case Study of the 5-4-3-2-1 Go! Childhood Obesity Prevention Campaign Evaluation

Campaign Background

The Consortium to Lower Obesity in Chicago Children (CLOCC; http://www.clocc.net) developed a public health education initiative to bolster ongoing local efforts addressing Chicago's childhood obesity epidemic through healthy eating and physical activity (Evans et al., 2007). CLOCC is a citywide coalition of over 500 organizations representing virtually all social sectors. CLOCC and its partners have developed the *5-4-3-2-1 Go!* social marketing initiative. The 5-4-3-2-1 Go! initiative involves community youth and partners across Chicago in development and dissemination of the core messages. After completing a training process, youth ambassadors deliver these messages through community outreach activities. The campaign is based on healthy eating and active living messages for children: Consume 5 or more fruits and vegetables, 4 servings of water, and 3 servings of low-fat dairy a day; spend no more than 2 hours watching television or similar sedentary behavior; and engage in at least 1 hour of physical activity per day.

The ongoing 5-4-3-2-1 Go! initiative uses a healthy lifestyles *branding* strategy aimed at improving family food choices and increasing utilization of community physical activity resources (Evans et al., 2007). It was aimed initially at six vanguard community areas linked to census boundaries in Chicago: Englewood, Humboldt Park, Lower West Side, Rogers Park, West Garfield Park, and West Town. These areas were targeted based on high pediatric obesity prevalence (Mason et al., 2006). The campaign later expanded to become a citywide initiative (Gustat et al., 2012).

The theoretical foundation of this initiative lies in a socioecological approach to health (Green & Kreuter, 2005). Recognizing that multiple social and physical environmental factors affect obesity prevalence in the targeted Chicago communities, the program developed strategies at multiple levels of social ecology, ranging from policy to family- and individual-level messages (Evans et al., 2010). Activities at each level of ecology followed multiple 4P (place, price, product, and promotion) social marketing strategies, as shown in Figure 6-1.

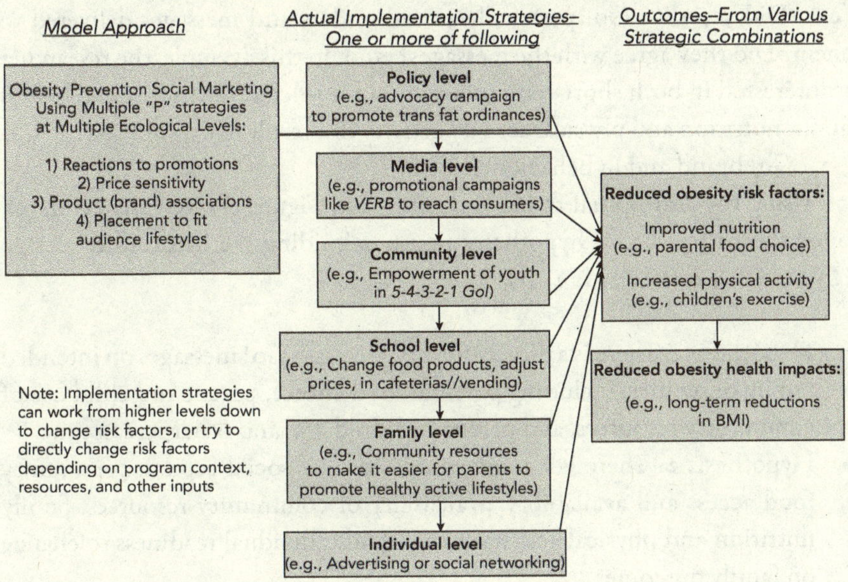

FIGURE 6-1 Conceptual Framework for 5-4-3-2-1 Go! obesity prevention social marketing. BMI, body mass index.

Source: Evans, Christoffel, Necheles, et al., 2010.

Evaluation Background

Parents in six Chicago neighborhoods were surveyed before and after possible exposure to the 5-4-3-2-1 Go! social marketing program to prevent childhood obesity behavioral risk factors. Parents were randomized to get the 5-4-3-2-1 Go! program in their community prior to follow-up data collection or to receive it at a later time (lagged comparison design; Evans, Christoffel, et al., 2011). Researchers compared the effects of exposure on the five behavioral outcomes targeted by 5-4-3-2-1 Go!

The surveys were conducted 1 year apart. Parents were surveyed on their families' nutrition and physical activity behavior (their own and children's). They were also asked about exposure to the 5-4-3-2-1 Go! campaign and specific messages, products, and placements; other social influences; and changes in their communities.

Developing the Evaluation Hypotheses: How do we work from the campaign strategy and conceptual framework to the design of the evaluation study? First, researchers started by defining the outcomes of interest. What would be evidence that the campaign had been effective? This comes from the communication or behavioral objectives of the campaign. In a process evaluation example, the researcher might look at communication objectives (e.g., Did 5-4-3-2-1 Go! parents hear and understand messages delivered to them? Did they agree with the messages? etc.). In this example, the researcher is interested in both short-term increases in knowledge, attitudes, and beliefs about nutrition and physical activity activity as a result of exposure to the 5-4-3-2-1 Go! brand and in behavior change.

Using the conceptual framework shown in Figure 6-1, researchers developed these three broad hypotheses to use in guiding the M&E study design (Evans, Christoffel, et al., 2011):

- Hypothesis 1: There is a direct effect of 5-4-3-2-1 Go! messages on intended family outcomes, including parental food choice, parent and child use of community resources, and parent and child TV and other screen time.
- Hypothesis 2: There is a moderating effect of social capital, community food access and availability, availability of community resources, family nutrition and physical activity norms, and individual readiness to change on family outcomes.
- Hypothesis 3: There is a mediating effect of knowledge, attitudes, and beliefs about nutrition and physical activity on the relationship between 5-4-3-2-1 Go! messages and behavioral outcomes.

How Do Social Marketing Campaigns Influence Behavior?

Social marketing campaigns are designed based on formative research, the left-hand side of the research continuum. Designers settle on a conceptual framework, design their 4P strategies, develop activities to support the strategies, and then launch. At this point, and just prior in order to establish a baseline, researchers are engaged in M&E research. But, how exactly do we believe health messages influence behavior?

The theory underlying a campaign, such as the example of 5-4-3-2-1 Go! discussed previously, predicts changes in behavior occur through a process. Based on formative research, and most often also on tested, validated behavioral theory, such as the theory of planned behavior (Fishbein & Ajzen, 2010); social cognitive theory (Bandura, 2004); the transtheoretical model (Prochaska, DiClemente, & Norcross, 1992); the socioecological model (Green & Kreuter, 2005); or in some cases a combination of theoretical perspectives. In general, researchers hypothesize a change process driven by exposure to a "message" (where by the term *message*, we mean the campaign's call to action as embodied typically in multiple 4P strategies):

- exposure to the message at a certain level of dosage;
- reaction and some degree of receptivity to the message;
- acquisition of knowledge and formation of attitudes, beliefs, and intentions in relation to the message;
- acting on the message; and
- Adoption and maintenance of the behavior recommended by the message.

It is worth noting that, in some cases, campaign objectives may not go as far as behavior change. There are numerous examples of highly successful social marketing campaigns that seek to raise awareness, reframe issues in public discourse, or achieve other social or policy-level changes at levels of social ecology well beyond the individual (Kotler & Lee, 2008). But, for the current purposes, let us focus on the familiar scenario in which the campaign calls on the recipient of the message to change behavior, for instance, increase physical activity, consistently use a condom, do not start smoking.

Therefore, a drug use prevention campaign might use the theory of planned behavior, and its conceptual framework may include messages for adolescents that target the intention to avoid marijuana use. The logic model adopted by the evaluators predicts a process of intention formation based on message exposure at some level of dosage of the prevention message leading to avoidance of marijuana use behavior.

Consider a generalized logic model for the effects of social marketing on determinants of behavior and subsequent outcomes related to health communication and social marketing campaigns developed by the Centers for Disease Control and Prevention (CDC) and members of the Community Preventive Services Task Force (http://www.thecommunityguide.org/healthcommunication/index.html) (Figure 6.2). This generic logic model captures the features discussed previously. Campaigns potentially have inputs into multiple levels of social ecology—at the individual and multiple environmental levels. These can lead to effects on individuals or on the multiple targeted levels in the environment. In turn, these intermediate effects can produce individual behavior changes and have impacts on reduced morbidity and mortality.

Measures of Campaign Effectiveness

Now, let us explore each of the research questions and hypotheses framed previously in terms of measures used in campaign M&E. We can confirm or disconfirm our hypotheses, as a test of the M&E research logic model, based on collection and analysis of these measures.

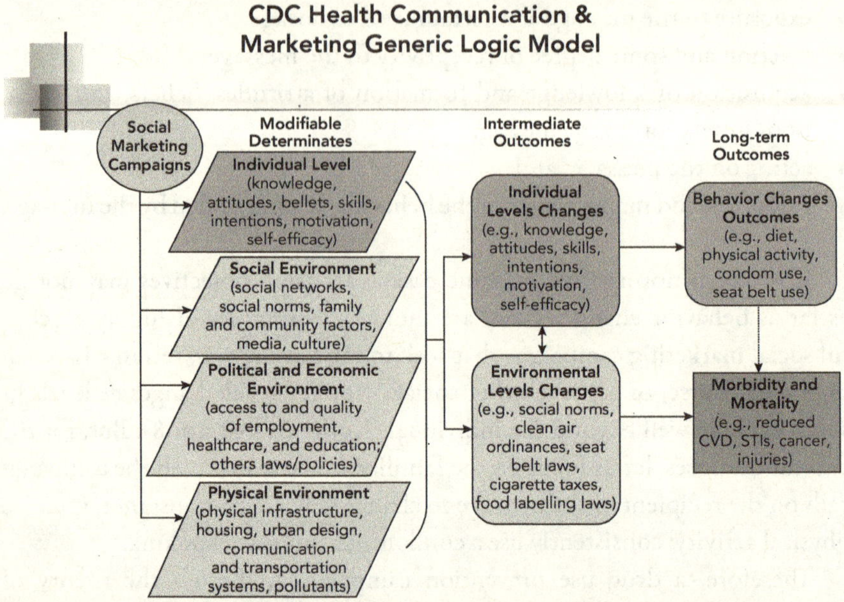

FIGURE 6-2 Generalized logic model for the effects of social marketing on determinants of behavior and subsequent outcomes related to health communication and social marketing campaigns. CVD, cardiovascular disease; STI, sexually transmitted infection. *Source: Adapted* from Robinson, M.N., Tansil, K.A., Elder, R.W., Soler, R.E., Labre, M.P., Mercer, S.L., Eroglu, D., Baur, C., Lyon-Daniel, K., Fridinger, F., et al. (2014). Health Communication Campaigns That Include Mass Media and Health-Related Product Distribution: A Community Guide Systematic Review. *American Journal of Preventive Medicine,* 47(3): 360–371.

Referring to the research continuum figure from Chapter 1, once the campaign launches, the first type of evaluation activity is monitoring of implementation (process evaluation). It is important to recognize that outcome evaluation activity is typically going on at the same time (e.g., a well-designed evaluation would have collected some form of baseline or pretest data related to the campaign and its outcomes immediately prior to the launch), but because monitoring activities are relevant to assessing campaign direction and immediate success and are also relevant to outcome evaluation, we start with them.

The first step is measuring exposure and monitoring social marketing implementation (e.g., were the planned campaign activities or inputs from the evaluation logic model actually implemented as planned?). There are two basic types of advertising exposure measures: respondent self-report and external (or environmental) measures. Self-report measures can be divided into recall and recognition measures (Evans, Davis, Umanzor, et al., 2012).

Recall measures capture individuals' aided (with verbal or similar prompts) or unaided (without prompts) awareness (Southwell et al., 2002; Southwell, 2005). They rely on cues to memory, such as a brief description of what an advertisement was about or some feature of it, which is clearly subject to the vagaries of memory and selective attention bias (MacLeod et al., 2002). To demonstrate exposure, respondents then provide a more detailed self-report (correctly describing some detailed feature of the ad) to demonstrate recall. Recognition measures rely on actual depiction of the advertisements through presentation via media such as TV, Internet, radio, or print. Respondents view, hear, or read the ads and indicate their recognition of the ad. Frequency of exposure may be asked for both recall and recognition.

External Measures of Exposure

External measures use extant data about the delivery of an advertised message, typically through mass media in a given geographic area (e.g., a designated market area, or DMA) or through social media (e.g., Google analytics). Using external data not collected directly from individuals but captured through media-monitoring tools, such as social media metrics and traditional media organizations such as Nielsen for mass media, researchers can develop estimates of media exposure data for a population potentially exposed to a social marketing campaign.

As a simple illustration, consider the idea of media impressions, made up of two components: reach and frequency. The reach is the number of people exposed (or estimated to be exposed) to a message (e.g., contained in an advertisement, or a set of advertisements, sometimes called a schedule). So, reach can be considered a percentage of a target audience:

- Reach (%): the number of people exposed to at least one issue in a schedule (as a percentage of the target)

The other component of media impressions is frequency. The average frequency is the number of advertisements seen by each person in the target audience who have seen at least one message. So, frequency is a total number of messages seen:

- Average frequency: the average number of issues read by each person in the target market who have been exposed to at least one issue in the schedule

Therefore, the gross impressions seen (or gross opportunities to see an advertisement) by the audience would be the total opportunities to see the campaign or a specific advertisement. For example, if an advertisement reaches 1,000 people (i.e., the reach), and the average frequency (i.e., the average number of times a person will see the campaign or schedule) is 5, then the gross impressions would be 5,000 (CDC, 2010).

The next concept from the mass media world is GRPs (gross rating points). These are the gross impressions expressed as a percentage of the target market. So, for example, if the gross impressions are 5,000 and the population of the target is 25,000, then the GRPs are 20. GRPs are a widely used measure of dosage and exposure to mass media campaigns. More information about these measures and their uses in social marketing M&E studies is available online (http://www.orau.gov/cdcynergy/soc2web/).

Self-Reported Exposure

The other category of communication and marketing exposure data is self-reported exposure. It is important to distinguish between *recognition* and *recall* of (1) messages and (2) advertising executions. Myriad recent studies provide evidence that advertising campaigns can be effective in changing health-related attitudes, intentions, and behavior, such as tobacco use (Farrelly et al., 2005; Hersey et al. 2005; Sly et al., 2001) and other health or problem behaviors (Hornik, 2002). Studies have examined measures of exposure to or memory of televised advertisements. Measures of *recognition* typically used in laboratory forced exposure designs have participants view an ad and indicate whether they have seen the message before, whereas *recall* measures provide study participants with only a minimal verbal cue (Evans, Davis, et al., 2009; Singh and Rothschild, 1983). These studies have shown that recognition and recall measures are strongly correlated, and researchers generally agree that both measures require respondents to access their long-term memory for at least minimal remnants of ad exposure (Southwell, 2005).

In recent years, recognition measures have also been used in field studies in which respondents are shown ads that have recently (e.g., in the past 1–2 months) aired on TV or on radio or appeared in print in their DMA. They are then asked to indicate whether they have seen the ad(s) and, if so, with what frequency on an ordinal scale.

Case Study: M&E Study of the 2010 US National Census Media Campaign

Campaign Background

The 2010 Census Integrated Communication Campaign (ICC) was sponsored by the US Census Bureau, and the campaign evaluation was conducted by the National Opinion Research Corporation (NORC) at the University of Chicago. NORC conducted an evaluation of the full 2010 ICC, including community-level, partnership, and national paid media campaign activities. The objective of the study was to assess the extent to which the 2010 ICC achieved its goals of increasing mail returns and increasing cooperation with enumerators. The evaluation was also structured to investigate some of the mechanisms through which the campaign might or might not have succeeded in affecting people's census-related knowledge, attitudes, and behavior. The principal data source for the evaluation was a set of three nationally representative household surveys conducted between October 2009 and August 2010 to capture knowledge, attitudes, and exposure to the campaign. To increase the ability to understand person-specific response to the campaign, the surveys included a panel sample in which the same individuals were interviewed in each of the three waves.

Survey data collection for the 2010 Census Integrated Communications Program Evaluation (CICPE) took place at three points: Wave 1 was conducted mid-September 2009 through mid-January 2010, during early partnership activity (and prior to the launch of the paid media effort), to assess baseline levels of all measures of public attention and intentions that were the focus of the 2010 Census ICC. Wave 2 took place January through March 2010, during the peak of the paid media campaign and partnership (with local organization that promoted census participation) activities, but before the paper census forms were distributed to households. Wave 3 was conducted during a follow-up period called the nonresponse follow-up (NRFU) from April through July 2010 when people had made their decisions about participating in the census form mailback phase and had been exposed to the full course of the main paid media, community-level, and partnership campaigns.

Mirroring the structure of the paid media component (and thus satisfying the important criterion of *sensitivity* to the campaign design), the campaign evaluation also focused on specific racial/ethnic origin groups. Specifically, survey samples included approximately equal numbers of individuals from five traditionally hard-to-count (meaning that previous research has shown that they tend to be underrepresented in the total census data collection) groups: Hispanics, non-Hispanic blacks, American Indians and Alaska Natives, Asians, and Native Hawaiians and other Pacific Islanders. For comparison purposes, all others that had traditionally been hard to count were included as a sixth group. Table 6-1 provides (unweighted) completed case counts by race/ethnicity and wave.

The campaign evaluation survey interviews were conducted with sampled individuals by telephone or, if needed, in person. Panel respondents in the last two waves were first invited to complete the interviews by mail or web, then pursued using telephone and finally in-person modes for nonresponse follow-up. Items on census knowledge, attitudes, and intention to participate were adopted from earlier surveys where possible to enhance comparability across census years and with the 2008 survey that informed development of 2010 ICC messages and strategy. The questionnaires also collected detailed information on individuals' self-reported exposure to

Table 6-1 2010 Completed Cases by Race/Ethnicity Group

	Total Cases Completed		
Race/Ethnicity	Wave 1	Wave 2	Wave 3
Hispanic	461	369	539
Non-Hispanic black	377	384	526
Non-Hispanic white[a]	404	358	472
American Indian	457	392	529
Asian	542	410	548
Native Hawaiian	430	350	494
Total	2,671	2,263	3,108

Source: Datta, A.R., Yan, T., Evans, W.D., Pedlow, S., Spencer, B., & Bautista, R. (2012). *2010 Census Integrated Communications Program Evaluation: Final Report.* Prepared for the US Bureau of the Census, US Department of Commerce. Chicago: NORC at the University of Chicago.

[a]This category included all non-black, non-Hispanic individuals, including Asians, Native Hawaiians and other Pacific Islanders, and American Indians and Alaska Natives. This "non-Hispanic white" category, together with the Hispanic and non-Hispanic black category, constitutes a nationally representative sample of all Americans in households. The remaining three categories—Asians, Native Hawaiians and other Pacific Islanders, and American Indians and Alaska Natives—are independent supplemental samples fielded to collect adequate numbers of interviews from rare populations.

2010 ICC components. Operational data on actual 2010 census participation were combined with survey data to determine households' actual census behavior.

Campaign Evaluation Conceptual Model and Hypotheses

The campaign evaluation design did not support estimation of a "total" effect of the campaign. Rather, the evaluation analyses sought to determine the relationship, if any, between increased "dosage" of campaign exposure and changes in interim or final outcomes, such as knowledge, attitudes, beliefs, or census mailback behavior.

Figure 6-3, the CICPE conceptual model (repeated from Chapter 3, where it was used to illustrate campaign theory development) visually depicts relationships between campaign exposure, the outcomes of primary interest, and other relevant factors of interest to evaluation design and measurement. The conceptual model provides a framework within which to consider the objectives for the 2010 CICPE and provides a basis for hypotheses to be tested in analysis of outcome data.

The model reflects well-supported theoretical assumptions from health communication (Evans, Uhrig, et al., 2009; Hornik, 2002; Southwell, 2005). The reception phase involves campaign exposure, campaign message recall, and message receptivity (MR). Three types of exposure are assumed in the model: paid and earned media, partnership and school activities, and word of mouth and social interactions. This case study focuses on the paid media component.

The first hypothesis (H1) is that exposure intensity affects message recall, which we measured with questionnaire items. Following exposure, researchers hypothesized that there is a degree of receptivity to 2010 ICC messages. Message receptivity (MR) is a construct that represents rational and affective reactions to messages (Evans, Yan, & Datta, 2012). A number of studies in health communication have established measures of "receptivity" to public service advertising that capture audiences' subjective appraisals of message persuasiveness, believability, and other aspects of cognitive processing (Dillard, Shen, & Vail, 2007; Bruner, 1998). These measures are often used as proxies of ad effectiveness. They have been shown to predict changes in attitudes toward the social and health issues, behaviors and other subject matter of public service advertising (Davis et al., 2011). Such measures can be used to assess effectiveness of campaign messages during development and prior to implementation. They can also be used as mediators to test the theory

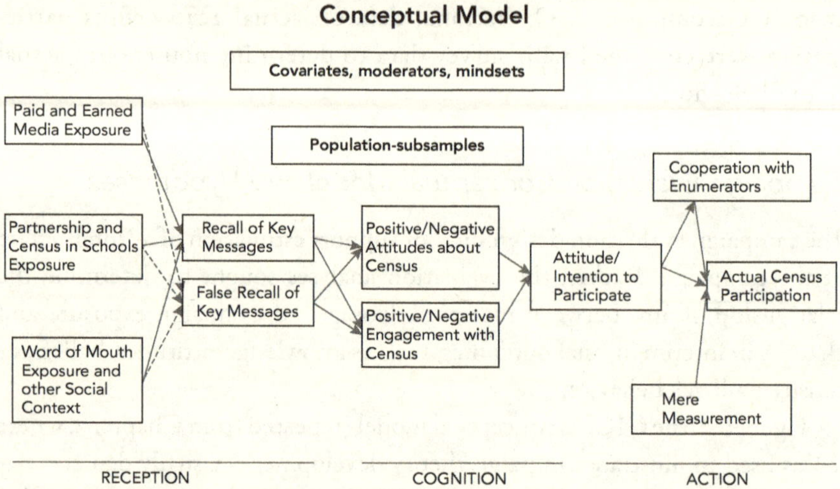

FIGURE 6-3 The 2010 Census media campaign evaluation conceptual model.
Source: Datta, A.R., Yan, T., Evans, W.D., Pedlow, S., Spencer, B., & Bautista, R. (2012). *2010 Census Integrated Communications Program Evaluation: Final Report.* Prepared for the US Bureau of the Census, US Department of Commerce. Chicago: NORC at the University of Chicago.

of change underlying a campaign during and after implementation (Evans, Uhrig, et al., 2009).

The cognition phase involved the processing of the received messages and their integration into views held by the individual regarding the census in particular and the public good more generally. Knowledge and attitudes targeted by the 2010 ICC advertising were expected to increase as a function of exposure and receptivity to census messages. Researchers hypothesized (H2) that the specific targeted knowledge and attitudes promoted in 2010 ICC advertising would be higher among respondents who had higher exposure and among those who had higher MR, compared to those with lower exposure or lower MR (Evans, Yan, & Datta, 2012).

The cognition phase of the model had two elements that measured the effect of messages on attitudes toward and knowledge of and engagement with the census, respectively. The former (attitudes and knowledge) covered inherent positive or negative aspects of participating in the census, such as the time required or the potential invasion of privacy. The latter (engagement) pertained to the motivations for participation that stem from the individual's broader views about the public good. For example, one belief measured in the campaign evaluation was that "answering and sending back the Census matters for my family and community." These two elements then informed the intention of the individual to participate.

However, intention alone did not entail census participation. In the action phase, individuals translated their attitudes and beliefs about the census and the public good into concerted behavior. Census campaign evaluators had access to a record of actual participation behavior from the Census Bureau (individuals who had mailed back their form and identifying information to link those individuals to the data collected in the evaluation). The third hypothesis (H3) was that increased knowledge of or positive attitudes toward the census would translate to increased likelihood of census participation (i.e., knowledge and attitudes mediate the effects of campaign exposure on census participation).

Spanning the full conceptual model, researchers further hypothesized (H4) that greater exposure to 2010 ICC advertising would be associated with greater census participation as measured both by self-report and by Census Bureau records.

Finally, the Figure 6-3 model specifies mediating variables between 2010 ICC exposure and census participation. Specifically, we hypothesized that MR, census attitudes, and knowledge targeted in 2010 ICC advertising and intentions to participate each mediate the pathway from exposure to participation.

Researchers derived and examined four research questions in the light of the conceptual framework:

1. Did exposure to the 2010 ICC, including group-specific advertising, lead to improved reception of census messages?
2. Did improved reception of census messages lead to more positive beliefs, attitudes, and intentions to participate?
3. Were more positive beliefs and attitudes associated with greater observed census participation?
4. Did more exposure to the ICC have a direct impact on the observed census participation?

Dosage and Exposure Measures for the 2010 Census ICC

For the 2010 Census ICC campaign evaluation, researchers used both measures of recognition and GRPs for paid advertising in the media campaign. For advertising, this included both aided and unaided awareness. Researchers created aided awareness measures for new media, partnership, and word of mouth, although little is known about validity and reliability of these measures from previous research (Evans et al., 2014). Researchers also had access to external data sources that provided additional information to develop estimates of exposure sources. Exhibit 6-1 provides a summary of each domain of measures.

Exhibit 6-1

Example of Self-Reported Recall Questions

ITEM A. Have you recently seen an advertisement that showed everything frozen in time (construction sites, schoolyards, hospital rooms, and chambers of Congress) until a man dropped his census form into a mailbox?

- **1 ☐ YES**
- **2 ☐ MAYBE, NOT SURE**
- **3 ☐ NO → [SKIP TO NEXT AD]**
- **99 ☐ REFUSED → [SKIP TO NEXT AD]**

ITEM B. What happens in the ad? For example, can you tell me anything in detail about the people in the ad? (DO NOT READ RESPONSE CATEGORIES AND CODE ALL THAT ARE MENTIONED.)

- A BRIDGE CONSTRUCTION FROZEN IN TIME
- CONCRETE STOPPED IN MIDAIR
- SCHOOLCHILDREN IN A KICKBALL GAME FROZEN IN TIME
- IN A HOSPITAL ROOM, NURSE FROZEN WITH A BLANKET OVER A CHILD
- CONGRESSMEN/LEGISLATOR STOPPED IN DEBATES
- MAN WALKS TO MAILBOX
- MAN PUTS CENSUS FORM IN MAILBOX
- EVERYTHING COMES TO LIFE
- PHRASE: THE ANSWERS YOU PROVIDED TO THE CENSUS HELP DETERMINE WHAT OUR FUTURE WILL BE
- PHRASE: YOUR CENSUS ANSWERS HELP IMPROVE OUR HEALTHCARE, STRENGTHEN OUR SCHOOLS, DESIGNATE REPRESENTATIONS, AND BUILD OUR COMMUNITIES

- SLOGAN: WE CAN'T MOVE FORWARD UNTIL YOU SEND IT BACK
- SLOGAN: IT'S IN YOUR HANDS
- NO SPECIFICS MENTIONED, GENERAL COMMENTS ONLY

EXPOSURE LOCATION AND FREQUENCY

- **Item C. During the past 30 days, how often have you seen this advertisement?**

  Would you say . . .

  1. Often
  2. Sometimes
  3. Rarely
  4. Never
- **Item D. Where did you see this ad?**
  1. On TV
  2. At the movies
  3. Magazine
  4. Online
  5. Newspaper
  6. Other (specify): ____________
  7. Both
  8. Not sure, don't know
  9. Refused

SLOGAN RECALL

- **Item E. Do you remember any slogan or phrase being used about the census?**

  1. ☐ YES

  2. ☐ NO

  77. ☐ DON'T KNOW

  99. ☐ REFUSED
- **Item F. Can you tell me what the slogan or phrase was?**
  - [FILL IN SLOGAN HERE] ____________________
  - 77 ☐ DON'T KNOW
  - 99 ☐ REFUSED

Another technique that is used to validate self-reported recall is so-called false exposure measures (or "ringers"). This type of measure involves a self-reported recall question where the ad or message referenced *was never actually aired or made available to the target audience* (Valente, 2002). The items in Exhibit 6-2 illustrate how this was done for the 2010 Census ICC campaign evaluation.

The advertisement asked about in these questions never actually ran in the 2010 Census ICC. Yet, when asked, some percentage of respondents may say yes or maybe to item G and then actually pick out one of the response options in the confirmation item H. What would a researcher do with false recall data? If false recall is high, what then? Do people really recognize the campaign?

The answer lies in using the false recall data as a diagnostic tool (Valente, 2002; Davis, Evans, Kamyab, 2012). Researchers can look for signs that true recall is occurring and compare it to the rate of false recall. If a campaign is being implemented in the field and the total amount of dosage (e.g., as measured through an external measure such as GRPs) is rising as more and more advertisements air over time, researchers would expect to see changes in true confirmed recall. For example, in the evaluation by Davis and colleagues (2012) of the Parents Speak Up National Campaign (PSUNC), which promoted parent-child communication about sex, researchers conducted analyses to determine the magnitude of differences between false and true recall recognition over time (i.e., does false recall decline as cumulative GRPs increase?) and between true confirmed recall and cumulative GRPs. A finding of increasing significant correlation between true recall (not false) and GRPs would validate the self-report measure and also provide evidence to rule out the threat of selective attention bias (Davis, Evans, Kamyab, 2012).

Case Study of Measuring Dose-Response Relationships and Effects on Communication and Behavioral Objectives

Campaign Background

Launched nationally in June 2007, PSUNC targeted parents of children 10 to 14 years old; it primarily used televised public service announcements (PSAs) supplemented by radio and print advertising. In 2007, the campaign initially relied on PSAs, aired during donated advertising time on local television

Exhibit 6-2

Example of Self-Reported False Exposure Recall Questions

- **Item G. Have you recently seen an ad about the 2010 Census that shows an elderly Hispanic woman asking herself why it's important to return the Census form?**
  1. Yes
  2. Maybe, not sure
  3. No [SKIP TO NEXT AD]
  4. Refused [SKIP TO NEXT AD]
- **Item H. What happens in this ad? (DO NOT READ RESPONSE CATEGORIES AND CODE ONE ONLY)**
  1. She asks how the census can help her family.
  2. She thinks about improvements needed in her community.
  3. She imagines community projects only possible if she returns her census form.
  4. She thinks the census form is complicated, but she can do it anyway.
  5. She thinks she should complete and return the census form even though it takes a long time.
  6. She realizes that the census is responsible for $10 billion per year in federal funding.
  7. She fills out the census form.
  8. She walks out the door with her completed census form in hand.
  9. She goes to the mailbox and mails her census form.
  10. Other, specify ____________________.

networks. Increased campaign resources in 2008 and 2009 allowed for national paid advertising in addition to PSAs during those years. This example illustrates the effectiveness evaluation of PSUNC and builds on discussion of efficacy evaluation of the campaign in Chapter 5.

The campaign's advertisements address common barriers and parent fears about talking about sex and encourage parents to talk "early and often" with their children. Between 2007 and 2009, the campaign used four television advertisements: "Muffinhead," "Talk to Me," "Gadgets," and "Mimes." The first two ads were the first ads used during the campaign's initial airing in 2007 and featured age-appropriate youth letting their parents know that they want to talk to them about sex and that they should talk "early and often." These ads also depict youth saying to their parents "tell me you want me to wait." The last two ads were parent-voiced ads that featured parents portraying the barriers and difficulties parents face in initiating conversations about sex with their children. These ads also feature youth saying to their parents "tell us to wait to have sex." The television advertisements were supplemented with a radio ad called "S-Word" that also aired in local media markets across the country. This ad also focused on addressing parent barriers to communication about sex and encouraged parents to talk early and often with their children. All campaign PSAs also promoted the PSUNC website, which provided parents information and guidance on how to talk with their children about sex.

A recent study using a randomized trial found that parents who were exposed to the campaign under controlled conditions were more likely to initiate conversations about sex with their children (Evans, Davis, et al., 2009). Further results from this trial showed that parents' exposure to the campaign was associated with norms related to appropriate child age for sexual initiation and outcome expectations that communication would be successful (Davis et al., 2010). These cognitions were also found to be predictive of future parent-child communication, validating the campaign's strategy for behavior change by first targeting cognitive precursors to parent-child communication. A follow-up study of children of parents who participated in the randomized trial confirmed the aforementioned findings, showing that children of parents who received PSUNC exposure were more likely to report having conversations about sex with their parents (Evans, Davis, et al., 2009). While these studies strongly suggest that the campaign is efficacious, their external validity is limited due to the controlled nature of parents' exposure to PSUNC. Researchers thus designed and implemented a field-based effectiveness evaluation to measure campaign exposure and response to advertising under real-world conditions.

Evaluation Background

This M&E study explored the relationships between exposure to the campaign and multiple measures of parent-child communication about sex among parents nationwide. Specifically, we examined whether exposure to the campaign was related to (1) parent initiation of conversations about sexual activity with their children; (2) frequency of parent-child conversations about sex; and (3) parent recommendations to his or her child to wait to have sex.

This study used an online survey of parents sampled from the Knowledge Networks panel (now GfK Knowledge Panel; http://www.gfk.com/products-a-z/knowledgepanelr-north-america/) online panel and was conducted in fall 2009. The study sample was limited to parents of 10- to 14-year-old children, the target audience of PSUNC. A total of 2,258 parents responded to the study invitation and were eligible to participate. Among those, 1,804 parents (1,253 mothers and 551 fathers) completed the survey (total cooperation rate = 53.3%) (Blitstein et al., 2012).

Exposure was measured through both self-reported recognition and GRPs. Parents' awareness of specific PSUNC ads was assessed with a validated procedure that measures ad recognition (Southwell, 2005). Each parent was first shown a 30-second version of each PSUNC television ad, streamed within the online survey. Participants who were not able to view the ad were instead shown a series of screenshots from the ad.

Researchers also used external data from the campaign's media contractor to measure potential exposure to PSUNC at the market level. This additional data on PSUNC exposure serves two purposes. First, it allows us to examine in more detail the reach of the campaign across media markets in the United States. Second, it provides an alternative measure of exposure to PSUNC that is exogenous to the parent. This helps address the potential limitations of selective attention bias that may be present with self-reported awareness: Parents who already communicate at higher levels with their children may also be more attentive to PSUNC ads and thus more likely to indicate ad recognition (Davis, Evans, & Kamyab, 2012).

Overall, 59.4% of parents in the sample reported awareness of PSUNC. We found that higher market-level PSUNC GRPs were associated with greater frequency of communication and increased recommendations for the child to wait to have sex. Similar relationships were observed between self-reported awareness of PSUNC and increased frequency of communication and recommendations to wait (Davis, Evans, & Kamyab, 2012).

Self-reported frequency of awareness of PSUNC was also strongly associated with the media market "dose" of the campaign in multivariable logistic regressions for self-reported awareness of PSUNC. Higher total PSUNC GRPs at the media market level were associated with increased frequency of awareness of any PSUNC ad ($b = 0.14, p < .001$). This relationship was present among both mothers ($b = 0.11, p < .001$) and fathers ($b = 0.38, p < .05$). This tended to both confirm true campaign awareness in the recognition measures and provide evidence to rule out selective attention bias.

Case Study of Measuring Exposure and Evaluating Outcomes: The Role of Monetary and Nonmonetary Pricing in Social Marketing

Campaign Background

Monetary and nonmonetary (e.g., convenience, effort, time) price are among the four Ps that social marketing tries to influence. Price is often neglected in evaluations of social marketing campaigns. The following case study of the Population Services International (PSI) Protector Plus (P+) condom brand evaluation provides an example of measuring and evaluating price in social marketing (Evans, Taruberekera, et al., 2011).

The PSI-Zimbabwe's marketing objectives for P+ are to

- distribute an affordable brand of condoms in traditional, nontraditional, and high-risk outlets (condom social marketing);
- promote condom use among high-risk groups and sexually active youth; and
- develop behavior change communication programs that address the dynamics of high-risk behavior among target groups.

PSI-Zimbabwe's goals are to measure current brand equity in its P+ lines, actively manage brand equity, and increase equity through future brand repositioning, marketing, and management.

Specific aims of this research were to

- determine current brand equity in P+ as a baseline for future M&E;
- identify opportunities to improve P+ brand equity by addressing specific audience segments and brand attributes;
- evaluate the effect of the price increase and examine the relationship between product price points and brand equity; and
- examine whether former P+ users switched or lapsed from condom use due to the brand's price.

The study employed a simple observational design, with data collected at one time point in November 2010 from a random, nationally representative sample of Zimbabwean men aged 18–49 residing in rural and urban areas. The sample was stratified to compare current P+ users to users of free/government-provided condoms and lapsed users (those who had not used P+

condoms in the past 3 months). Sample size was based on a set of power analysis assumptions: (1) Design effect = 1.5 Alpha (5%) = 1.64; 50% brand equity among current P+ users at the time of data collection; 15% difference in brand equity to be detected between current and former P+ users. These assumptions yielded sample sizes as shown in Table 6-2.

Quantitative data were collected from a 46-item, interviewer-administered questionnaire that was fielded using a laptop computer. Researchers also drew a random sample of 8 participants (n = 32) from each cell in the survey study for additional participation in a follow-up qualitative in-depth interview (IDI) that was done to gather more in-depth information about reasons behind responses given on the questionnaire and emotional reactions and connection to the P+ brand and condom use as a category of behavior. This mixed-method approach helped to interpret quantitative findings in the analysis phase of the study.

Researchers conducted descriptive analyses, factor analysis of brand equity factors, and estimated multivariate logistic regression models for the questionnaire data to answer the research questions. The qualitative data were coded by hand to identify major thematic responses. Outcome measures included the following categories:

- Market barriers/supports
- Price willing to pay
- Condom use
- Risk perceptions
- Knowledge, attitudes, beliefs, social norms
- Behavioral intentions
- Media exposure and use
- Brand awareness
- Brand equity (associations with the brand, as discussed in Chapter 4 of this volume) in each brand in the Zimbabwe market
- Sociodemographics

Table 6-2 Protector Plus Study Design and Sample Sizes by Condition

Brand	Current Users	Lapsed Users
Protector Plus	200	200
Free/government sector	200	XXX
Lapsed Protector Plus users	XXX	200

Major results of this study (see Evans, Taruberekera, et al., 2011 for details) were as follows:

- There was high brand equity across all factors for P+, much higher for P+ than a free/government brand.
- Overall, no major differences were observed between current and lapsed users' brand equity in P+.
- The greatest preferences for brand extensions were for flavors; some colors were also of interest.
- Willingness to pay varied by user status:
  - Most current P+ users said they would pay 15 cents (current price 10 cents).
  - Lapsed users were not significantly different; a higher price was not the decisive factor in condom use decision.
- Current P+ users had higher loyalty and lower perceived market barriers compared to all others and compared directly to lapsed P+ users.
- Lapsed P+ users had lower loyalty and reported higher perceived market barriers than others.
- Lapsed users may be possible "switchers" who could have their loyalty raised and market barriers lowered through social marketing efforts.
- The price of P+ could potentially be raised given the high willingness to pay.

In conclusion, the study found that P+ had a strong brand equity and market position. There was observed potential to grow the total market by persuading lapsed P+ users to switch back to P+. Some government brand users (including lapsed P+ users) appeared to be willing to switch; raising their brand equity in P+ through repositioning and promotion would potentially lead to switching. Price did not appear to be a major barrier to condom use, and the total market for condom sales could be increased through switching (Pollard, 2014). The market potentially could be grown at an even higher price point than the level at the time of the study in 2010.

Case Study: Use of Social Media and Mobile Phone Technologies for Monitoring and Evaluation

New media, defined here as digital technologies, including the Internet, social media, and apps and other mobile phone–based technologies, are both tools for research and program evaluation (i.e., platforms on which research can be conducted) and intervention channels for social marketing that need to be evaluated (Evans, 2015). The following is a case study of one use of social media that includes both implementation of a social marketing campaign and evaluation using a digital platform.

Campaign Background

Consider the case of recent social marketing research using online and mobile technologies to evaluate efforts by not-for-profit organizations to prevent child abuse and neglect (CAN). Prevent Child Abuse America (PCAA) has developed a National Movement for America's Children. This project involved several steps:

- A pretesting study was conducted of reasons why people join the PCAA Cause and behaviors related to preventing abuse.
- The PCAA Cause at the time (2011) had over 3 million members.
- It implemented a 55-item pretesting survey made available to all members (convenience sample) to evaluate new promotions for the National Movement for America's Children.
- It received a total of 1,199 completed surveys.

The survey included a series of questions about reasons for visiting the cause website and what participants did when they went there. Table 6-3 provides examples of the results of these questions.

Based on the Facebook Causes pretesting research, researchers developed a follow-up evaluation of the National Movement brand and associated messaging. The National Movement represented a major change from earlier child abuse prevention social marketing efforts, which focus on parenting skills and family intervention before abuse begins (Prevent Child Abuse America, 2004). Messaging for primary prevention focused on the seriousness of the issue, the importance of parenting skills, and intervention by the community, state, and local agencies to prevent abuse from occurring. By contrast, the main focuses of the National Movement and its messaging are volunteerism; building public will for collective action; and outlining specific steps that government, philanthropies, businesses, and private citizens can take to change public discourse and ultimately prevent child abuse. The brand seeks to build a sense of shared responsibility and provide an outlet for collective action for CAN prevention (Evans, Falconer, et al., 2012).

Table 6-3 Sample Results From the Facebook Causes National Movement for America's Children Survey

10. What do you do when visiting the Prevent Child Abuse America Cause site? (Please check all that apply)		
Post comments	209	20%
Respond to other members' comments	229	22%
Attach files	18	2%
Post weblinks	49	5%
Stay active with the cause	538	53%
Other, please specify	338	33%
12. Please indicate your level of agreement: My participation in the Society Against Child Abuse Cause site will make a difference in reducing child abuse and neglect in the real world.		
Strongly agree	175	15%
Agree	549	48%
Disagree	87	8%
Strongly disagree	21	2%
Don't know	323	27%
Total	1,155	100%

To begin the process of building brand awareness and engagement with the National Movement, PCAA and partners created a website (http://www.movementforchildren.org/). The site offers a variety of avenues for engagement with the brand and to become involved in CAN prevention efforts and thus applies three of the 4Ps: a place P (multiple online channels), promotion P (prevention messaging), and product P (preventing child abuse and policy action). There is a pledge document, which lays out basic principles of the National Movement and defines roles public actors (e.g., Congress, state governments, businesses) can play in changing policy and building public support for prevention and changing discourse on CAN. There are social media tools, including a Twitter feed and links to Facebook and other online engagement resources. Finally, there are direct messages about CAN itself, the movement's purposes and objectives, and ways that different segments of society can become involved and benefit both individually and collectively.

As a first step to quantitatively evaluate receptivity to the National Movement brand, researchers conducted an MR evaluation of National

Movement branded messages as delivered through the movement's new website. MR is the extent to which a message recipient finds a message to be rationally or emotionally appealing (Evans, Davis, et al., 2011). Receptivity was based on previous psychological research on factors influencing message processing through central and peripheral cognitive functions and on the elaboration likelihood model (ELM) of cognitive processing (Petty & Cacioppo, 1986).

Researchers implemented the evaluation through an online survey hosted at the National Movement website. The design was an observational study (no comparison group) of all users of the website during this time period. We opened the survey (i.e., made the survey weblink active) to site visitors and invited them to complete the survey between October 2011 and January 2012. We anticipated this time period would be sufficient to collect a convenience sample of approximately 300 participants. However, the total sample fell short of this target number, as described in the material that follows. All visitors to the site were recruited to take a survey and, once they clicked on the survey link, were taken to the SurveyMonkey hosted site, where they completed an informed consent and the survey.

The sample included all visitors to the National Movement website who agreed to participate. Thus, the sample represented self-selected visitors to the site, not a randomly selected or representative sample of the US population. Many visitors were among those for whom CAN is a personal or moral issue, not necessarily the broad US public with which the National Movement hoped to engage over time. Researchers measured the respondent's reason for visiting the site and used those data in the analysis, as it was hypothesized that the reason for visiting was correlated with receptivity to movement messages.

The overall goal of the data analysis was to answer the evaluation questions noted previously and to begin to explore the draft National Movement logic model (which hypothesizes increased participation in the movement as a result of reframed child abuse prevention messages). The data will allow us to assess short-term relationships among the MR, brand associations, and behavioral precursors (e.g., self-efficacy to prevent child abuse through the National Movement social movement) described previously. Another key element of this research agenda is to begin a longer-term process of studying relationships between exposure to National Movement messages and social movement behavioral outcomes, including volunteer efforts, actions based on the recommendations in the pledge, advocacy with elected officials, and financial contributions.

For this pilot evaluation, researchers conducted descriptive and bivariate analyses of associations between audience characteristics, including sociodemographic characteristics such as having children at home and psychosocial characteristics such as reason for visiting the website. Analyses included frequencies, cross-tabulations, and chi-square statistics to examine the sample characteristics, explore potential for inferential analyses, and test for potential between-group differences (e.g., between those who visited the site due to dedicated moral interest in CAN prevention and those interested in pragmatic reasons for prevention, such as economic progress, or between members of older and younger generations who may have differing views on social causes or parents versus individuals without children).

Based on these findings, researchers developed multivariable logistic regression models comparing differences in willingness to engage in future National Movement activities based on sociodemographic differences and reasons for being involved in CAN (e.g., those visiting the website for moral versus pragmatic reasons, age, those with and without children living at home). Analyses reported here examined single time point tests of association between hypothesized independent, mediating, moderating, and dependent variables (as conceptualized in the movement logic model).

Table 6-4 summarizes the National Movement domains of measures evaluated in this study. Each of these domains represents a section of the questionnaire, for which multiple items were asked. The total questionnaire comprised 48 items, some asked as multi-item scales.

Table 6-5 summarizes MR to National Movement messages and provides an example of data analyzed in this study. The table shows data on receptivity to a series of statements about the potential for various social and political actors to take action, promote policy change, and be effective in bringing about changes in CAN by participating in the National Movement.

Overall, respondents were highly receptive to the messages with some variation (see Table 6-5). Individuals and communities were the articles in the National Movement statement (e.g., related to actions that the president of the United States could and should take to support the movement) that were found most convincing and most supported overall. Overall, belief that messages "grabbed your attention" was lower than other receptivity measures. Belief that the statements "said something important" was generally higher than other receptivity measures.

Researchers found that most respondents had positive knowledge, attitudes, and beliefs about CAN prevention (over 80% positive agreement, and many items over 90%). The lowest response (just under 73%) was the belief that members of the respondents' community were actively engaged in prevention. While this result is still fairly high and may reflect the sample of people who are themselves mostly actively involved, it suggests an opportunity for movement messages to increase the sense that community participation is important and will be effective.

Table 6-4 Domains of National Movement Evaluation Measures

Domains	Comments
Demographics	Limited items, including age, gender, race/ethnicity, and presence of children under 18 in participant's home
Interest and background in child abuse and neglect prevention	Includes perceived seriousness of the problem, actions taken, reasons for actions
Participation in social media and social networking • Social media as a channel to engage in the Movement • Social media use as a predictor of Movement-related attitudes, beliefs, behaviors	Segmentation variables
Knowledge, attitudes, beliefs, social norms about child abuse and neglect • Measures of cognitions targeted by movement that may change through message exposure and engagement	Short-term outcomes of the movement
Brand equity in the movement • Moral and pragmatic reasons for engaging in the movement	Recognition and value placed in brand
Reactions to National Movement messaging and promotion • Beliefs in credibility, likability of messages	Independent variables (campaign effects on outcomes)
Social movement engagement behaviors, including volunteering, donating, sharing information in social networks, etc.	Intermediate outcomes of the movement
Beliefs about potential solutions to CAN	Intermediate outcomes of the movement

Respondents generally had positive reactions to movement messages (the eight articles referring to social and political actors) and expressed willingness to take recommended actions to become involved and participate. We found no statistical variation in responses when we examined overall agreement. However, when we examined strong agreement (the strongest statement of support for an article or intention to take a recommended action), we found some

Table 6-5 Receptivity to National Movement Messages: Overall Agreement (Respondent Indicated Agree or Strongly Agree as Response Option)

	% Agreement	Standard Error (%)	95% Confidence Interval: Low (%)	95% Confidence Interval: High (%)
Article 1. The President of the United States				
Convincing	79.5	6.2	67.1	92.0
Grabbed your attention	65.9	7.5	50.7	81.0
Good reasons to support	73.8	6.9	59.9	87.7
Said something important	86.7	5.1	76.3	97.0
Article 2. The Congress of the United States				
Convincing	86.0	5.3	75.3	96.8
Grabbed your attention	71.4	7.1	57.2	85.7
Good reasons to support	81.0	6.1	68.6	93.3
Said something important	90.5	4.6	81.2	99.7
Article 3. State Governors				
Convincing	83.3	5.8	71.6	95.1
Grabbed your attention	68.3	7.4	53.4	83.2
Good reasons to support	71.1	7.5	55.9	86.2
Said something important	90.2	4.7	80.8	99.7
Article 4. State Legislatures				
Convincing	89.5	5.0	79.3	99.7
Grabbed your attention	61.3	8.9	43.1	79.5
Good reasons to support	77.8	7.0	63.5	92.0
Said something important	91.7	4.7	82.2	100.0

Table 6-5 Continued

	% Agreement	Standard Error (%)	95% Confidence Interval: Low (%)	95% Confidence Interval: High (%)
Article 5. Local Communities				
Convincing	87.2	5.4	76.2	98.2
Grabbed your attention	78.4	6.9	64.5	92.3
Good reasons to support	83.8	6.1	71.3	96.2
Said something important	89.7	4.9	79.8	99.7
Article 6. The Business Sector				
Convincing	77.8	7.0	63.5	92.0
Grabbed your attention	69.4	7.8	53.6	85.3
Good reasons to support	65.7	8.1	49.2	82.3
Said something important	82.9	6.5	69.7	96.0
Article 7. Communities of Faith				
Convincing	89.5	5.0	79.3	99.7
Grabbed your attention	70.3	7.6	54.8	85.7
Good reasons to support	77.1	7.2	62.5	91.8
Said something important	91.9	4.5	82.7	100.0
Article 8. Individuals				
Convincing	91.9	4.5	82.7	100.0
Grabbed your attention	78.4	6.9	64.5	92.3
Good reasons to support	78.9	6.7	65.4	92.5
Said something important	88.9	5.3	78.1	99.7

interesting differences. Individuals were the ones most perceived as able to make a difference in CAN prevention, followed by communities. Strong agreement in statements about other actors was generally much lower. This may reflect the current political and media environment and public discourse. Public satisfaction with and trust in many institutions of government (e.g., Congress) and business (e.g., banks and Wall Street) may be low due to effects of the Great Recession of 2008–2009 and long-term aftereffects on economic and political conditions in the United States. Strong agreement is generally more predictive of subsequent action in response to a message. If the underlying factors (e.g., beliefs about the role of individuals, communities, and other institutions) could be uncovered through qualitative research (e.g., focus groups), this may help PCAA to develop refined and potentially more effective messages.

Conclusions and Future Directions

Monitoring and evaluation of social marketing represent a rich domain of research that is rapidly growing. The evidence base is growing, but there remain gaps and the need for enhanced and more rigorous evaluation methods. There are many valuable case studies from M&E of social marketing efforts that researchers can use and build on in future studies. New media technologies offer opportunities to build the evidence base. As seen in subsequent chapters, the methods described in this chapter are applicable to, but may require significant adaptation, different settings and to varying topics in social marketing research. For example, M&E methods may need to be modified in the context of new media technologies, as discussed in Chapter 7. In addition, adaptations are often required, and opportunities for methodological innovation arise in low-resource settings, such as in low- and middle-income countries, as seen in Chapters 8 and 9.

Additional Resources: Literature

- Andreasen, A. (2002). *Marketing Research That Won't Break the Bank: A Practical Guide to Getting the Information You Need* (2nd ed.). New York Wiley.
- Esser, F., & Hanitzsch, T. *The Handbook of Comparative Communication Research*. New York: Routledge.
- Evans, W.D., Davis, K.C., Umanzor, C., Patel, K., & Khan, M. (2011). Evaluation of Sexual Communication Messages. *BMC Reproductive Health*, 8(15). doi:10.1186/1742-4755-8-15

- Hayes, A., Slater, M., & Snyder, L.B. (2008). *The Sage Sourcebook on Advanced Data Analysis Methods for Communication Research*. Thousand Oaks, CA: Sage.
- Rice, R.E., & Atkin, C.K. (2013). *Public Communication Campaigns* (4th ed.). Thousand Oaks, CA: Sage.

References

Bandura, A. (2004). Health Promotion by Social Cognitive Means. *Health Education & Behavior,* 31(2): 143–164.

Blitstein, J.L., Evans, W.D., Davis, K.C., & Kamyab, K. (2012). Impact of Repeated Exposure to Media Messages Encouraging Parent-Child Communication: Longitudinal Change in the Parents Speak Up National Campaign (PSUNC). *American Journal of Health Promotion,* 27(1): 43–51.

Bruner, G.C. (1998). Standardization and Justification: Do Ad Scales Measure Up? *Journal of Current Issues and Research in Advertising,* 20: 1–18.

Centers for Disease Control and Prevention. (2010). CDCynergy. Retrieved on September 1, 2015, from http://www.cdc.gov/healthcommunication/index.html

Chapman, S., Ayers, J., LeTouze, O., & Renard. (2013). Branding and Social Marketing. In *Psychology of Branding,* W.D. Evans (Ed.). Hauppage, NY: Nova Science. Chapter 10.

Datta, A.R., Yan, T., Evans, W.D., Pedlow, S., Spencer, B., & Bautista, R. (2012). *2010 Census Integrated Communications Program Evaluation: Final Report.* Prepared for the US Bureau of the Census, US Department of Commerce. Chicago: NORC at the University of Chicago.

Davis, K.C., Blitstein, J., Evans, W.D., & Kamyab, K. (2010). Impact of a parent-child sexual communication campaign: results from a controlled efficacy trial of parents. *BMC Reproductive Health*, 7: 1, DOI:10.1186/1742–4755-7–17.

Davis, K.C., Evans, W.D., & Kamyab, K. (2013). Effectiveness of a National Media Campaign to Promote Parent-Child Communication About Sex. *Health Education and Behavior*, 40(1): 97–106. doi:10.1177/1090198112440009

Davis, K.C., Nonnemaker, J.M., Farrelly, M.C., & Niederdeppe, J. (2011). Exploring Differences in Smokers' Perceptions of the Effectiveness of Cessation Media Messages. *Tobacco Control,* 20(1): 26–33.

Dillard, J.P., Shen, L., & Vail, R.G. (2007). Does Perceived Message Effectiveness Cause Persuasion or Vice Versa? 17 Consistent Answers. *Human Communication Research,* 33(4): 467–488.

Evans, W.D. (Ed.). (2015). *Social Marketing: Global Perspectives, Strategies, and Effects on Consumer Behavior*. Hauppauge, NY: Nova Science.

Evans, W.D., Blitstein J., & Hersey, J. (2008). Evaluation of Public Health Brands: Design, Measurement, and Analysis. In *Public Health Branding: Applying*

Marketing for Social Change, W.D. Evans & G. Hastings (Eds.). London: Oxford University Press. Chapter 3.

Evans, W.D., Christoffel, K.K., Necheles, J., Becker, A.B., & Snider, J. (2011). Outcomes of the 5-4-3-2-1 Go! Childhood Obesity Community Trial. *American Journal of Health Behavior*, 35(2): 189–198.

Evans, W.D., Davis, K.C., & Farrelly, M.C. (2008). Planning for a Media Evaluation. In *A Practical Guide to Program Evaluation Planning*, D. Holden & M. Zimmerman (Eds.). Thousand Oaks, CA: Sage. Chapter 6.

Evans, W.D., Davis, K.C., Ashley, O., Blitstein, J., Koo, H., & Zhang, Y. (2009). Efficacy of Abstinence Promotion Media Messages: Findings From an Online Randomized Trial. *Journal of Adolescent Health*, 45(4): 409–417.

Evans, W.D., Davis, K.C., Umanzor, C., Patel, K., & Khan, M. (2012). Evaluation of Sexual Communication Messages. *BMC Reproductive Health*, 8:15. doi:10.1186/1742-4755-8-15

Evans, W.D., Falconer, M.K., Khan, M., & Ferris, C. (2012). Efficacy of Child Abuse and Neglect Prevention Campaign Messages: Results From an Online Evaluation of the Florida Winds of Change Campaign. *Journal of Health Communication*, 17(4):413–431. doi:10.1080/10810730.2011.626502

Evans, W.D., Necheles, J., Becker, A.B., Christoffel, K.K., & Snider, J. (2010). Social Marketing as a Childhood Obesity Prevention Strategy. *Obesity*, 18(S1): S23–S26.

Evans, W.D., Necheles, J., Longjohn, M., & Christoffel, K. (2007). The 5-4-3-2-1 Go! Intervention: Social Marketing for Nutrition. *Journal of Nutrition Education and Behavior*, 39(2)(S1): S55–S59.

Evans, W.D., Nielsen, P., Szekely, D., Wallace, J., Murray, E., & Snider, J. (2014). Initial Outcomes From a 4-Week Follow-Up Study of the Text4baby Program in the Military Women's Population: Randomized Controlled Trial. *Journal of Medical Internet Research*, 16(5): e13. doi:10.2196/jmir.3297

Evans, W.D., Taruberekera, N., Longfield, K., & Snider, J. (2011). Brand Equity and Willingness to Pay for Condoms in Zimbabwe. *BMC Reproductive Health*, 8: 29. doi:10.1186/1742-4755-8-29

Evans, W.D., Uhrig, J., Davis, K., & McCormack, L. (2009). Efficacy Methods to Evaluate Health Communication and Marketing Campaigns. *Journal of Health Communication*, 14(3): 244–254.

Evans, W.D., Yan, T., & Datta, R. (2012). Receptivity to 2010 US Census Media Messages. *Journal of Mass Communication and Journalism*, 2: 9. doi:10.4172/2165-7912.1000126

Farrelly, M.C., Davis, K.C., Haviland, M.L., Messeri, P., & Healton, C.G. (2005). Evidence of a Dose-Response Relationship Between "truth" Antismoking Ads and Youth Smoking. *American Journal of Public Health*, 95(3): 425–431.

Fishbein, M., & Ajzen, I. (2010). *Predicting and Changing Behavior: The Reasoned Action Approach*. New York: Psychology Press.

Green, L., & Kreuter, M. (2005). *Health Program Planning: An Educational and Ecological Approach* (4th ed.). New York: McGraw-Hill.

Guba, E.G., & Lincoln, Y.S. (1994). Competing paradigms in qualitative research. In *Handbook of Qualitative Research*, N.K. Denzin & Y.S. Lincoln (Eds.). Thousand Oaks, CA: Sage. Chapter 6.

Gustat, J., Rice, J., Parker, K.M., Becker, A.B., & Farley, T.A. (2012). Effect of Changes to the Neighborhood Built Environment on Physical Activity in Low-Income African Neighborhood. *Preventing Chronic Disease*, 9: 110165.

Hersey, J., Niederdeppe, J., Evans, W.D., Nonnemaker, J., Blahut, S., Holden, D., Messeri, P., & Haviland, M.L. (2005). The Theory of truth®: How Counterindustry Campaigns Affect Smoking Behavior Among Teens. *Health Psychology*, 24(1):22–31.

Hornik, R.C. (2002). *Public Health Communication: Evidence for Behavior Change.* Mahwah, NJ: Erlbaum.

Kotler, P., & Lee, N. (2008). *Social Marketing: Influencing Behaviors for Good* (3rd ed.). Los Angeles: Sage.

MacLeod, C., Rutherford, E., Campbell, L., Ebsworthy, G., & Holker, L. (2002). Selective Attention and Emotional Vulnerability: Assessing the Causal Basis of Their Association Through the Experimental Manipulation of Attentional Bias. *Journal of Abnormal Psychology*, 111(1): 107.

Mason, M., Meleedy-Rey, P., Christoffel, K.K., LongJohn, M., Garcia, M.P., & Ashlaw, C. (2006). Prevalence of Overweight and Risk of Overweight 3- to 5-Year-Old Chicago Children, 2002–2003. *Journal of School Health*, 76(3): 104–110.

Petty, R.E., & Cacioppo, J.T. (1986). *Communication and Persuasion: Central and Peripheral Routes to Attitude Change*. New York: Springer-Verlag.

Pollard, R. (2014). Total market approaches to the social marketing of health services and commodities in low-income countries. *Cases in Public Health Communication & Marketing*, 8(suppl 1): S4–S18.

Prevent Child Abuse America. (2004). Reframing Child Abuse and Neglect for Increased Understanding and Engagement: Defining the Need for Strategic Reframing. Retrieved on September 2, 2015, from http://2011.preventchildabuse.org/about_us/reframing/downloads/reframing%20revised.pdf.

Prochaska, J.O., DiClemente, C.C., & Norcross, J.C. (1992). In Search of How People Change: Applications to Addictive Behaviors. *American Psychologist*, 47(9): 1102–1114.

Robinson, M.N., Tansil, K.A., Elder, R.W., Soler, R.E., Labre, M.P., Mercer, S.L., Eroglu, D., Baur, C., Lyon-Daniel, K., Fridinger, F., et al. (2014). Health Communication Campaigns That Include Mass Media and Health-Related Product Distribution: A Community Guide Systematic Review. *American Journal of Preventive Medicine*, 47(3): 360–371.

Rossi, P., & Freeman, R. (1993). *Evaluation: A Systematic Approach*. Thousand Oaks, CA: Sage.

Singh, S.N., & Rothschild, M.L. (1983). Recognition as a Measure of Learning From Television Commercials. *Journal of Marketing Research*, 20(3): 235–248.

Sly, D.F., Hopkins, R.S., Trapido, E., & Ray, S. (2001). Influence of a Counteradvertising Media Campaign on Initiation of Smoking: The Florida "truth" Campaign. *American Journal of Public Health*, 91(2): 233–238.

Southwell, B.G. (2005). Between Messages and People: A Multilevel Model of Memory for Television Content. *Communication Research*, 32(1): 112–140.

Southwell, B.G., Barmada, C.H., Hornik, R.C., & Maklan, D.M. (2002). Can We Measure Encoded Exposure? Validation From a National Campaign. *Journal of Health Communication*, 7: 445–453.

Valente, T.W. (2002). *Evaluating Health Promotion Programs*. Oxford, UK: Oxford University Press.

7

Social Marketing Research in the Digital Media Age

W. Douglas Evans

Summary Points

- Social marketing research continues to change as campaign strategies evolve due to new technologies.
- Single new media approaches, such as text messaging campaigns and apps, represented the early model.
- Multimedia approaches have become the paradigm.
- Research on the effectiveness of multiple modalities, and optimization of channel combinations, is needed to fully integrate new technologies into social marketing.

Introduction and Background

Just as social marketing has changed from a marketer-consumer top-down relationship to one of multimodal marketing nested within social environments due to technologies such as social media and mobile phones (Lefebvre, 2011), so social marketing research has rapidly changed in recent years (Evans, 2015). Social marketing campaigns have new tools to build relationships with audiences, and research and evaluation studies need to measure those relationships and exposure to and engagement with new media technologies that increasingly drive campaign implementation (French et al., 2010). Exposure to new media and diffusion of messages within social networks are critical independent variables to account for in campaign evaluations, and effective use of these strategies is an important topic for formative research and message testing. These phenomena are occurring in both developed and developing markets, but the mix of the 4Ps (place, price, product, and promotion) is often different, and the resources and constraints on both campaign implementation and evaluation differ (Chapman et al., 2013; Agha, 2003).

New media technologies also increase the range of methods available for social marketing research and evaluation, especially through increased experimental and quasi-experimental control, as seen in Chapters 5 and 6. This chapter explores the development of new social marketing programs and new research and evaluation measures, methods, and growth of evidence in the field.

Another change in the social marketing landscape that has emerged in part due to the widespread use of new technologies for behavior change is the proliferation of campaigns competing for attention and the emergence of more robust categories of competing social marketing product offerings. This change has been noted in the international development arena with the growth of interest in "total market approaches" (TMAs) or "whole market approaches" to behavior change (Pollard, 2014; Population Services International [PSI], 2015). TMA has been defined as a system "to improve the financial sustainability of health services in low- and middle-income countries, with an emphasis on commodities provision" (Pollard, 2014, p. 1). This approach is typically promoted by social marketing organizations in under- or undeveloped markets for essential social commodities, such as condoms, bed nets, and family planning products. TMA seeks to match market segments with appropriately priced and distributed products: free for those in the poorest communities, partially subsidized products for those with somewhat greater resources, and commercially priced products from the private sector for those who can afford them. This approach has the overall goal of growing the market by encouraging product use and eventual transition to private sector sales and distribution as the local market matures and the economy grows; the approach also is to avoid socially marketed products "crowding out" or eliminating the private-sector offerings due to subsidized prices (PSI, 2015). Recent studies suggested the TMA has been effective in achieving these goals in some recent case examples from emerging economies that are in economic and epidemiological transition from less developed to more developed markets (Drake, Vail, & Stewart, 2014).

In addition, even in wealthy countries such as the United States, those in Europe, and Japan, where social marketing programs more frequently target behavior change not related to physical product sales, distribution, and use, there has been a trend toward development of "behavioral product" categories (Evans, 2015). (Note: It should also be said that there are certainly physical product-based social marketing efforts in wealthy countries, such as for injury prevention, but they are not predominant as in low- and middle-income markets; see Robinson et al., 2014.) In the case of a behavioral product category, multiple social marketing efforts are ongoing within the same market space aimed at the same or overlapping audiences. For example, in the case of tobacco control, countermarketing campaigns aimed at youth smoking prevention operate in a competitive environment with multiple concurrent social marketing activities by different organizations. Consider the example discussed next.

In 2014, the American Legacy Foundation (now known as Truth Initiative) launched the most recent version of its famous and highly acclaimed *truth*® campaign, which was originally launched in 2000 (Farrelly et al., 2009). Truth Initiative has "[positioned] truth 3.0 [the new campaign] as an updated brand for teens and young adults it designed to develop a relationship with this audience, who will build an affinity for the brand and its attributes over time via campaign messages and other truth activities, internalize truth brand attributes, self-identify as a truth supporter, and reduce intentions to smoke and longer-term smoking behavior" (Source: Internal Truth Initiative memo).

But, the most recent *truth* campaign (*FinishIt*) operates in a vastly altered tobacco control and tobacco industry marketplace from the one it faced in 2000 (when *truth* 1.0 was first launched). In 2014, there were *three* major organizations sponsoring countermarketing campaigns in the United States: Truth Initiative (*FinishIt*), the Centers for Disease Control and Prevention (CDC; TIPS), and the Food and Drug Administration (FDA; The Real Cost). This represents competition within the *category* of tobacco control brands that needs to be accounted for in future research. Finally, the tobacco industry continues to sponsor its own alleged tobacco control campaigns, which have been shown to be ineffective or to encourage youth smoking (Wakefield et al., 2006).

Further, tobacco industry marketing continues to evolve and now heavily relies of online and social media promotion. In addition, the presence of alternative tobacco products, such as electronic cigarettes (e-cigarettes), changes the marketplace of tobacco-related product options for youth. Recent studies suggest that e-cigarette use is rapidly increasing among adolescents and may actually exceed traditional cigarette use among some subgroups (Johnston et al., 2015). These changes also may affect response to the *truth* 3.0 brand and the category of tobacco use countermarketing campaigns that needs to be studied as part of new social marketing research.

Thus, changes in new technologies such as social media and mobile phones change not only the questions, methods, and designs used in social marketing research but also the nature of markets and social marketing strategies. This chapter considers these trends and extends recent analysis of the changes in social marketing due to social media and mobile phones (Evans, 2015) by exploring recent examples of new and emerging programs that use multiple media modalities to affect behavior change. Major changes in the field center on strategic use of multiple new technology platforms to create rich media environments where social marketing campaigns can reach consumers in multiple places with complimentary products and promotions. Social context can interact with new media technologies, as their use can be augmented by peer relationships, and in some cases those relationships shape use and behavior change resulting from media exposure. Multiple case studies illustrate these trends. The chapter concludes with implications and future expectations for the field.

Social Context and New Technologies: Case Study of the Self-Help Obesity Prevention Program

Project Background

The *Self-Help Obesity Prevention Program in Stokvels* (SHOPPS) is a wellness program comprising a healthy diet, increased physical activity (PA), and a self-help cognitive-behavioral intervention for black South African women in stokvels (informal credit unions that are formed by small groups and are widespread among black South Africans; African Response, 2012). The stokvel social context offers an opportunity to reach groups of similar individuals who can both participate in a technology-based obesity prevention intervention and provide mutual social support (Stokols, 1996). Mobile phones and evidence-based, web-based weight control programs are promising approaches for obesity prevention, and SHOPPS will demonstrate its potential in conjunction with social support activities. This example presents the conceptual framework, methods, protocol, and intervention strategy using digital media. SHOPPS will use mobile and Internet technologies to provide a cognitive-behavioral feedback to promote healthy eating and active living (HEAL). The primary outcome of interest is weight loss of 5% among SHOPPS participants compared to control.

SHOPPS will be evaluated in a cluster randomized controlled trial (RCT). Participants will get detailed, tailored feedback on nutrition and PA through their mobile phones and online regarding how to overcome barriers to HEAL behavior change in their community and help to track progress in managing their weight. Tailoring will occur through customized text messaging and online feedback based on individual progress. This will include making a personal resolution to lose 5% of their body weight, the target for this intervention, and will include a financial incentive for the stokvel group (group reward if each member reaches her individual goal). Participants will use the website to track personal progress and receive tailored feedback.

The hypothesis underlying SHOPPS is that increased engagement with the program, feedback, and creation of a program "brand identity" to represent a "trusted friend and advisor" will promote HEAL behaviors (Evans et al., 2010; Shaw et al., 2005). SHOPPS is based on cognitive-behavioral therapy (CBT) (Cooper et al., 2010), and social cognitive theory (SCT) (Bandura, 2004). Outcomes include changes in HEAL behaviors and weight loss.

Studies have shown that health promotion in community and social group settings can improve adults' morale, health, fitness, and dietary intake (Anderson et al., 1998; Aldana et al., 2005). One reason for this may be that within-group social dynamics (e.g., support, mutual accountability, friendly competition) help group members to achieve personal or group health goals (Burke et al., 2004). Thus, a wellness program for stokvel members comprising a healthy diet, increased PA, and a self-help cognitive-behavioral intervention may reduce or prevent obesity risk behaviors, and related chronic non-communicable diseases (NCD), as advocated by the World Health Organization (WHO, 2008).

Evaluation Background

A cluster RCT will evaluate SHOPPS. A total of 22 stokvels (average 20 members per stokvel) will be randomized to a SHOPPS treatment group and a control group (11 stokvels in each). Stokvel members in both conditions will receive SHOPPS plus standard printed South African Department of Health (DOH) information on nutrition, PA, and wellness. Participants assigned to the control group will receive the DOH information only. We will recruit stokvels based on (1) comparable size (15–25 members), (2) location in the Johannesburg metro area, and (3) exclusively black African female membersship.

In addition, the protocol requires that all individual participants have a body mass index (BMI) of greater than 25 kg/m^2 (i.e., be overweight or obese). The goal is to maximize internal validity rather than external validity. As the stokvel is the sampling unit, all members of a group will be in one study condition. Researchers will include all members of a stokvel who meet group criteria *in the intervention activities.* However, investigators will separately analyze those members who meet minimum individual BMI criteria for outcome evaluation purposes. This will enable full group participation by all members but maintain intent-to-treat principles for analysis.

The evaluation has two primary aims. Aim 1 is to conduct formative research with African women to tailor SHOPPS to the target population. For hypothesis (H) 1.1, participants will have positive message receptivity to SHOPPS based on a validated scale (Petty & Cacioppo, 1986). Aim 2 is to conduct a 6-month cluster RCT of SHOPPS in Johannesburg area stokvels. For H2.1, compared to control, SHOPPS participants lose 5% more weight after 6 months; for H2.2, SHOPPS brand equity will mediate intervention effects on HEAL and weight loss outcomes.

Data will be collected from (1) anthropometric measures from in-person physical examinations; (2) self-reports through an in-person questionnaire at baseline and after 6 months; and (3) online recording of weight status and participation in intervention activities (e.g., providing shopping lists). To ensure comparability and sufficient numbers of participants, the research team will only sample from Johannesburg stokvels. The research team has a list of Johannesburg registered stokvels from the South African National Stokvels Association (SANSA), which provides background information on these groups. Only stokvels meeting inclusion criteria will be included. This will ensure relative homogeneity of stokvel group environments.

The research team calculated the required sample size for analysis of covariance in a cluster-randomized trial (Teerenstra, Eldridge, Graff, de Hoop, & Borm, 2012). Required baseline sample size was determined to be 131 participants, or 11 stokvels averaging 13 members. This is similar to other web-based weight loss studies (Neve et al., 2010).

On obtaining institutional review board (IRB) approval and before the recruitment, the research team will visit in person each sampled stokvel at its monthly meeting in the Johannesburg metro area and ensure that all group members fully agree to terms of the study and sign a written agreement to participate. Next, the research team will conduct a second visit to the stokvel at its subsequent monthly meeting, conduct group orientation of all members, describe the study using a predeveloped script, and recruit members. An initial 24-hour dietary intake recall will be done at this time, on a weekday. This will be conducted as a fun event with refreshments. At the second visit, the baseline assessment, including all instruments and a second 24-hour dietary intake recall, will be done, all on a weekend day. After the baseline interview, all participants will receive the South African DOH basic dietary guidelines on a printed brochure, a $5 equivalent gift card, and a T-shirt. Then, the intervention will begin, and SHOPPS participants will receive password-protected access to the website. After 6 months, the team will follow up using the same procedures, and the participants will receive another $5 gift card.

After 6 months, the research team will return to each stokvel and administer the follow-up assessments. We will administer a physical exam, as in the baseline assessment. The interviews will include a supplemental module of questions on intervention exposure and reactions with the two treatment groups. The supplemental module will be used to measure self-reported dosage of SHOPPS received and satisfaction/preferences for specific intervention components. All interviews will be conducted in person by the investigators. To ensure retention, researchers will contact a representative of the stokvel by phone, e-mail, and text 1 week before follow-up. Participants will be tracked via unique case ID for confidentiality.

SHOPPS will be tailored both to the individual's HEAL and weight loss goals and success or specific needs as the individual progresses. Tailoring will be based on (1) individual response to keywords through the mProve texting platform (based on an algorithm programmed by mProve that triggers individually tailored feedback texts) and (2) information provided by participants and goal progress captured through the SHOPPS website.

The website includes detailed information, self-help advice, and progress-monitoring tools on diet, PA, and weight status. The program includes a CBT component to assist the participant in adopting positive behaviors to follow the program successfully. The website comprises the following sections of information: (1) health benefits of weight loss; (2) an explanation of a reasonable body weight and what it comprises; (3) methods of changing current eating and PA behaviors; (4) a healthy eating plan that can be individualized; (5) a PA guide; (6) weight loss strategies; (7) how to maintain weight loss and a PA program; and (8) weight, diet, and PA self-monitoring tools. Participants will be required to monitor their weight status and record this on a weekly basis. The website also includes weekly activities that the participant follows to engage actively with every aspect of the program. The website will also link to numerous other wellness websites, including those dealing with stress and tension. As the participants follow the program from week 1 through to week 26, they will receive feedback on PA and weight status.

Texts will be delivered through a platform that supports interactive SMS (short message service) using a content management system that delivers texts. The SHOPPS protocol will be an application on the platform that captures keyword responses to texts received and includes an algorithm that calculates a tailored SHOPPS text response based on the participants' history. The research team will design a branching tree structure of tailored texts to be delivered based on participant response. For example, if a participant has a history of replying to keywords for PA texts, the participant may receive in-depth suggestions for convenient daily exercise options in the local community on weekdays and weekends. Thus, the SHOPPS protocol will provide tailored text feedback and complement tailored website feedback on progress.

Researchers will use a "group contest" approach with a prize equal to the annual contribution for a member of the stokvel if all overweight (BMI > 25) group members reach the outcome of 5% weight loss. If each overweight member of the group meets the goal of 5% weight loss, the research team will deposit US$200 (about the average for a Johannesburg stokvel individual member's annual contribution) into the group's collective stokvel account, proportionally increasing the value of each member's share of the account. The contribution will only be made if every overweight group member meets her goal, providing added incentive for achievement of intervention goals according to behavioral economic theory (Patrick et al., 2009), following the successes of similar health promotion programs using texting (Fjeldsoe et al., 2009; Franklin et al., 2006; Haapala et al., 2009; Lim et al., 2008; Logan et al., 2007; Rodgers et al., 2005; Whittaker et al., 2009). All members will benefit from the incentive, including those who were not overweight at baseline, as it is a group benefit.

The SHOPPS intervention represents an example of using both social context and digital media to leverage behavior change. These two factors can be mutually reinforcing, and evaluation of SHOPPS will shed light on how future social marketing campaigns can capitalize on the interrelationship between context and technology use, as well as the power of incentives and social support.

Using Digital Media to Enhance Diffusion of Social Marketing: Case Study of Using Social Media and Storytelling for Prevention

Campaign Background

The Mentor Foundation USA currently conducts the Shattering the Myths youth rally (STM rally; http://www.mentorfoundationusa.org/shattering-the-myths-2015/), an interactive in-person event with high school students designed to dispel the myths surrounding drug abuse. By focusing on their own innate talents and strengths, youth become advocates for staying drug free. The Substance Abuse and Mental Health Services Administration (SAMHSA) noted that interactive youth activities can improve social norms regarding prevention (Center for Behavioral Health Statistics and Quality, 2012). The STM rally raises awareness of *risks* surrounding substance use, *specifically marijuana*, and is based on recent neuroscience (Jacobus et al., 2014). It creates new mental associations with the benefits of avoiding substance use and may reduce social norms supporting use and use intentions. STM is an experiential learning approach to prevention and applies principles from social marketing (Evans & Hastings, 2008).

Positive antidrug brand representations can also be promoted using social media and social networking strategies to complement the STM in-person, event-based approach. The *#STM4U* is a novel program that will consist of tailored, in-person video design activities based on the Adobe Youth Voices (AYV; https://youthvoices.adobe.com/) platform, followed by youth sharing of their own video narrative content via their preferred social media platform, thereby creating a prevention brand for peers in their social network (Table 7-1).

This approach to branding an alternative, healthy behavior, or "countermarketing" as it has been termed in tobacco control (CDC, 2014), has been highly effective and is recognized as one of the main elements in effective, comprehensive tobacco control programs according to the CDC (2014). However, this approach has not been applied in marijuana use, largely because the concept of an "industry" (e.g., the tobacco industry) has not truly existed until recent changes in marijuana laws created a legal marijuana industry. Recent estimates suggest that the value of the medical marijuana industry alone will be $8 billion in the United States by 2018 and could be as high as $35 billion by 2020 if more states legalize the drug (Huffington Post, 2014). In this new marijuana market context, countermarketing for prevention using a

Table 7-1 #STM4U Evaluation Study Design

	Data Collection Time Point	
Experimental Condition	Baseline	6-Month Follow-up
Social media + STM (#STM4U)	80	64
STM Rally only	80	64

branding strategy is a significant approach that may be able to leverage strategies used in tobacco control. Evaluation of the #STM4U program will provide needed evidence for the potential of countermarketing in the new prevention environment.

Social media have become major drivers of public debate and perceptions of marijuana and prevention. Organizers of the drives for legalization in Colorado and Washington used social media to influence public opinion (Pew Research Center, 2014). There are numerous ongoing social media forums that promote legalization. Such forums likely affect public opinion and social norms, especially of teenagers, but little is known about these processes or effects (Neighbors et al., 2013). #STM4U aims to reduce pro-marijuana social norms, potentially counteracting the effects of relaxed laws and change in social environment.

In addition, campaigns such as Above the Influence (ATI), at the national level, and at the state and local level have used social media (ATI, 2015). There is now evidence that these efforts can be effective in changing knowledge, attitudes, and beliefs about marijuana use among targeted population groups such as teenagers (Slater et al., 2011; Carpenter & Pechmann, 2011). Following prospect theory, research on message framing (Rothman et al., 2006; O'Keefe & Jensen, 2007) and on prevention messages for preteens and teenagers (Evans et al., 2004) suggests that gain-framed messages may be effective. The use of graphic imagery has been found to contribute to uptake of gain-framed health messages (Mays et al., 2014). Social media are effective tools through which to share graphic, multimedia content, and #STM4U will apply this approach to prevention.

Despite large-scale social media efforts such as ATI and its large Facebook presence and efforts to create a social community of youth sharing narratives related to avoidance of marijuana use (Andrade et al., 2015), relatively little has been published demonstrating the effectiveness of social media for prevention. SAMHSA has funded a number of state media campaigns for prevention, some of which, including Colorado's Speak Now! campaign focused on teen drinking prevention, have used social media activities (http://www.samhsa.gov/capt/tools-learning-resources/prevention-media-campaigns). However, these are early efforts, and #STM4U will be an effort to design and rigorously test a systematic intervention for prevention driven by social media.

Schools are a common context for interventions given their almost-universal access to youth. School-based interventions have an established history with an emerging cadre of successful interventions documented on SAMSHA's National Registry of Evidence Based Programs and Practices

(NREPP) (SAMHSA, 2015). Previous research provides a basis for adding media to school interventions. In the conceptual framework behind Slater et al.'s in-school media intervention, Be Under Your Own Influence, the adolescent's experience was embedded in the experience of school, community, and the larger social world (Slater et al., 2006). That project emphasized the combination of school and community media. #STM4U extends this approach as youth will create their own authentic video narratives for dissemination through social media. This approach will complement and extend the reach of the existing STM youth in-person rally. Social media provides access to the larger social world that is inaccessible to direct experience (Chou et al., 2009). Social media messages will echo the branded STM rally messages in school, thus reinforcing and amplifying antiuse norms.

Evaluation Background

The research team will conduct in-person program activity sessions throughout the intervention period. There will be STM rally-only activities at one of the two schools and social media plus STM rally activities at the other. For the STM rally, Mentor Foundation USA staff will lead a one-time, interactive youth rally during project month 13 designed to dispel marijuana use myths (e.g., that most peers use marijuana and approve of use) and encourage positive peer influence (http://www.mentorfoundationusa.org/what-we-do/prevention-programs/). The STM rally aims to help youth become personal advocates for avoiding marijuana use.

For the #STM4U condition, researchers will conduct an STM rally as noted previously and visit the #STM4U school monthly for 6 months during the intervention period and use the AYV platform to train youth to create their own video-based narrative stories to disseminate over social media. AYV offers a free online course, Adobe Youth Voices: Create Change. The course is designed to prepare educators to lead youth media development. Many health topics have previously been included in AYV projects, including marijuana use and addiction (https://youthvoices.adobe.com/youth-media-gallery/). AYV has also been used in school settings and capitalizes on the power of digital media to allow youth to express their own stories in exportable video format, ready made for sharing over social media such as YouTube, Facebook, Twitter, and Instagram. Researchers will use the AYV Youth Media Fundamentals course in #STM4U and will select 3 or 4 lessons per school visit from the suite of lessons available in the category, focused on working with youth to create video media and the creative process. The intervention will consist of a self-expression component by which students will learn techniques for expressing their ideas about marijuana use. Expressive segments will be created as videos for social media.

Teens who participate in the social media activities will be asked to disseminate the video-based narratives they create throughout their social media networks using all platforms to which they are current members. Researchers will also create and ask youth to post to a dedicated project YouTube channel. Youth must also use at least one platform (and create or already have an account) to share videos (e.g., Twitter, Instagram, Facebook, kik).

Due to the intervention activities taking place on social media, eliminating all possible contamination is unlikely. However, researchers will document all participant exposure to #STM4U social media metrics captured on the Hootsuite social media management platform (https://hootsuite.com) and through survey responses from all participants and control for potential contamination in the analyses. The project will use the Hootsuite platform to capture social media process (implementation) data.

After obtaining active parental consent (take-home consent that must be returned signed) and student assent (completed at school), researchers will administer the survey in school as per procedures approved by IRB review. After the survey, all teens will participate in the activities for their study condition. Teens in the #STM4U condition will participate both in the AYV-based social media training activities on a monthly basis (one research team visit to school per month) and participate in a single STM rally. Teens in the STM rally will participate only in the rally.

In addition to marijuana and other drug-related knowledge, attitudes, beliefs, intentions, and behavioral outcomes, the evaluation will collect extensive implementation and process data in the feasibility pilot. This will both include social media metrics and in-person activity attendance, participation/engagement, and satisfaction (STM rally and media activities). We also collect process data related to duration of in-person activities, topics covered, deviations from the activity plan, and implementation challenges. Process data assist in determining feasibility and acceptability of #STM4U.

Six (6) months after the pretest, teens will be surveyed again. Participants in the social media conditions will be asked to follow the #STM4U project on Twitter and to like us on Facebook. This will enable us to track their posting of videos and other project-related activity on Hootsuite. Researchers will use the social media metrics data (number of video posts, shares, retweets) to (1) quantity participants' video narrative activity by type in the AYV categories and (2) code the content of video narratives created by adolescents for qualitative analysis. These data will be used both to quantify the diffusion of prevention messages in the program and to use as dosage measures in the outcome analyses. In the latter analyses, researchers will calculate changes in behaviors, intentions, and social norms given exposure to #STM4U or STM rally-only conditions. Main hypotheses will be examined using multiple regression analysis with study condition as the independent variable and marijuana use intentions and 30-day marijuana use as the dependent variables.

Behavior Change Using Multiple Digital Channels: Integrating the 4Ps

Digital media are highly complementary to the 4Ps and social marketing applications. Many of the early digital health interventions have used relatively simple messaging, such as SMS texts, e-mail, websites, and other essentially single "promotion P" approaches (Abroms, Padmanabhan, & Evans, 2012; Evans, 2015). However, the future trend appears to much more widespread use of multiple Ps (beyond simple messaging, such as through SMS), to include context-specific applications (place P using the GPS feature of the mobile phone to provide feedback and reinforcement when an individual is at a specific place or at a certain time), nonmonetary incentives (price P using reinforcement based on self-monitoring of behavior or achievement of a specific personal objective, such as for daily PA), or offering of various behavioral choices (product P, including use of digital tools themselves, which represent new and in many cases immediately reinforcing behaviors).

The following provides an example of a novel program, the *Pregnancy Book Suite* (PBS), which both builds off previous SMS text interventions and uses mobile phones and multiple P strategies for behavior change. This example provides a potential future model for digital health and social marketing interventions.

Case Study of the Pregnancy Book Suite Mobile App

Campaign Background

There is growing evidence that mHealth programs are effective in promoting chronic disease self-management (e.g., diabetes), promoting treatment adherence (e.g., medication adherence and smoking cessation), and promoting health behavior (e.g., reminder systems for healthy behavior) (Free et al., 2013). The *text4baby* program is an example of a successful mHealth solution. An RCT linked the text4baby program to increased patient belief in the importance of prenatal care vitamins, compliance to prenatal care visits, and reduced alcohol use (Evans, Wallace Bihm, et al., 2014). The program demonstrates the opportunity to change the behavior of pregnant women by following the defined time stages of pregnancy to provide specific healthcare guidelines at the point of decision (e.g., when folic acid is recommended) to complement or reinforce the messages delivered by healthcare providers (Evans, Wallace Bihm, et al., 2014). However, SMS programs like text4baby demonstrate a limited solution only based on text messaging but do not capitalize on the full potential and capabilities of mobile devices to deliver tailored, easily accessible, 4P social marketing interventions (Jordan et al., 2011; Evans et al., 2015; Whittaker et al., 2012; Gutierrez, 2014).

The PBS aims to provide personalized *social marketing* of healthy pregnancy behaviors; provide *context-aware* and *theory-driven* prenatal care information based on existing pregnancy guidelines used in the military health system (Poropatich, 2010) to increase knowledge; increase utilization of prenatal care content (Kotelchuck, 1994); and increase intention to follow prenatal care guidelines by pregnant users. The innovations include

- ***Social marketing*** using text messages, notifications, and content branded to represent an engaging and appealing persona of a trusted companion who is there to guide and support (Department of Defense and US Department of Veterans Affairs [DOD], 2012; Whittaker et al., 2012; Cole-Lewis & Kershaw, 2010).
- ***Context aware*** care using user information, time, activity, location, and environmental variables from mobile devices to learn about users' individual needs and to tailor guidance and content to deliver timely prenatal care information (Figure 7-1).
- ***Theory-driven design*** utilizing social marketing principles and behavioral theory to promote positive, meaningful, and sustainable behavior change.

Pregnancy Book Suite will provide different layers of prenatal care communication and user engagement from information "cards" providing timely microlearning content on prenatal care to health tips and reminder services. The project has two overall objectives:

- ***Phase 1:*** Researchers will (1) develop a context-aware framework including microlearning content based on the *Pregnancy and Childbirth* guidebook

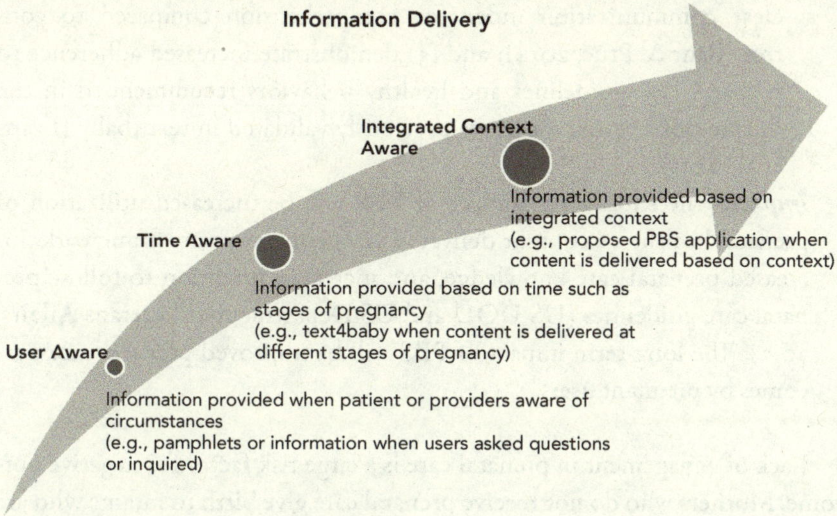

FIGURE 7-1 Context-aware content delivery.

(Purple Book) (US DOD and US Department of Veterans Affairs, 2012) and develop the prototype PBS application using user-centered design (UCD) methodology and (2) conduct usability pilot testing.

- *Feasibility measures for phase 1:* (1) Complete prototype for PBS application with context-aware content delivery; (2) obtain at least an average score of 68 from participants' System Usability Scale (SUS) responses (Bangor, Kortum, & Miller, 2008); (3) demonstrate continuous usage of PBS and content with at least 60% of participants; and (4) demonstrate a 20% increase from pretest to posttest among participants in their intention to follow prenatal care guidelines timed to the point in their pregnancy based on pretest/posttest intention survey (primary study outcome).

- ***Phase 2:*** Researchers will (1) complete development of a fully functional PBS application and (2) conduct randomized pilot evaluation of PBS application with 300 patients at Madigan Army Medical Center (MAMC).
  - *Efficacy measures for phase 2:* (1) Obtain improved average SUS score of 75 on PBS's usability; (2) Demonstrate continuous use of PBS application by 75% of participants at 28-weeks' gestational age follow-up; (3) demonstrate an increase of 30% from pretest to posttest in knowledge of and intent to follow prenatal care guidelines in PBS compared to control; (4) demonstrate 20% higher score on the modified CDC

clear communication index for comprehension compared to control (Baur & Prue, 2014); and (5) demonstrate increased adherence to prenatal care guidelines and healthy behaviors recommended in the Purple Book, using measures previously validated in text4baby (Evans et al., 2015).

- ***Impact:*** The short-term impact of PBS will be increased utilization of prenatal healthcare content delivered via a context-aware framework, increased prenatal care knowledge, and increased intention to follow prenatal care guidelines (US DOD and US Department of Veterans Affairs, 2012). The long-term impact of PBS will be improved prenatal care outcomes by pregnant users.

Lack of engagement in prenatal care is a large risk factor for negative outcome. Mothers who do not receive prenatal care give birth to infants who are five times more likely to die and exhibit three times the likelihood of being born at a low birth weight (Health Resources and Services Administration [HRSA], 2015). Low health literacy is a barrier to effective patient utilization of prenatal care (Whittaker et al., 2012).

Improvement in health literacy is a strong predictor of increased prenatal care utilization. There is evidence showing that adequate timely delivery of content offered with standard prenatal care can help mitigate negative pregnancy outcomes and behaviors, such as by reducing poor pregnancy outcomes such as low birth weight (Kogan et al., 1994) or preterm birth in smokers, along with introducing positive pregnancy behavioral outcomes, such as increased attendance at childbirth classes and dietary improvements (Olds et al., 1986). The proposed PBS system is significant because it will help to improve adherence to prenatal care guidelines and improve care delivery by offering multiple modes of information delivery, such as short videos or visual "card" aids.

Information and app overload for prenatal care makes it difficult to digest information. The DOD and US Department of Veterans Affairs implements the *Pregnancy and Childbirth* guidebook (Purple Book) in military-affiliated healthcare facilities to provide guidelines for both patient and provider to improve care, comfort, and health outcomes related to pregnancy in military women or spouses of active duty military (US DOD and US Department of Veterans Affairs, 2012). The classic paper format for this support tool is cumbersome, hard to search through, and not optimized to provide user information relevant to the developmental timeline of pregnancy. This can cause difficultly in effective and timely adherence to Purple Book guidelines. According to information-processing theory, readers can only handle a limited amount of information at one time. (By grouping information into meaningful "chunks" of reasonable size, we can save our audience from experiencing information overload and improve their ability to organize and recall the material; Miller, 1956.) Offering microcontent on prenatal care in varying delivery media (video, text, visual cards, audio formats), such as our proposed PBS application will provide, can make it easier for audiences with varying levels of health literacy to understand health information relating to prenatal care.

Military women face many of the same healthcare challenges as civilian women, with additional burdens due to the stress, mobility, and workload associated with military life (Mulhall, 2009; Committee on Health Care for Underserved Women, 2012). These barriers make the availability of an easy-to-use, mobile tool such as PBS highly significant as a potential solution to improve both military and civilian women's health behaviors and care during pregnancy. PBS will be tested in a military setting but is highly applicable to civilian settings. Women veterans will immediately benefit from PBS (Committee on Health Care for Underserved Women, 2012). In addition, low-income and working civilian women face many of the same barriers to accessing and utilizing healthcare information during pregnancy—time, complexity, health literacy—that make PBS an effective solution. The tool will be readily adaptable for civilian uses.

The high usability of mobile devices will help bridge the gap in practicality of information and prenatal support tools, as demonstrated in the text4baby evaluation at MAMC (Evans et al., 2015). Mobile devices are becoming a popular medium for delivering content for learning at the right time (Agboola et al. 2014). Through microlearning, teachable moments are presented that provide an opportunity to offer a nugget of insight to learners in an engaging way. Recent advances in digital pedagogy point to this approach as especially salient and effective for millennial generation learners (McHaney, 2011), who represent the MAMC pregnant patient population.

The novelty of PBS lies in its (1) context-aware mobile framework, which can respond to environmental and situational factors such as time, location, temperature, mood, health status, diet, and activity to deliver prenatal care information; (2) microlearning delivered via bite-size multimedia perinatal care information to pregnant women to improve knowledge; (3) existence as a behavior change communication (BCC) tool using card notification to encourage behavior change for perinatal care; (4) cross-platform mHealth interface that provides digestible bit-size information based on the Purple Book; and (5) practicality as an easy-to-navigate tool.

The BCC of PBS using cards" to encourage behavior change is novel (Figure 7-2). According to both the health belief model (Becker & Maiman, 1979; Cox, 2009) and the information, motivation, and behavioral skills model (Gavgani, Poursharifi, & Aliasgarzadeh, 2010) on which PBS is built, knowledge is a major construct of health beliefs and behaviors. Pregnant women can more readily accept and act on information or helpful hints that are introduced in a timely manner. For example, reminding a pregnant woman to begin folic acid supplementation and discussing her birth defect screening plan with her doctor would be more helpful early in her pregnancy rather than later.

Overall, timing of recommendations and adherence to prenatal guidelines is crucial. This has been the foundation of previous successful mHealth

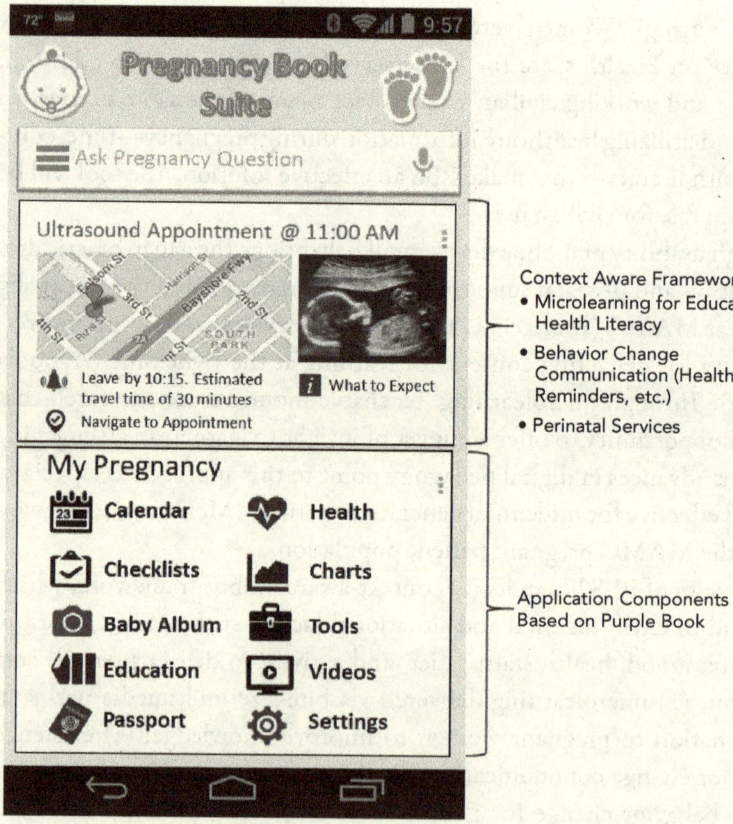

FIGURE 7-2 "Cards" communication for microlearning and behavior change.

programs, such as text4baby. PBS will implement this via cards similar to Google Now, which provides health tips (e.g., not eating raw meats when at a Japanese restaurant), reminders (e.g., to take prenatal vitamins daily), and advice (e.g., planning for a safe delivery or avoiding unhealthy work) for a healthy pregnancy.

A cross-platform, user-centered, mobile health solution will be provided by PBS. PBS will leverage cross-platform mobile health technologies to provide small bite-size packets of relevant perinatal care information that is easy to absorb and can improve knowledge and understanding of the Purple Book guidelines. By creating a cross-platform application, PBS will be available to a variety of cell phone users through compatibility with Apple, Android, and Windows devices. PBS will leverage mobile health technologies to help increase pregnancy care skills by offering reminders, care management assistance, and skills-based knowledge.

Practicality, ease of use, and portability will be offered by PBS for seamless integration in the lives of pregnant women. Pregnant women, especially those on active duty, often do not have the time to deal with the sheer volume of perinatal information, including that contained in the voluminous Purple Book. They are busy with duty, work, family, and outside responsibilities in addition to completing necessary readings for their pregnancy. One way to enhance traditional perinatal information found on the web and in the Purple Book includes the use of microlearning tools. Microlearning via multimedia microcontent allows for "learning on the go" that can be processed in small and manageable segments of content. Examples of multimedia microcontent include short podcasts (1–5 minutes in length) and short video clips (1–5 minutes in length) (Pollak et al., 2010). Information that is provided in simple, bite-size, pieces is more digestible and has been linked to improved use of prenatal care (Bennett et al., 2006) and increased health literacy (Gazmaranian et al., 2012).

Evaluation Background

After initial development of a fully functional prototype of PBS, the research team will proceed with pilot testing using an RCT to evaluate the PBS application at MAMC in a 12-month, phase 2 pilot study. Recruitment criteria will be first presentation for prenatal care at MAMC, between 10th and 14th week of pregnancy, and owning either a smartphone (defined as a phone with app capabilities) or mobile tablet device. In the previous text4baby study at MAMC, 100% of pregnant women presenting for care had a cell phone, and approximately 60% had smartphones (Evans, Wallace Bihm, et al., 2014). Given the rise in smartphone usage overall, this number will likely be higher by the time of our study.

Treatment group participants will engage in a usability assessment, and all participants will participate in a prenatal care knowledge assessment based on Purple Book content and the modified CDC clear communication index to measure for communication comprehension. Control participants will receive the printed Purple Book, following standard obstetrics/gynecological (OB/GYN) practice at MAMC. Recruitment for the study will occur over a 2-month period.

For estimating the minimum sample size, researchers used $\alpha = .05$, Cohen's medium effect size ($f = 0.25$), with power at 80% (Cohen, 1992). The power analysis for an estimated total sample size for a randomized two-group (PBS vs. usual care) repeated-measure analysis of covariance (ANCOVA) with two observations (baseline and 6-month follow-up) per subject, with four covariates, and tests of interactions require a minimum of 150 subjects for the study. A sample size of 75 subjects per group provides greater than 80% power to detect medium effects over time, accounting for anticipated attrition of 20% of the original sample. To ensure sufficient statistical power, and given more than adequate availability of eligible participants at MAMC, researchers planned to recruit 150 pregnant women per condition (total of 300).

The treatment participants will receive access to PBS for use on their own smartphones. Control participants will not receive access to the PBS application. They will receive a follow-up from the research team after intake at each postbaseline follow-up (approximately at 6 and 9 months of pregnancy) regarding their intentions to implement the recommendation and actual implementation of the recommendation in the PBS application. The expected testing for the participants will include 6–7 months of pilot testing of the PBS application, depending on the stage of pregnancy the participants are recruited (between 10 and 14 weeks).

Using multivariable longitudinal analysis to control for potential confounding influences, researchers will analyze the relationship between experimental condition and PBS usability and utilization outcomes. Age, race/ethnicity, income, and other sociodemographic and individual variables will be examined for their potential inclusion as covariates in these models. This procedure is similar to methods used in previous studies by myself and colleagues on response to mHealth and online health message delivery (Evans 2015; Evans, Holtz, & Snider, 2014).

By estimating multivariate logistic regression models, researchers will calculate the odds of improved knowledge and intent to follow pregnancy guidelines given participation treatment condition compared to control. The main hypothesis that participation in PBS and use of the app will significantly increase knowledge and intent will be examined using logistic regression analysis in which study condition will be the independent variable and a factor developed through factor analysis for pregnancy knowledge and intent to follow guidelines as the dependent variable. The hypothesis is that higher knowledge and intent will be associated with participation and PBS app use in the treatment condition.

Evaluating Digital Media–Based Social Marketing: Future Considerations

Evaluating any individual-level digital technology program presents design challenges. Very high percentages of the population are now social media users (some 80% of women according to a 2015 Pew Research Center survey; http://www.pewinternet.org/files/2015/08/Social-Media-Update-2015-FINAL2.pdf). At the same time, mobile communications are by nature pervasive. They can be accessed and utilized 24 hours a day, 7 days a week, anywhere there is cellular coverage. This creates significant obstacles in designing controlled studies. If large portions of the population can become contaminated by easily being able to access a message, social media, or app content that social marketing researchers want to evaluate, how do we ensure fidelity to program delivery and prevent control participants in evaluations from enrolling in mHealth services?

One approach is the natural experiment (Rossi & Freeman, 1993). In natural experiments, naturally occurring variation in penetration of an intervention within a program delivery area (e.g., community, city, or nationwide) can be used for a quasi-experimental design (Valente, 2002). Differences in dosage that occur naturally within the program delivery area can be used to model dose-response effects (Farrelly et al., 2005; Evans, Blitstein, et al., 2008). However, because mHealth delivered through text messaging or newer technologies such as Twitter cannot be monitored for reading receipt, determining actual exposure to messages in a population is difficult. In Chapter 8, this topic is explored in much more depth in the context of quasi-experimental designs overall, specifically the use of "heavy-up" experiments to manipulate the dosage of social marketing efforts and examine dose-response effects as a form of quasi-experimental control.

Another promising approach is to use "location" or "place-based" approaches, such as in clinics, schools, or workplaces, to control exposure and dosage of mHealth programs to intervention and not control participants. For example, an mHealth program can be tested and evaluated first within a central location like a hospital or healthcare clinic. Dissemination can be controlled through the healthcare provider staff, and individuals can be recruited to participate in the program based on a randomization scheme identified in advance (e.g., participants can be randomly assigned to get an mHealth intervention, such as text messaging, based on when they enter the care setting for treatment). Evaluation and data collection can be done in the healthcare setting and through follow-up once participants leave (e.g., through surveys conducted by mobile phone).

The growing popularity of mHealth programs creates a number of opportunities and challenges to evaluation. First, dissemination of mHealth programs, and the nature of mobile phones as devices, creates many naturally occurring conditions in which evaluation can be conducted, such as national, regional, or local dissemination of quit lines for smoking cessation. Second, dissemination of these programs also makes them more accessible to more people, and thus makes experimental control and comparison more difficult because it is hard to create groups that are distinct from treatment. These issues have always arisen in evaluating mass media campaigns—the difficulty in controlling dosage and attributing observed behavior changes to campaign exposure (Hornik, 2002)—but are more pronounced in mHealth due to the ubiquity of the medium.

Based on these considerations, a number of issues and fundamental questions arise in evaluating mHealth programs:

- How do we best design studies with rigorous control conditions?
- What designs can best be used to maximize rigor of social marketing research that involves digital technologies?
- What threats to internal and external validity arise?
- How do we measure exposure to digital social marketing using each of the 4Ps?
    - Self-reported recall to text messages
    - Participant interaction with the digital technology system
    - Computer-measured interaction
- What are the mediators of behavior change and social marketing exposure?
- What are the behavioral outcomes of interest? What human-digital device interactions are of interest to social marketing research?

Additional Resources: Literature

- Evans, W.D. (Ed.). (2015). *Social Marketing: Global Perspectives, Strategies, and Effects on Consumer Behavior.* Hauppauge, NY: Nova.
- Hicks, N., & Nicols, C. (Eds.). (2011). *Health Industry Communication: New Media, New Methods, New Messages,* N. Hicks & C. Nichols (Eds.). Boston: Jones and Bartlett.
- Noar, S., & Harrington, N.G. (Eds.). (2012). *eHealth Applications: Promising Strategies for Health Behavior Change.* New York: Routledge.

References

Above the Influence. (2015). Drug Facts. Retrieved on September 2, 2015, from http://abovetheinfluence.com/

Abroms, L.C., Padmanabhan, N., & Evans, W.D. (2012). Mobile Phones for Health Promotion. In *Interactive Health Communication Applications: Promising Strategies for Health Behavior Change,* S. Noar and N.G. Harrington (Eds.). New York: Routledge. Chapter 9.

African Response. (2012). Stokvels—A Hidden Economy. Retrieved June 23, 2015, from http://www.africanresponse.co.za/PressReleases/Documents/2012Stokvel Hidden Economy.pdf

Agboola, S., Kamdar, M., Flanagan, C., Searl, M., Traeger, L., Kvedar, J., & Jethwani, K. (2014). Pain Management in Cancer Patients Using a Mobile App: Study Design of a Randomized Controlled Trial. *JMIR Research Protocols,* 3(4): e76.

Agha, S. (2003). The Impact of a Mass Media Campaign on Personal Risk Perception, Perceived Self-Efficacy and Other Behavioral Predictors. *AIDS Care,* 15: 749–762.

Aldana, S.G., Greenlaw, R.L., Diehl, H.A., Salberg, A., Merrill, R.M., Ohmine, S., & Thomas, C. (2005). Effects of an Intensive Diet and Physical Activity Modification Program on the Health Risks of Adults. *Journal of the American Dietetic Association,* 105(3): 371–381.

Anderson, A.S., Cox, D.N., McKellar, S., Reynolds, J., Lean, M.E., & Mela, D.J. (1998). Take Five, a nutrition education intervention to increase fruit and vegetable intakes: impact on attitudes towards dietary change. *British Journal of Nutrition,* 80(2): 133–140.

Andrade, E., Evans, W.D., Edberg, M., Cubana, I., & Cleary, S. (2015). Victor and Erika Webisodes for the Adelante Brand: An Innovative Audience Engagement Strategy for Prevention. *Journal of Health Communication,* 20(12): 1465–1472. doi:10.1080/10810730.2015.1018648

Andreasen, A. (1995). *Marketing Social Change.* San Francisco: Jossey-Bass.

Bales, S.N. (2009). *Summary Research Memo: FrameWorks' Analysis of Frame Effects on PCAA Policies and Implications for Messaging.* Washington, DC: FrameWorks Institute.

Bandura, A. (2004). Health Promotion by Social Cognitive Means. *Health Education & Behavior,* 31(2):143–164.

Bangor, A., Kortum, P.T., & Miller, J.T. (2008) An Empirical Evaluation of the System Usability Scale. *International Journal of Human-Computer Interaction*, 24(6): 574–594.

Baur, C., & Prue, C. (2014).The CDC Clear Communication Index Is a New Evidence-Based Tool to Prepare and Review Health Information. *Health Promotion Practice*, 15(5): 629–637.

Becker, M., & Maiman, L. (1979). Patient Perceptions and Compliance; Recent Studies of the Health Belief Model. In Compliance in Health Care, R.B. Haynes, D.W. Taylor, & D.L. Sackett (Eds.). Baltimore, MD: Johns Hopkins University Press; 78–112.

Bennett, I., Switzer, J., Aguirre, A., Evans, K., & Barg, F. (2006). "Breaking It Down": Patient-Clinician Communication and Prenatal Care Among African American Women of Low and Higher Literacy. *Annals of Family Medicine*, 4(4): 334–340. Retrieved on September 6, 2015, from http://www.annfammed.org/content/4/4/334

Burke, V., Giangiulio, N., Gillam, H.F., Beilin, L.J., & Houghton, S. (2004). Changes in Cognitive Measures in a Randomized Controlled Trial of a Health Promotion Program for Couples Targeting Diet and Physical Activity. *American Journal of Health Promotion*, 18(4): 300–311.

Carpenter, C.S., & Pechmann, C. (2011). Exposure to the Above the Influence Antidrug Advertisements and Adolescent Marijuana Use in the United States, 2006–2008. *American Journal of Public Health*, 101(5): 948–954.

Center for Behavioral Health Statistics and Quality. (2012). *Results From the 2011 National Survey on Drug Use and Health: Summary of National Findings* (HHS Publication No. SMA 12-4713, NSDUH Series H-44). Rockville, MD: SAMHSA.

Centers for Disease Control and Prevention (CDC). (2014). *Best Practices for Comprehensive Tobacco Control Programs*. Atlanta: US Department of Health and Human Services, Centers for Disease Control and Prevention, National Center for Chronic Disease Prevention and Health Promotion, Office on Smoking and Health.

Chapman, S., Ayers, J., LeTouze, O., & Remard, B. (2013). Branding and Social Marketing. In *Psychology of Branding*, W.D. Evans (Ed.). New York: Nova Science.

Chou, W.Y.S., Hunt, Y.M., Beckjord, E.B., Moser, R.P., & Hesse, B.W. (2009). Social Media Use in the United States: Implications for Health Communication. *Journal of Medical Internet Research*, 11(4): e48. doi:10.2196/jmir.1249

Cohen, J. (1992). A Power Primer. *Psychological Bulletin*, 112(1): 155–159. doi:10.1037/0033-2909.112.1.15

Cole-Lewis, H., & Kershaw, T. (2010). Text Messaging as a Tool for Behavior Change in Disease Prevention and Management. *Epidemiologic Reviews*, 32(1): 56–69.

Committee on Health Care for Underserved Women, American College of Obstetricians and Gynecologists. (2012). Health Care for Women in the Military and Women Veterans. Committee Opinion No. 547. *Obstetrics and Gynecology*, 120: 1538–1542.

Cooper, Z., Doll, H.A., Hawker, D.M., Byrne, S., Bonner, G., Eeley, E., O'Connor, M.E., & Fairburn, C.G. (2010). Testing a New Cognitive Behavioural Treatment for Obesity: A Randomized Controlled Trial with Three-Year Follow-up. *Behaviour Research and Therapy*, 48(8): 706–713.

Cox, L.E. (2009). Predictors of Medication Adherence in an AIDS Clinical Trial: Patient and Clinician Perceptions. *Health and Social Work*, 34(4): 257–264.

Drake, J.K., Vail, J.G., & Stewart, J.R. (2014). Best Practices for Fostering Family Planning Total Markets in Indonesia, Mexico, Romania, Thailand, and Turkey: A Retrospective Analysis. *Cases in Public Health Communication & Marketing*, 8(suppl 1): S19–S41. Retrieved from http://www.casesjournal.org/volume8_suppl1

Evans, W.D., Necheles, J., Becker, A.B., Christoffel, K.K., & Snider, J. (2010). Social Marketing as a Childhood Obesity Prevention Strategy. *Obesity*, 18(S1): S23–S26.

Evans, W.D. (2013) Branding Social and Health Behavior: An Education and Research Agenda. In *Psychology of Branding*, W.D. Evans (Ed.). New York: Nova Science.

Evans, W.D. (Ed.). (2015). *Social Marketing: Global Perspectives, Strategies, and Effects on Consumer Behavior.* Hauppauge, NY: Nova Science.

Evans, W.D., Blitstein, J., Hersey, J., Renaud, J., & Yaroch, A.L. (2008). Systematic Review of Public Health Branding. *Journal of Health Communication*, 13(8): 351–360.

Evans, W.D., Christoffel, K.K., Necheles, J., Becker, A.B., & Snider, J. (2011). Outcomes of the 5-4-3-2-1 Go! Childhood Obesity Community Trial. *American Journal of Health Behavior*, 35(2): 189–198.

Evans, W.D., & Hastings, G. (2008). Public Health Branding: Recognition, Promise, and Delivery of Healthy Lifestyles. In *Public Health Branding: Applying Marketing for Social Change*, W.D. Evans & G. Hastings (Eds.). London: Oxford University Press.

Evans, W.D., Holtz, K., & Snider, J. (2014). Effects of the Above the Influence Brand on Adolescent Drug Use Prevention Normative Beliefs. *Journal of Health Communication*, 19(6): 721–737. doi:10.1080/10810730.2013.837559

Evans, W.D., Longfield, K., Shekhar, N., Rabemanatsoa, A., Snider, J., & Reerink, I. (2012). Social Marketing and Condom Promotion in Madagascar: A Case Study in Brand Equity Research. In *Handbook of Global Health Communication*, R. Obregon & S. Waisboard (Eds.). New York: Wiley.

Evans, W.D., Wallace Bihm, J., Szekely, D., Nielsen, P., Murray, E., Abroms, L., & Snider, J. (2014). Initial Outcomes From a 4-Week Follow-Up Study of the Text4baby Program in the Military Women's Population: Randomized Controlled Trial. *Journal of Medical Internet Research*, 16(5): e13. doi:10.2196/jmir.3297

Evans, W.D., Nielsen, P.E., Szekely, D., Wallace Bihm, J., Murray, E.A., Snider, J., & Abroms, L.C. (2015). Dose-Response Effects of the text4baby Mobile Health Program: Randomized Trial *Journal of Medical Internet Research: mHealth uHealth*, 3(1): e12. doi:10.2196/mhealth.3909

Evans, W. D., Price, S., Blahut, S., Hersey, J., Niederdeppe, J., & Ray, S. (2004). Social imagery, tobacco independence, and the truthsm campaign. *Journal of Health Communication*, 9(5): 425–441.doi:10.1080/10810730490504143

Farrelly, M.C., Davis, K.C., Haviland, M.L., Messeri, P., & Healton, C.G. (2005). Evidence of a Dose-Response Relationship Between "Truth" Antismoking Ads and Youth Smoking Prevalence. *American Journal of Public Health*, 95(3): 425–431.

Farrelly, M.C., Nonnemaker, J., Davis, K.C., & Hussin, A. (2009). The Influence of the National truth® Campaign on Smoking Initiation. *American Journal of Preventive Medicine*, 36(5): 379–384.

Fjeldsoe, B.S., Marshall, A.L., & Miller, Y.D. (2009). Behavior Change Interventions Delivered by Mobile Telephone Short-Message Service. *American Journal of Preventive Medicine*, 36: 165–173.

Franklin, V.L., Waller, A., Pagliari, C., & Greene, S.A. (2006). A Randomized Controlled Trial of Sweet Talk, a Text Messaging System to Support Young People With Diabetes. *Diabetes Medicine*, 23: 1332–1338.

Free, C., Phillips, G., Galli, L., Watson, L., Felix, L., Edwards, P., Patel, V., & Haines, A. (2013). The Effectiveness of Mobile-Health Technology-Based Health Behavior Change or Disease Management Interventions for Health Care Consumers: A Systematic Review. *PLoS Medicine*, doi:10(1):e1001362

French, J., Blair-Stevens, C., McVey, D., & Merritt, R. (2010). *Social Marketing and Public Health*. Oxford, UK: Oxford University Press.

Gavgani, R.M., Poursharifi, H., & Aliasgarzadeh, A. (2010). Effectiveness of Information-Motivation and Behavioral skill (IMB) Model in Improving Self-Care Behaviors and Hba1c Measure in Adults With Type 2 Diabetes in Iran-Tabriz. *Procedia—Social and Behavioral Sciences*, 5: 1868–1873.

Gazmaranian, J.A., Yang, B., Elon, L., Graham, M., & Parker, R. (2012). Successful Enrollment in Text4Baby More Likely With Higher Health Literacy. *Journal of Health Communication*, 17(S3): 303–311. doi:10.1080/10810730.2012.712618

doiGutierrez, K. (2014, April 15). The Age of Bite-Sized Learning: What Is It and Why It Works. Shift Disruptive Elearning. http://info.shiftelearning.com/blog/bid/342367/The-Age-of-Bite-sized-Learning-What-is-It-and-Why-It-Works

Haapala, I., Barengo, N. C., Biggs, S., Surakka, L., & Manninen, P. (2009). Weight Loss by Mobile Phone: A 1-Year Effectiveness Study. *Public Health Nutrition*, 12(12): 2382–2391.

Health Resources and Services Administration (HRSA). (2015). Prenatal Services. Retrieved on February 27, 2015, from http://mchb.hrsa.gov/programs/womeninfants/prenatal.html

Hornik, R. (2002). *Public Health Communication: Evidence for Behavior Change*. Mahwah, NJ: Erlbaum.

Huffington Post. (2014). US Pot Sales to Hit $8 billion a Year in 2018: Report. Retrieved on January 29, 2015, from http://www.huffingtonpost.com/2014/04/11/marijuana-industry-8-billion_n_5133863.html

Jacobus, J., Squeglia, L.M., Sorg, S.F., Nguyen-Louie, T.T., & Tapert, S.F. (2014). Cortical Thickness and Neurocognition in Adolescent Marijuana and Alcohol Users Following 28 Days of Monitored Abstinence. *Journal of Studies on Alcohol and Drugs*, 75(5): 729–743.

Johnston, L.D., O'Malley, P.M., Miech, R.A., Bachman, J.G., & Schulenberg, J.E. (2015). *Monitoring the Future National Survey Results on Drug Use: 1975–2014: Overview, Key Findings on Adolescent Drug Use.* Ann Arbor: Institute for Social Research, University of Michigan.

Jordan, E.T., Ray, E.M., Johnson, P., & Evans, W.D. (2011). Early Results: Text4baby Program Reaches the Intended Audience. *Nursing for Women's Health*, 15(3): 206–212.

Kogan, M.D., Alexander, G.R., Kotelchuck, M., & Nagey, D.A. (1994). Relation of the Content of Prenatal Care to the Risk of Low Birth Weight: Maternal Reports of Health Behavior Advice and Initial Prenatal Care Procedures. *Journal of the American Medical Association*, 271(17): 1340–1345. doi:10.1001/jama.1994.03510410052032.

Kotelchuck, M. (1994). Overview of the Adequacy of Pre-Natal Care Utilization Index. Retrieved on February 21, 2016, from http://www.mchlibrary.info/databases/HSNRCPDFs/Overview_APCUIndex.pdf

Lefebvre, R.C. (2011). An Integrative Model for Social Marketing. *Journal of Social Marketing*, 1: 54–72.

Lim, M.S.C., Hocking, J.S., Hellard, M.E., Aitken, C.K. (2008). SMS STI: A Review of the Uses of Mobile Phone Text Messaging in Sexual Health. *International Journal of STD & AIDS*, 19(5): 287–290.

Logan, A.G., McIsaac, W.J., Tisler, A., Irvine, M.J., Saunders, A., Dunal, A., Rizo, C.A., Feig, D.S., Hamill, M., Trudel, M., et al. (2007). Mobile Phone-Based Remote Patient Monitoring System for Management of Hypertension in Diabetic Patients. *American Journal of Hypertension*, 20(9): 942–948.

Mays, D., Niaura, R.S., Evans, W.D., Hammond, D., Luta, G., & Tercyak, K.P. (2014). The Impact of Graphic Cigarette Warning Label Message Framing and Plain Packaging on Motivation to Quit Among US Young Adult Smokers. *Tobacco Control*. doi:10.1136/tobaccocontrol-2013-051234

McHaney, R. (2011). *The New Digital Shoreline: How Web 2.0 and Millennials Are Revolutionizing Higher Education*. Sterling, VA: Stylus.

Miller, G.A. (1956). The Magical Number Seven, Plus or Minus Two: Some Limits on Our Capacity for Processing Information. *Psychological Review*, 63(2): 81–97. http://dx.doi.org/10.1037/h0043158

Mulhall, E. (2009). *Women Warriors: Supporting She Who Has Borne the Battle.* Washington, DC: Iraq and Women's Veterans of America (IAVA).

Neighbors, C., Foster, D.W., Walker, D.D., Kilmer, J.R., & Lee, C.M. (2013). Social Identity as a Moderator of the Association Between Perceived Norms and Marijuana Use. *Journal of Stuides on Alcohol and Drugs*, 74(3): 479–483.

Neve, M., Morgan, P.J., Jones, P.R., & Collins, C.E. (2010). Effectiveness of web-based interventions in achieving weight loss and weight loss maintenance in overweight and obese adults: a systematic review with meta-analysis. *Obesity Review*, 11(4): 306–321.

O'Keefe, D.J., & Jensen, J.D. (2007). The Relative Persuasiveness of Gain-Framed Loss-Framed Messages for Encouraging Disease Prevention Behaviors: A Meta-Analytic Review. *Journal of Health Communication: International Perspectives*, 12(7): 623–644.

Olds, D.L., Henderson, C.R., Tatelbaum, R., & Chamberlin, R. (1986). Improving the Delivery of Prenatal Care and Outcomes of Pregnancy: A Randomized Trial of Nurse Home Visitation. *Pediatrics*, 77(1): 16–28.

Patrick, K., Rabb, F., Adams, M.A., Dillon, L., Zabinski, M., Rock, C.L., Griswold, W.G., & Norman, G.J. (2009). A Text Message-Based Intervention for Weight Loss: Randomized Controlled Trial. *Journal of Medical Internet Research*, 11(1): e1.

Petty, R.E., & Cacioppo, J.T. (1986). The elaboration likelihood model of persuasion. *Advances in Experimental Social Psychology*, 19: 123–205.

Pew Research Center. (2014). Views of Marijuana—Legalization, Decriminalization, Concerns. Retrieved on January 26, 2015, from http://www.people-press.org/2014/04/02/section-2-views-of-marijuana-legalization-decriminalization-concerns/

Pollak, K.I., Denman, S., Gordon, K.C., Lyna, P., Rocha, P., Brouwer, R.N., Fish, L., & Baucom, D.H. (2010). Is Pregnancy a Teachable Moment for Smoking Cessation Among US Latino Expectant Fathers? A Pilot Study. *Ethnicity & Health*, 15(1): 47–59. doi:10.1080/13557850903398293. Retrieved on March 6, 2015, from http://www.ncbi.nlm.nih.gov/pmc/articles/PMC3637962/

Pollard, R. (2014). Total Market Approaches to the Social Marketing of Health Services and Commodities in Low-Income Countries. *Cases in Public Health Communication & Marketing*, 8(suppl 1): S4–S18.

Population Services International (PSI). (2015). Total Market Approach in Six African Countries. Retrieved on August 26, 2015, from http://www.psi.org/publication/total-market-approach/

Poropatich, R. (2010). The Use of Mobile Phones in Health Care: Selected US Army Medical Department Projects and Research Focus. Presented at the Institute of Medicine Annual Meeting, Fort Detrick, MD. Retrieved on September 1, 2015, from http://www.iom.edu/~/media/Files/Activity%20Files/PublicHealth/AnnualMeeting/2010-OCT-11/POROPATICH.pdf

Purple Book Pregnancy Passport. VA/DoD. Featured in conjunction with Pregnancy and Childbirth: A Goal Oriented Guide to Prenatal Care. VA/DoD February 2012. Versions 3.1. Accessed February 21, 2016 from http://www.pregnancyatoz.org/PregnancyAtoZ/media/PregnancyAtoZ/Resources/Pregnancy-Passport.pdf

Robinson, M.N., Tansil, K.A., Elder, R.W., Soler, R.E., Labre, M.P., Mercer, S.L., Eroglu, D., Baur, C., Lyon-Daniel, K., Fridinger, F., et al. (2014). Health Communication Campaigns That Include Mass Media and Health-Related

Product Distribution: A Community Guide Systematic Review. *American Journal of Preventive Medicine*, 47(3): 360–371.

Rodgers, A., Corbett, T., Bramley, D., Riddell, T., Wills, M., Lin, R.B., & Jones, M. (2005). Do U Smoke After TXT? Results of a Randomized Trial of Smoking Cessation Using Mobile Phone Text Messaging. *Tobacco Control*, 14(4): 255–261.

Rossi, P.H., & Freeman, H.E. 1993. *Evaluation: A Systematic Approach*. London: Sage.

Rothman, A.J., Bartels, R.D., Wlaschin, J., & Salovey, P. (2006). The Strategic Use of Gain- and Loss-Framed Messages to Promote Healthy Behavior: How Theory Can Inform Practice. *Journal of Communication*, 56: S202–S220.

Seeman, N. (2008). Web 2.0 and Chronic Illness: New Horizons, New Opportunities. *Electronic Healthcare*, 6(3). http://www.electronichealthcare.net

Shaw, K., O'Rourke, P., Del Mar, C., & Kenardy, J. (2005). Psychological Interventions for Overweight or Obesity. *Cochrane Database of Systematic Reviews*, (2): CD003818.

Slater, M.D., Kelly, K.J., Edwards, R.W., et al. (2006). Combining In-School and Community-Based Media Efforts: Reducing Marijuana and Alcohol Uptake among Younger Adolescents. *Health Education Research*, 21(1): 157–167.

Slater, M.D., Kelly, K.J., Lawrence, F.R., Stanley, L.R., & Comello, M.L. (2011). Assessing Media Campaigns Linking Marijuana Non-Use With Autonomy and Aspirations: "Be Under Your Own Influence" and ONDCP's "Above the Influence." *Prevention Science*, 12: 12–22. doi:10.1007/s11121-010-0194-1

Stokols, D. (1996). Translating Social Ecological Theory Into Guidelines for Community Health Promotion. *American Journal of Health Promotion*, 10: 282–298.

Substance Abuse and Mental Health Services Adminstration (SAMHSA). (2015). National Registry of Evidence-Based Programs and Practices. Retrieved on February 3, 2015, from http://www.nrepp.samhsa.gov/

Teerenstra, S., Eldridge, S., Graff, M., de Hoop, E., & Borm, G.F. (2012). A simple sample size formula for analysis of covariance in cluster randomized trials. *Statistics in Medicine*, 31: 2169–2178. DOI: 10.1002/sim.5352.

US Department of Defense and US Department of Veterans Affairs. (2012). *Pregnancy and Childbirth: A Goal Oriented Guide to Prenatal Care* (Version 3.1). Washington, DC: Department of Defense and the Department of Veterans Affairs.

Valente, T.W. (2002). *Evaluating Health Promotion Programs*. Oxford, UK: Oxford University Press.

Wakefield, M., Terry-McElrath, Y., Emery, S., Saffer, H., Chaloupka, F. J., Szczypka, G., Flay, B., O'Malley, P.M., & Johnston, L. D. (2006). Effect of Televised, Tobacco Company–Funded Smoking Prevention Advertising on Youth Smoking-Related Beliefs, Intentions, and Behavior. *American Journal of Public Health*, *96*(12): 2154–2160. http://doi.org/10.2105/AJPH.2005.083352

Whittaker, R., Borland, R., Bullen, C., Borland, R., Rodgers, A., & Gu, Y. (2009). Mobile Phone-Based Interventions for Smoking Cessation. *Cochrane Database of Systematic Reviews*, 11: CD006611.

Whittaker, R., Matoff-Stepp, S., Meehan, J., Kendrick, J., Jordan, E., Stange, P., Cash, A., Meyer, P., Baitty, J., Johnson, P., et al. (2012). Text4baby: Development and Implementation of a National Text Messaging Health Information Service. *American Journal of Public Health*, 102: 2207–2213. doi:10.2105/AJPH.2012.300736.

World Health Organization. (2008). WHO Global Strategy on Diet, Physical Activity and Health: A Framework to Monitor and Evaluate Implementation. Geneva, Switzerland: WHO.

8

Quasi-experiments and Heavy-up Experiments in Social Marketing

W. Douglas Evans

Summary Points

- Use of natural experiments and other quasi-experimentation techniques such as heavy-up studies and propensity score matching (PSM) are growing outcome evaluation approaches in social marketing.
- There are several considerations in choosing from the range of quasi-experimental designs explored in this chapter.
- The case study of the Saleema campaign for women and girls' health in Sudan is an example of combined quasi-experimental and heavy-up methodologies conducted in a low-resource setting.

Introduction

As discussed in Chapters 2 and 6, social marketing campaign evaluation often requires quasi-experimental methods, as randomized trials are not feasible in real-world settings. For purposes of this chapter, let us broadly consider quasi-experiments to be a family of methods used to identify or create a non-randomized comparison group for campaign evaluation. Quasi-experiments are about identifying a "quasi-independent" variable that is used to define treatment and comparison groups, which are then compared for differences in an outcome (i.e., dependent variable) targeted by the social marketing campaign, such as smoking behavior or condom use (Shadish, Cook, & Campbell, 2002). This chapter examines different ways of creating comparison groups and focuses on one major example of such a quasi-experiment in a low-resource country setting.

Social marketing campaigns are typically developed and implemented independently from the evaluation, often on different schedules. Campaigns in some cases may have existed for an extended period of time prior to the evaluation, making an unexposed comparison group difficult or impossible to identify. The socially marketed condom brands of Population Services International (PSI) (e.g., see discussion in Chapter 4) are good examples of this: Evaluations of new branding and rebranding efforts were faced with the existing awareness and brand equity and thus could not use a randomized experimental design. The best, most rigorous, alternative was some form of quasi-experiment.

Quasi-experiments, and different approaches to creating quasi-experimental comparisons, have various strengths and weaknesses. In some designs, the researcher has control over assignment to the treatment condition but uses nonrandom assignment (e.g., a cutoff score) to determine which participants receive the treatment (e.g., the regression discontinuity design; Shadish, Cook, & Campbell, 2002). Or, the researcher may have no control over the treatment condition assignment and relies on naturally occurring conditions to determine treatment and comparison conditions. The latter represents a "natural experiment," such as in campaign evaluation that uses exposure to the campaign (either external or self-reported measures) to identify high- and low- (or no-) exposure groups (see Chapter 6 for examples).

In social marketing research, quasi-experiments may also be used for pre-post comparisons, as in a random assignment study, to evaluate effects of a campaign. These data can be compared as part of the study or the pretest data can be included in an explanation for the actual experimental data. Quasi-experiments have independent variables that already exist, such as age, gender, race/ethnicity, income, and so on. Naturally occurring variables are typically measured within quasi-experiments either to create the experimental conditions or to use as covariates in the analysis (Morgan, 2000).

Some examples of quasi-experiments typically used in social marketing research are (1) heavy-up experiments, (2) propensity score matching (PSM) and similar matching methodologies, and (3) natural experiments. These are all examples of robust quasi-experimental designs for campaign evaluation.

A heavy-up experiment is the manipulation of media or other implementation activities in a campaign during a defined period of time in order to evaluate an effect on an outcome. Advertisers routinely modify implementation of product promotion campaigns, such as in the time period leading up to a major holiday like Halloween or Christmas when advertising ramps up. When this is done for purposes of designing a study to evaluate campaign effects, it represents a heavy-up methodology.

A good example of a heavy-up experiment is one component of the overall 2010 National Census Media Campaign evaluation, also discussed in Chapter 2. A key feature of the National Opinion Research Corporation (NORC) evaluation was the Paid Advertising Heavy-Up Experiment (PAHUE). For this experiment, pairs of designated market areas (DMAs) were matched on indicators, such as how difficult it had historically been to count the population in that DMA, Census 2000 completion (postal return) rates, race/ethnicity, local poverty rates, urbanicity, language, and number of households. One of the identified DMAs in each pair was randomly assigned to receive a 50% increase in the media purchase compared to the initial census media levels, or a heavy-up of paid advertising (Evans, Datta, & Yan, 2014).

Another good example of a heavy-up experiment is the American Legacy Longitudinal Tobacco Use Reduction Study (ALLTURS), which aimed at examining variation in the *truth*® campaign exposure across media markets and over time. ALLTURS was a 3-year, school-based longitudinal study of adolescents age 12–18, and it was conducted between 2000 and 2002 as a substudy of the overall national *truth* campaign evaluation (Davis et al., 2009). ALLTURS used a questionnaire modeled on the national *truth* evaluation that measured youth smoking knowledge, attitudes, beliefs, intentions, and behaviors and related sociodemographic variables (Farrelly et al., 2005). The survey was administered to approximately 35,000 students in grades 6 through 12 located in seven communities in 10 school districts and 83 schools in the United States (Davis et al., 2009). The study communities were selected for a community-level, heavy-up, quasi-experiment designed to isolate dose-response effects of the *truth* campaign on adolescent smoking outcomes. The communities all received an initial dosage of *truth* media as measured by Nielsen ratings–based gross ratings points (GRPs). One year later, communities were randomly assigned to receive either increases or no increases in the media market–level dose of *truth* (Davis et al., 2009). All but one of the seven study communities received relatively low amounts of *truth* campaign advertising prior to ALLTURS. Market levels of *truth* GRPs were then increased from between 100% and 120% of the national average of the campaign as a whole in two of the study communities.

Published analyses of the ALLTURS data showed that, although the media increases produced sharp differences in *truth* GRPs between the communities that received the heavy-up dosage and those that did not, there were only small community-level differences in self-reported awareness of the campaign (Davis et al., 2009). In other words, the heavy-up did not produce a large difference in campaign awareness at the community level, and it was not associated with significant community-level differences in tobacco-related outcomes of interest. However, there was significant individual-level variation in self-reported recall of *truth* within the experimental communities. The Davis and colleagues (2009) study was able to use this observed individual-level variability to study effects of self-reported dose-response effects on tobacco use outcomes of interest.

By contrast, a natural experiment is another form of quasi-experiment often used in social marketing research that differs from person-by-treatment assignment studies in a way that there is no variable manipulated by the experimenter (i.e., no independent variable that determines assignment). Instead of controlling at least one variable like the person-by-treatment design, experimenters do not use random assignment and leave the experimental control up to environmental circumstances, hence the name "natural" experiment.

The *truth* campaign evaluation, discussed in Chapter 6 and elsewhere in this volume, is a good example of a natural experiment. The national *truth* evaluation used natural variation in GRPs at the media market level to identify a dose-response effect of campaign exposure on smoking outcomes of interest among youth and young adults (Farrelly et al., 2005).

Another good example is the *VERB: It's What You Do* national evaluation (Huhman et al., 2010). In 2002, the Centers for Disease Control and Prevention (CDC) launched the VERB campaign. Its call to action was for children aged 9 to 13 years (i.e., tweens) to be physically active every day (Wong et al., 2004) and to build a positive relationship with the VERB brand (Gronroos, 1997). VERB was a social marketing campaign that used mass media, school and community promotions, the Internet, and partnerships with national organizations and local communities and ran from 2002 to 2006, with cumulative funding of some US$339 million (Huhman et al., 2010). VERB is one of the largest social marketing campaigns ever conducted and had significant resources for evaluation.

The VERB evaluation collected both self-reported measures of aided and unaided awareness (see discussion of these measures in Chapter 6) and external or objective measures of exposure through GRPs. These measurements were validated by a study that found positive correlation observed between the self-report and external exposure (Berkowitz, Huhman, & Nilan, 2008). These measures were used to compare exposed and unexposed youth and to measure the effects of VERB dosage on physical activity outcomes among the target audience. The study used PSM to adjust the exposed and unexposed groups for potential confounding variables so that both groups were statistically equivalent for subsequent analysis (Judkins et al., 2007).

Survey results indicated consistently high awareness of the VERB campaign among tweens during the 4-year study period (Huhman et al., 2010). At the endpoint, in 2006, children aged 10 to 13 years with high levels of exposure were significantly more likely to report being active on the day before the survey compared to youth with low exposure, and there was a dose-response relationship between exposure and physical activity. VERB campaign effects were lower as the children's age increased beyond the target of age 13, but the dose-response relationship persisted in 2006 for outcome expectations and free-time physical activity (Huhman et al., 2010). Thus, the quasi-experimental methodology was successful in identifying validated campaign effects.

Researchers studying campaigns conducted in low- and middle-income countries have noted the challenges in conducting social marketing evaluations in such settings and the importance of quasi-experimental methods (Chapman et al., 2013). Issues include the ongoing nature and widespread diffusion of many social marketing activities, including product distribution, such as condoms, malaria-preventing bed nets, and water purification systems (Evans et al., 2014). In addition, randomization in the context of campaign implementation is often impossible, and low-resource settings raise challenges in terms of the logistics of maintaining experimental control. Exceptions include group randomized studies in which, for example, villages or districts can be randomized before an intervention begins to treatment or control (Eldridge & Kerry, 2012). While possible in the case of social marketing campaigns, most often this approach is not a viable option, and thus quasi-experimental methods are of great value and importance to researchers.

Saleema is a new evaluation that aims to conduct a highly rigorous quasi-experiment in a low-resource, politically challenging situation. This project, currently being implemented in Sudan, uses a quasi-experimental design and offers a good example of this form of evaluation design.

Background on the Saleema Campaign

The overall goal of the Saleema Communication Initiative (http://www.unicef.org/sudan/protection_6092.html) is to promote long-term abandonment of female genital mutilation and cutting (FGMC) through changing social norms, attitudes, and intentions related to the practice. The immediate measureable objective of the program is to increase social acceptance of uncut girls, as reflected in increased use of the positive term *Saleema* and in normative beliefs about the acceptability of being uncut.

In Sudan, as in many African and Middle Eastern countries, FGMC is a highly accepted social practice with deep cultural roots. It is based on social normative beliefs about how individuals in the community should behave (subjective norms, beliefs about what should be)—what most people in the community actually do (descriptive norms, empirical beliefs) (Kahneman & Miller, 1986; Cialdini, 2007). When a social norm such as FGMC is in place, families and individuals engage in the practice because they believe that it confers social status, is expected of them, and is prevalent. Without these perceptions, the social norm would be weakened, and the practice would become less widespread and may eventually cease to exist. Changing both subjective and descriptive social norms is thus a key step in social norm change (Cialdini, 2007). When subjective and descriptive norms are in conflict, many people follow descriptive norms, what they perceive the prevalent behavior to be (Fekadu & Kraft, 2002). Recent experimental studies have shown that people tend to have conditional preferences for following prosocial norms, and those preferences can be modified through interventions, which may lead to substantial behavior changes (Bicchieri, 2010). Even if a norm is considered subjectively important (what should be), if individuals observe nonconformity or otherwise undergo a change in conditional preferences, they will be less likely to follow the norm (Bicchieri, 2010).

In the case of FGMC, families practice it to ensure the marriageability and status of their daughters within the community of potential marriage partners. In this situation, what one family chooses to do, such as practice FGMC, is to a substantial degree dependent on what other families in the community do. In the absence of some change in social norms, no individual family is likely to abandon the practice. The perception is that to do so would ruin the marriageability of daughters and the status of the family. The hypothesis underlying Saleema is that, to change the social norm in Sudan, abandonment of FGMC must be promoted as a new social norm that is widespread and conveys greater benefits to families and individuals within the community.

The new social norm of abandonment must be promoted and in a sense "outcompete" the old norm of practicing FGMC.

Within practicing communities, the subjective norm of doing the best for one's children motivates a parent's decision to engage in FGMC because the consequences of not complying with the social practice are seen as grave for both the girl and her family. It is essentially a cost-benefit perception. However, this also represents an opportunity to change perceptions and ultimately behavior. The same motivation to do what is best for one's children can also lead parents to stop FGMC once a better alternative choice and perceived social environment are promoted and accepted as the prevailing norm in the community. For example, if introduced by credible figures in a credible manner in the community, and abandonment is perceived as more beneficial and less costly, the norm may be changed.

Social marketing uses marketing principles and processes to design and implement programs to promote socially beneficial changes, including social norms and behavior (Kotler & Lee, 2008; Evans, 2006). In public health, social marketing attempts to increase healthy behaviors in a population by using proven marketing techniques used to promote commercial products. Social marketers analyze their competition (e.g., social norm of FGMC practice) and use persuasive techniques such as creating social models (i.e., socially desirable individuals engaging in FGMC abandonment), evocative imagery, and in some cases messages tailored for individuals using information about personal preferences and behavior. In recent years, social marketers have applied branding principles to create *health brands,* creating a representation of the branded behavior as more beneficial and less costly for the audience (Evans & Hastings, 2008). Social marketers have successfully branded numerous health behaviors worldwide (Evans et al., 2008).

In social marketing terms, FGMC is a widely accepted "product," with an established market base (Calkins, 2005), and thus is in competition with behavioral alternatives such as abandoning the practice. Social marketing treats behaviors as being product-like in the sense that they have established benefits and costs and operate within market environments that are subject to competition. Any socially marketed alternative must address this competition by providing a beneficial exchange and raising awareness and acceptance of the benefits of abandonment and that they outweigh the perceived costs (change in established, culturally grounded practice).

Saleema is a health brand in that it seeks to create a beneficial exchange and a positive identity for abandonment of FGMC, a more positive alternative to the old social norm and FGMC practice (Evans & Hastings, 2008).

It seeks to reframe and change the use of language by associating the word *Saleema* with abandonment and promoting the health and well-being of girls and women. As such, it should be evaluated as a branded campaign. In recent years, health researchers have applied branding principles to the challenging task of changing social and health behavior. The basic idea is to treat behaviors like FGMC, condom use, or drug abuse like products: Consumers perceive benefits and costs to both products and behaviors and to an extent decide whether to use or engage in them on that basis. Health branding is a new theory of disease prevention that posits building brand equity—positive associations on the part of the consumer with the branded product or behavior (i.e., a sense of identification with the product or behavior)—to promote healthy behaviors such as abandonment of FGMC or condom use (Evans, Holtz, & Snider, 2014). Health behavior can be branded using methods like those used successfully with products and services because each of these types of brands share common characteristics of promoting a beneficial exchange and relationship between consumer and object (Evans & Hastings, 2008).

Theory and Study Design

As discussed in Chapter 4, brand personality is the expression of the point of differentiation (PoD) of the brand, the social and emotional features that distinguish the brand and its identity from others (Ngoc et al, 2011). It can be expressed in adjectives such as "fun," "helpful," "happy," or "serious," like describing a person. At the same time, behavioral choices that are in competition with unhealthy alternatives have been branded in terms of the benefits they provide the consumer, much like products (Evans, Price, & Blahut, 2005). For example, in the *truth* campaign, the psychological construct of *need for uniqueness* (i.e., a personality characteristic associated with self-orientation and positively associated with the need for autonomy) was used as a basis to brand living tobacco free as normative behavior for adolescents (Snyder & Fromkin, 1977). Similarly, Saleema is creating positive associations with the term and the behaviors associated with FGMC abandonment. It seeks to associate the word *Saleema* with a positive perception of abandonment.

Brand execution is how the brand is implemented in the real world. It is the images, colors, symbols, logo, tag lines, and other physical manifestations of the brand position and personality used to represent and market it to consumers. It is what the consumer experiences when he or she comes in contact with the brand and what shapes brand associations. Thus, like personality, it can be measured and evaluated: How did consumers experience the brand execution, and what were their reactions? Do they follow the Saleema messages? In the Saleema evaluation, an adapted brand equity scale is being used to measure reaction to the campaign and hypothesize that the same effects observed in previous health brand evaluation will be found with Saleema: The hypothesis is that higher brand equity in the program is associated with more positive social norms toward abandonment of FGMC and intentions to abandon the practice.

The Saleema evaluation aims to answer several broad research questions (RQs):

- RQ1: Is Saleema effective in improving normative beliefs about FGMC abandonment?
- RQ2: Is there a dose-response relationship between higher exposure to Saleema implementation and improved normative beliefs about FGMC abandonment?
- RQ3: Does brand equity in Saleema mediate the relationship between Saleema exposure and normative beliefs about FGMC abandonment?
- RQ4: How do different populations and regions within Sudan respond to Saleema, and what relationship is there between these variations and Saleema outcomes?

These questions are reflected in Figure 8-1, the current Saleema conceptual framework. The hypothesis is that there is a causal pathway from Saleema exposure through message reactions and receptivity (Cacioppo & Petty, 1989),

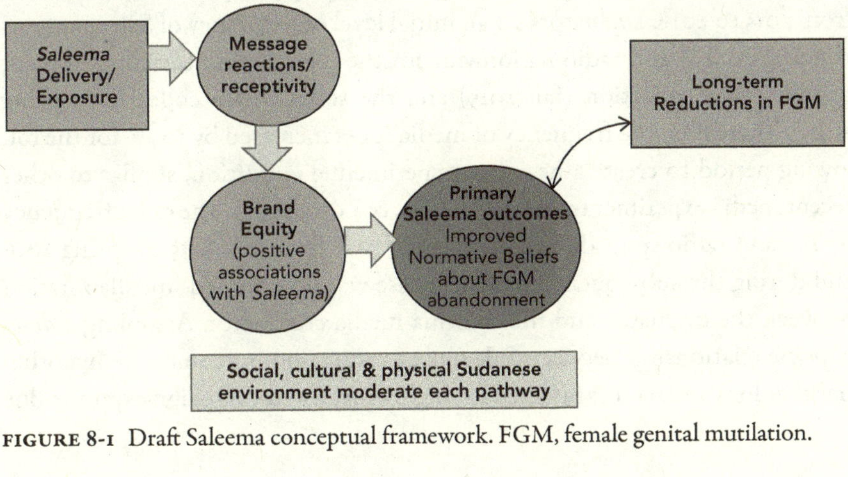

FIGURE 8-1 Draft Saleema conceptual framework. FGM, female genital mutilation.

to brand equity (Evans, Price, & Blahut, 2005), ad to improved normative beliefs (Bicchieri, 2010). The evaluation is designed to test these relationships.

The underlying assumption of this evaluation framework is that levels of Saleema exposure will vary by geographic location within Sudan. There are currently 18 states (provinces) within the country. As in previous social marketing campaigns, there will be natural variation in exposure to community-level and media-based Saleema campaign activities and implementation among the regional population. This is due to variable resources and efforts of local Saleema partners and variable capability to implement the campaign by location. As a function of higher and lower levels of exposure, measured outcomes will vary.

It is important to note that media exposure data (as measured by GRPs) available for other large campaigns discussed in this volume, such as the 2010 US Census, VERB, and *truth*, are not available in Sudan. These data are not collected in the country or the Middle East region in general. However, *reach* of Saleema to individuals across Sudan will vary due to variable levels of TV ownership and access. Generally, rural areas have lower levels of TV accessibility than urban areas. The evaluator works directly with UNICEF (United Nations Children's Fund) and state and local officials to quantify TV accessibility rates and design a standard measure for each location from which the study sample is drawn. This natural variation in TV penetration by location will be used as a proxy measure of reach in the outcome analysis. For radio, evaluators assume virtual universal access and no natural variation in reach in the analysis.

While evaluators could directly control reach of the campaign, they used a heavy-up methodology to experimentally control the *frequency* of delivery of Saleema mass media spots during the campaign implementation period from 2015 to 2018. Evaluators set an initial level of frequency of Saleema spots running on TV and radio nationwide for the period from the conclusion of baseline data collection (fall 2015) and the second data collection (spring 2016). Thereafter, the frequency of media spots increased by 100% for the following period to create a heavy-up experimental condition, similar to other recent media experiments (Bates, McCue, & Lotti, 2011). The exact frequency of TV and radio spots during the initial phase from fall 2015 to spring 2016 and during the subsequent heavy-up phase was determined in collaboration between the evaluator and the Saleema media contractor. Assuming a *dose-response* relationship between Saleema exposure and outcomes, we hypothesize that locations across Sudan with higher measured campaign exposure due to local activities combined with national-level media exposure (a combined measure of dosage) will achieve greater changes in FGMC social norms and other measured outcomes of the campaign.

The study has five data collection time points: a baseline in fall 2015, followed by a spring 2016 follow-up (T2), and a fall 2016 follow-up (T3; when initial effects of the heavy-up started in spring 2016 will first be observed). In fall 2017 (T4) and fall 2018 (T5), final outcome data will be collected. Table 8-1 provides a summary.

The strategy for the Saleema heavy-up media buys is to increase the media frequency level by 100% during the period between the second and third data collection time points (T2 and T3, respectively) and by a similar amount between subsequent time points up to T5. Previous research has found that commercial media studies typically use a 50%–100% increase in media level (reach and frequency). In a systematic review, Lodish and colleagues (1995) reported an average increase of 85% for established brands over 141 studies analyzed. Thus, Saleema uses a 100% increase after T2 (as shown in Table 8-1) to maximize the odds of substantial media effects at T3 and beyond.

The evaluation further specified and elaborated the Saleema conceptual framework in Figure 8-1. Specifically, evaluators identified individual variables and scales representing the constructs hypothesized to mediate the relationship between Saleema delivery and exposure (the main independent variable [IV] in the model) and the primary outcome (dependent variable, or DV) of interest, which is improved normative beliefs about FGMC abandonment. Reduction in FGMC is a *long-term* outcome, meaning that it is beyond the scope of the current evaluation but is the ultimate objective of Saleema. If the campaign is successful, over time beyond the planned evaluation period from

Table 8-1 Summary of Saleema Evaluation Design

Study Activity	Baseline	Mass Media Delivery X1 (Initial Phase)	T2	Mass Media Delivery X2 (Heavy-Up)	T3	T4	T5
Observation (O)	O		O		O	O	O
Media implementation (X)		X		X	X	X	X

2014 to 2018, the hypothesis is that the practice will be reduced and reduced to a greater extent in high-exposure areas based on evidence from the heavy-up experiment.

The overall study design is a quasi-experiment in which evaluators use (1) the heavy-up media experiment described previously, along with (2) natural variation in exposure to TV accessibility (reach) within communities and (3) variation in community-level Saleema activities to compare outcomes for surveyed individuals across Sudan with lower levels of campaign exposure to those with higher levels of exposure. Evaluators also monitor progress in campaign implementation and use these data as moderating variables to help understand observed changes in outcomes. As part of the campaign monitoring, local researchers also gather qualitative research to understand reactions to Saleema and to help identify campaign activities and messages that are most effective (and those that are ineffective) in promoting changes in FGMC social norms and other outcomes.

Methods

The Saleema evaluation operates on two levels within a project monitoring-and-evaluation (M&E) framework: (1) national-level changes in popular discourse within Sudan attributable to exposure to Saleema communications and (2) effectiveness of Saleema messages, materials, and social marketing activities in supporting face-to-face communications (or interpersonal communications) related to FGMC in popular discourse. The evaluation employs a mixed-methods approach (Creswell & Plano Clark, 2011) and a quasi-experimental design to evaluate dose-response effects of Saleema exposure on FGMC social norms. In a mixed-methods approach, both qualitative and quantitative methods are used to triangulate on program outcomes and to provide both depth of qualitative data and statistical estimates of outcomes derived from quantitative data (Rossi & Freeman, 1993). This approach is recommended in health campaign evaluation in which multiple data sources are typically needed to evaluate outcomes (Rice & Atkin, 2013).

Evaluators conduct a series of qualitative data collection activities to capture program implementation (process) data and to assist in interpretation of quantitative data. This will be coupled with the quasi-experimental longitudinal data collection based on annual monitoring of campaign exposure, reactions to campaign messages, and FGMC social norms and related cognitive outcomes. Evaluators also capture information about placements of Saleema media and community outreach, including follow-on activities to the basic components of the campaign (for details, see http://www.unicef.org/sudan/protection_6092.html): (1) Sufara Saleema Campaign, (2) Saleema Colors Campaign, (3) community dialogue, and (4) Born Saleema Project.

Monitoring (Process Evaluation) System Development

The evaluator has developed a Saleema Evaluation and Monitoring System (SEAMS). SEAMS is a database with a user-friendly data entry interface to allow the local State Council for Child Welfare (SCCW) in Sudan to capture major activities under each of the basic Saleema initiatives, Sufara, Colors, community dialogue, and Born Saleema. SEAMS data are uploaded to a central data registry to be maintained for M&E purposes.

Table 8-2 provides a summary of the core data elements for community-level activity monitoring. Note that Saleema TV broadcasts include both national and state levels. The types of broadcasts include Saleema advertisements, drama series, and moderated round-table discussions. Of these, the ads run most often, followed by drama series and then round tables. SEAMS records all information on national- and state-level broadcasts, including quantity, date/time, location, and type. The combined TV exposure data vary by location and by time as a result of the heavy-up design and media buy.

Table 8-2 Minimum SEAMS Data Elements[a,b]

Type of Event/ Activity	Event/ Activity ID	Activity Content	Location	Date/ Time	Duration	Number of Participants	Local Partners Participating
List of events/ activities							
Event 1							
Event 2							
Event 3, etc.							

[a] All variables are precoded in database, entered by selection from menu of options.
[b] SEAMS also includes national- and state-level media data, as noted above.

Qualitative Evaluation

For the qualitative component, evaluators use several data collection methodologies. First, they conducted site visits during the evaluation planning phase and conducted interviews with key informants (in-depth interviews or IDIs) to gain an in-depth understanding the FGMC in Sudan, the theoretical and practical basis of the Saleema initiative, plans for the campaign going forward, and other environmental and contextual information about the country and society that may affect campaign outcomes and need to be accounted for in the evaluation. Evaluators followed an interview guide that will be customized to anticipated stakeholders, including UNICEF staff, campaign developers, Sudanese policymakers, local community leaders involved in Saleema, and other interested groups. Results of these IDIs were used in development of the final conceptual evaluation framework, study design, and measures. During the evaluation implementation phase project, evaluators conducted additional IDIs with stakeholders to monitor progress of Saleema, identify potential challenges and solutions, and identify issues to be addressed in the quantitative evaluation.

During the implementation phase, evaluators and local researchers also captured the implementation of Saleema. Local researchers recruited community members to use *photovoice* techniques to capture campaign events, activities, and examples of how Saleema may have affected community social norms. Photovoice is a form of "participatory video methods" and a technique whereby members of a community capture pictures of their community to create a narrative of current conditions or change brought about by an intervention such as Saleema. Participants document visual changes in social norms about FGMC through this method. Photovoice has been recently used in other developing countries with success (Skovdal, 2011). Evaluators recruited both youth and adults to obtain varying perspectives on the program. They provided a semistructured protocol for the photovoice participants to follow in taking photos, following recent studies (Skovdal, 2011).

During annual site visits, evaluators also conducted direct observation of Saleema promotions and events and use ethnographic recording techniques. They worked with a local individual with experience in conducting qualitative research, to be contracted by UNICEF, to conduct focus groups with members of the community at events such as those sponsored in the Saleema Colors and Born Saleema campaign components. Evaluators developed a semistructured guide for the focus groups, and the local qualitative researcher will moderate the focus groups. These data helped to interpret quantitative findings regarding campaign reactions and outcomes. All of the quantitative outcome evaluation, qualitative, and implementation monitoring activities are or will be repeated at each of the evaluation time points (see Table 8-1) through 2018.

Quantitative Evaluation

For the quantitative component, evaluators conducted the previously described longitudinal quasi-experiment based on national surveys. The survey was administered by a third-party data collection organization contracted directly by UNICEF and supervised and trained by the evaluator. The evaluator delivered annual training on the data collection protocol and monitors the sampling methods and recruitment of participants and implementation of the study. Prior to baseline, the evaluator developed a human subjects' protection protocol and, in collaboration with UNICEF, obtained Institutional Research Board (IRB) approval in August 2015 from the Afhad University IRB (http://www.ahfad.net/), located in Khartoum, Sudan. Study implementation and research ethics are supervised and conducted with approval from the Afhad IRB.

In analysis of campaign longitudinal campaign data, evaluators modeled intended campaign effects on FGMC social norms based on level of estimated exposure, which will include data from the heavy-up design as well as monitoring data on exposure by location drawn from SEAMS. Regression models controlled for measured covariates, such as community, family, and individual characteristics, and estimate effects of campaign exposure on the dependent variable, FGMC social norms (a scale constructed from multiple questionnaire items). Evaluators also examined the dose-response relationship between Saleema exposure and changes in FGMC social norms. Using data on self-reported exposure and data from SEAMS, evaluators developed a Saleema dosage index (SDI) to estimate total exposure of each individual in the sample. Frequency data from the heavy-up design are combined with SEAMS data (to include the *reach index* based on TV accessibility by location), where each individual in the sample received an SDI score based on total exposure to campaign messages and activities in their local area.

Assuming natural variation in exposure to Saleema across regions over time, the evaluators' aim was to isolate the impact of the campaign on FGM social norms and related outcomes. This, combined with the heavy-up design, maximizes potential for variation in Saleema exposure and for comparisons between individuals receiving higher and lower dosages of campaign messages and activities over the evaluation study period.

Measuring Exposure

Evaluators used two types of data to measure exposure to Saleema: (1) self-reported recall of messages, the term *Saleema*, and campaign tag line; and (2) external data from multiple sources to measure potential exposure to Saleema at the community and media market levels. The former data were captured in the questionnaire and the latter through the Saleema media campaign implementation firm and their reported frequency of delivery of Saleema mass media through national TV channels according to the heavy-up design, as well as data captured through SEAMS. Evaluators also developed a TV accessibility, or reach index, that quantifies estimated availability of TVs per population member by state and locality. The reach index allows measurement of estimated natural variation in reach of Saleema ads, drama, and round tables by location.

This evaluation framework recognizes that there may be technical and logistical challenges in collecting the external data on Saleema community and media market exposure. Thus, evaluators planned for redundancy of measures, both self-report and external, to ensure that we will have some measures of campaign exposure to use in the outcome analyses. The goal was to collect all available exposure data to achieve the highest level of accuracy and validation of Saleema's effect on FGMC abandonment outcomes.

This additional external data on Saleema exposure served two purposes. First, it allowed evaluators to examine in more detail the reach of the campaign across regions of Sudan. Second, it provided an alternative measure of exposure to Saleema that is exogenous to the individual respondent. This helped to address the potential limitations of selective attention bias that may be present with self-reported awareness, where individuals may be more attentive to Saleema ads and thus more likely to indicate ad recognition. Thus, evaluators will be able to use these data to check the robustness of campaign effects across different measures of exposure and to examine the validity of individual self-reported measures of exposure. Following best practice, market-level potential exposure should be correlated with individual-level self-reported exposure (Davis, Evans, & Kamyab, 2013).

Saleema commercials will air on selected media channels, including TV and radio, in markets across the country through 2018. In the heavy-up study, evaluators varied frequency of ad delivery across the country between X1 (initial phase) and X2 (heavy-up phase) as shown in Table 8-1. Market-level exposure was estimated using a count of ad frequency over the time period covered per Table 8-1. For interim analyses, evaluators used frequency of exposure up to that point in the study and examine effects of the heavy-up experiment beginning at T3, after the first 100% increase in frequency at X2. For final outcome analyses, evaluators plan to examine total frequency of exposure across the study period.

Evaluators used separate measures for frequency of Saleema television video and frequency of radio spots. Reach (where the media are distributed) can only be measured in Sudan based on accessibility of channels. Radio was virtually always available, and was treated as a constant. TV varied by accessibility of a TV set and was generally lower in rural areas. Evaluators created a reach index to quantify this natural variation.

National-level media data were provided by the Saleema media contractor. State level data were provided by state contacts. While these data did not capture other Saleema advertising activities, such as community activities and print (e.g., outdoor) advertising, given the limited data on media delivery available in Sudan, frequency data and the planned reach index based on TV accessibility represent the best available data on the overall level of campaign "dose" delivered to each location.

Through SEAMS, evaluators collected separate data on community-level exposure and national and state-level media delivery and use that in combination with frequency data through the planned SDI construct to create composite external measures of exposure. Because media exposure was expected to take time to influence targeted behavioral outcomes, evaluators created cumulative measures of total Saleema SDI over the course of the evaluation for use in outcome evaluation. These data were then be merged into the survey data set based on standard geographic identifiers (at the lowest level of aggregation possible, community or village level) for each individual. A location-specific measure of SDI was assigned based on the geographic location of the respondent.

To illustrate the variability in Saleema exposure across the country, evaluators categorized total Saleema SDI into five levels and plot them geographically by regions and DMAs within region. Variation between regions created a natural experiment that could be used to examine how region-to-region variability in campaign exposure is associated with Saleema social norms and other outcomes at the individual level. This method of merging media exposure data to individual-level survey data for analysis of campaign effects on health outcomes has been used in multiple media evaluation studies in high-income countries (Davis, Evans, & Kamyab, 2013; Davis, Nonnemaker, & Farrelly, 2007; Farrelly et al., 2005, 2009; Terry-McElrath et al., 2007). However, the method is novel in low- and middle-income countries.

Sampling and Participant Recruitment

With assistance from Afhad University statisticians, evaluators drew a nationally representative sample stratified by the 18 states within Sudan. All households in all regions had an equal probability of selection, and local data collectors drew a list of households for individual recruitment. The data collectors sampled both the female *and* male head of household as the respondent to the survey, which will permit paired comparisons between males and females by household (Evans et al., 2011). The design is to sample approximately equal numbers of male and female respondents for the overall sample.

Statistical Power

Power was calculated based on descriptive normative beliefs about FGMC (i.e., that it is a widespread practice in the individual's community) given two time points of interest: at baseline and at 1 year postbaseline (at T3, after the heavy-up phase X2). This was to compare differences in that outcome between individuals with high versus low exposure to Saleema intervention and control conditions. Studies have shown that reductions in perceived norms of health behavior (descriptive norms) are associated with reductions in intentions and ultimately in behavior (Evans et al., 2007; Hecht et al., 1997). Evaluators assumed 25% descriptive social norms for FGMC abandonment at baseline (belief that abandonment is commonplace in my community), given the target population (Friedrich & Stein, 1975). They further assumed a 50% recruitment rate (i.e., success in enrolling participants) based on previous research (Alba & Hutchinson, 1987), 80% power (1-β) to detect a difference of 15% in descriptive norms between high and low Saleema exposure conditions, the standard deviation (SD) of descriptive norms as 1.5, and a two-sided significance level of 0.05, assuming 10% annual loss to follow=up (attrition). Based on these assumptions, we need a baseline sample of 199 participants per group. As the goal is to make comparisons between higher and lower exposure locations within Sudan, evaluators drew a baseline sample of this size from each state. To evaluate differences in Saleema outcomes based on the planned SDI measure of campaign dosage, the study will collect this sample *for each of the 20 states.* This resulted in 199 × 18 states = 3,582 participants drawn from across Sudan at baseline. The end-line sample after attrition will be 2,900. Table 8-3 illustrates the sampling plan based on this analysis (which may be adjusted during implementation).

Table 8-3 Illustrative Sampling Plan[a]

Baseline (T1)	T2 + T3 (end of year 2)	T4 (end of year 3)	T4 (end of year 4)
199 (× 18 = 3,582)	179 (× 18 = 3,222)	161 (× 18 = 2,898)	145 (× 18 = 2,610)

[a] Note that the sampling plan represents *households*. Evaluators collect both a male and a female head-of-household interview where available for each sampled household.

Measures and Instruments

Evaluators developed a questionnaire to be administered by trained interviewers in a field-based setting in communities across Sudan. The questionnaire was programmed into a tablet computer using Microsoft Access. The questionnaire included measures of aided and unaided awareness, message receptivity, scales for subjective and descriptive social norms about FGMC and related knowledge, attitudes, and beliefs, as well as sociodemographic information about community, family, and individuals. The questionnaire specifically asked about awareness of the Saleema messages, exposure to specific executions, including the TV and radio spots and community-level activities. The questionnaire included validation techniques to compare self-reported campaign awareness data to placement data from the mass media Surfara Saleema spots and community-level campaign components to develop reliable estimates of campaign exposure (McAfee et al. 2013; Davis, Evans, & Kamyab, 2013).

Table 8-4 summarizes the planned questionnaire measures. Additional measures may be added in subsequent rounds of data collection as a result of lessons learned from the IDIs conducted during the first two years of the project (through 2016). Also, as Saleema is a branded campaign and we hypothesized (Figure 8-1) that brand equity in the campaign would mediate FGMC social norms and other outcomes, evaluators developed a brand equity scale based on previous research (Evans, Price, & Blahut, 2005; Evans et al., 2011). Table 8-5 provides details on planned brand equity scale measures (included in the questionnaire).

Data Collection

The evaluators developed terms of reference to specify the responsibilities and scope of work for Afhad University to collect the monitoring, qualitative and quantitative evaluation data (including the SEAMS, questionnaire, IDI, and *photovoice* data), as described previously. The evaluators conducted an initial

Table 8-4 Questionnaire Measures

Measure (Number of Items)	Source	Reliability/Validity	Rationale
FGMC intentions			
Likelihood of practicing FGMC in future	Hecht et al, 2008	Scale α .81	Likelihood of engaging in behavior predicts use in other domains of public health (Elek et al., 2006)
Self-efficacy			
Confidence in ability to choose not to practice FGMC despite social pressure	Hecht, et al., 2003, 2008; modified from Kasen, Vaughan, & Walter, 1992	Scale α .79, .88	Increasing confidence in ability to abandon FGMC is a target of Saleema
Positive expectancies			
Agreement with positive consequences of FGMC abandonment	Hecht et al., 2003; modified from Hansen & Graham, 1991	Scale α .78	Found to predict health risk behavior avoidance (Miller-Day & Kam, 2010)
Descriptive norms			
Perceived prevalence of FGMC among peers	Hansen & Graham, 1991	Scale α .90	Directly targeted by Saleema (Elek et al., 2006)
Subjective norms			
Perceived acceptability of FGMC among peers	Hansen & Graham, 1991	Scale α .90	Directly targeted by Saleema (Elek et al., 2006)

Brand equity			
Four second-order constructs: brand loyalty, leadership/ popularity, brand personality, brand awareness (see details in Table 8-3)	Evans, Price, & Blahut, 2005, *truth* brand equity scale	Scale α .94	Brand equity mediates relationship between health media messages and attitudes/beliefs/ behavioral outcomes; will adapt *truth* scale to create Saleema brand equity scale
Media Use			
Structural access to media	Jordan et al., 2006, home media inventory	Parent and child ratings correlated ($r > .85$; Hersey et al., 2005)	Strong relationships between home media availability and hours of TV use (Wiecha et al., 2001; Saelens et al., 2002)
Hours of media use			
By category, see following measure of media use	Jordan et al., 2006, home media inventory	Parent and child ratings correlated ($r > .08$; Hersey et al., 2005; Wiecha et al., 2001; Robinson, 1999)	Evidence that it is important to assess differences between weekday and weekend TV and displacement from TV to video game and computer use (Hersey et al., 2005; Wiecha, et al., 2001; Robinson, 1999)
Media used			
• TV channels viewed • Video games played • Websites visited • Radio listened • Magazines and other print	Jordan et al., 2006, home media inventory	Moderator of campaign effects on FGMC beliefs	Evidence that exposure to content promoting health risk behaviors can promote emulation (Chandra et al., 2008)

(*continued*)

Table 8-4 Continued

Measure (Number of Items)	Source	Reliability/Validity	Rationale
Exposure and Reactions to Saleema Messages and Materials			
Saleema awareness • Awareness of Saleema language • (Aided) Awareness of campaign tag line • (Unaided) Awareness of campaign tag line	Developed by Saleema evaluators	Measured in previous national data collection and campaign tracking	Basic measure of campaign awareness and overall message
Recall			
Confirmed or independent awareness of • Ads • Website • Posters (in school or community)	Evans et al. (2008) Standardized measures of self-reported media recall	Corroborates with changes in campaign-related attitudes	Ability to corroborate exposure to the Saleema campaign

Recognition		
Ability to recognize having seen an advertisement when shown	Evans et al. (2009) recognition test scale	Additional measure of exposure validated in research on media campaigns
Argument credibility "Did this advertisement give you good reasons to agree with the Saleema message?" • Repeat for each channel	Evans et al. (2004) message receptivity scale	Mediates effects on brand equity and subsequent health risk attitudes and intentions (Evans, Price, & Blahut, 2005)
Affective reaction		
"Did this advertisement give you a positive emotional reaction to the Saleema message?" • Repeat for each channel	Evans et al. (2004) message receptivity scale	Mediates effects on brand equity and subsequent health risk attitudes and intentions (Evans, Price, & Blhaut, 2005)
Ratings of ads		
• Repeat for each channel		Assess reactions and appeal of Saleema ads

Table 8-5 Brand Equity Dimensions and Relevance to Saleema

Dimension	Saleema Relevance (Examples)
Price premium	Willingness to invest time/effort in participating in Saleema events and activities
Satisfaction/loyalty	Would individual recommend Saleema-promoted behaviors to friends?
Perceived quality	Value of *Saleema* behaviors compared to alternatives
Leadership/popularity	How "in" or popular are *Saleema* promoted behaviors?
Perceived value	Is the *Saleema* behavior perceived as adding value to the individual's lifestyle (social status)?
Brand personality	How the Saleema brand is differentiated from competing behaviors
Organizational associations	Is Saleema a trusted source of information?
Brand awareness	When you think of the Saleema brand, what do you think of?
Market share	Proportion of target population engaging in Saleema promoted behaviors
Market price	What is the cost of engaging in Saleema behaviors in light of behavioral alternatives (lost social status due to not practicing FGMC)?

training in 2015 and follow up in 2016, with Afhad. Evaluation plans call for follow-up trainings each year of the study.

Afhad University has extensive local experience in Sudan and expertise in qualitative and quantitative instrumentation and data collection. The training consisted of 2 days of orientation, in-depth presentation of the evaluation plan and instruments, and question-and-answer sessions on the following topics:

- Saleema program goals, objectives, conceptual framework, and major activities
- Saleema evaluation framework
- sampling plan
- data collection instruments—survey instrument and qualitative instruments (focus group and IDI guides)
- data management procedures

- data file delivery to evaluator
- follow-up data collection and related activities from 2015 to 2018 (T2–T5)

Data Analysis

Qualitative Data Analysis

Focus group and IDI data will be analyzed to identify additional variables for the questionnaire and to provide context for interpretation of subsequent quantitative findings. This will be done through the following sequence: (1) Text from interviews/focus groups is coded for content and major themes using QSR NVivo software, and (2) identified themes/content that have high consensus (they appear in a high proportion of interviews and focus groups relative to all coded themes/content) are converted to data items for inclusion in the quantitative instruments. Coded text can also be arrayed by respondent demographics to identify themes and contents that are unique to particular subgroups, which can provide data useful in the interpretation of quantitative results. Qualitative analysis has been or will be conducted after the evaluator's annual site visits from 2015 to 2018.

Quantitative Data Analysis

Questionnaire data will be analyzed by fitting fixed-effects regression models. This approach effectively adds a dummy variable for each study participant into a conventional regression model to represent the joint effects of all time-invariant respondent characteristics. As a result, regression coefficients represent the effects of changes in independent variables on changes in outcomes (Khandker, Koolwal, & Samad, 2010). Evaluators will use two different fixed-effects specifications, one designed to answer questions about population-level impacts and the other designed to measure impacts of individual exposure to Saleema.

Empirically, the approach is a *difference-in-difference* analysis using fixed effects to control for participant characteristics (Khandker, Koolwal, & Sama, 2010). Evaluators will create a person-period data set to which each sampled individual contributes two entries, one from T1 and the other from T*n* (where *n* is a given follow-up time point of interest, with the end line being T5). The parameter of primary interest is the extent to which social norms outcome measures increase between T1 and T*n*. This and other parameters in the model will be estimated via generalized least squares using the

XTREG, FE command in Stata 13 (College Station, TX) using the available options to adjust estimates and standard errors for the fact that the data come from a stratified cluster sample rather than a simple random sample. In effect, the analytical approach converts a one-group pretest-posttest preexperimental design into a natural experiment, thereby mitigating the primary sources of bias (history and testing) that normally characterize the former design (Shadish, Cook, & Campbell, 2002).

A further elaboration of this approach will be possible using the SDI construct based on locations in which our sample resides. Ideally, we would obtain this information for the study time periods (T1–T5) prior to each survey data collection time point. In that case, evaluators will conduct a fixed-effects analysis accounting for SDI score.

Conclusion: Potential Challenges and Constraints

Regarding potential challenges and constraints, first there are the substantial physical challenges of (1) effectively implementing the Saleema campaign and (2) capturing high-quality evaluation data. These challenges arise from the physical situation in a war-torn country facing endemic poverty, resource shortages, public health threats, and other social problems. The plans to implement the three major campaign components of Saleema, and fidelity of implementation, are issues that concern the evaluators. Evaluators need to spend considerable time and remain in regular contact with program designers, field-based implementers of the communication activities, and media planners and purchasers. The process evaluation, including qualitative research described previously, is critical for monitoring fidelity of implementation.

At the same time, Sudan has experienced tremendous disruption, which has been widely documented, due to conflict in the Darfur region. The conflict has had a disproportionate negative effect on women and girls. There may be challenges in collecting data to evaluate Saleema under these conditions. The evaluator needs to work closely with UNICEF, Afhad University (data collection organization), and Saleema designers and implementers to identify and work around these challenges. One example of this may be direct observation of the community-level campaign components in areas where unrest may have recently occurred.

Second, measuring and evaluating exposure is challenging due to available resources to measure exposure in mass media and at the community level. The evaluation design includes analysis of dose-response effects of Saleema; this requires adequate and reliable exposure data. Evaluators work closely with Saleema designers and implementers to determine the availability of exposure data and ensure that the campaign will collect and be able to provide these data for analysis.

Third, asking questions about a highly sensitive and culturally specific topic such as FGMC has the potential for social desirability bias (Stoeber, 2001). Social desirability bias leads respondents to give responses to survey questions that the respondents believe are socially acceptable. This bias can be reduced through data collection techniques that ensure the respondents' confidentiality. Evaluators work with the Afhad University to ensure that individual confidentiality is maintained to the maximum extent possible in light of conditions in communities where the survey is administered.

Fourth, the quality of the sampling plan is crucial. To conduct a media campaign evaluation and detect campaign effects, it is important to have variation in campaign exposure. The planned heavy-up study (see Table 8-1) is a response to this challenge, and the design aims to maximize measured variation in frequency of exposure over time for use in the outcome analysis. Related to the second point about exposure, evaluators and Afhad University need to understand where the campaign was implemented through community-level activities and to ensure representation of communities across Sudan that may have higher and lower levels of exposure to the campaign due to media buying and community-level campaign activities.

Additional Resources: Literature

- Bates, N., McCue, K., & Lotti, M. (2011). *The Paid Advertising Heavy-Up Experiment*. US Census Bureau: 2010 Census Program for Evaluations and Experiments. Washington, DC: US Department of Commerce, Census Bureau.
- Datta, A.R., Yan, T., Evans, W.D., Pedlow, S., Spencer, B., & Bautista, R. (2012). *2010 Census Integrated Communications Program Evaluation: Final Report*. Prepared for the US Bureau of the Census, US Department of Commerce. Chicago: NORC at the University of Chicago.
- Mpofu, E., Mpofu, N., Johnson, E., & Evans, W.D. (2014). Monitoring and Evaluation of Community-Oriented Health Services. In *Community Oriented Health Services: Practices Across Disciplines*, E. Mpofu (Ed.). New York: Springer; 117–133.

References

Alba, J.W., & Hutchinson, J.Y. (1987). Dimensions of Consumer Expertise. *Journal of Consumer Research*, 13: 411–454.

Bates, N., McCue, K., & Lotti, M. (2011). *The Paid Advertising Heavy Up Experiment.* Washington, DC: US Department of Commerce, Census Bureau. Retrieved on August 18, 2014, from https://www.census.gov/2010census/pdf/2010_Census_PAHUE.pdf

Berkowitz, J.M., Huhman, M., & Nolin, M.J. (2008). Did Augmenting the VERB Campaign Advertising in Select Communities Have an Effect on Awareness, Attitudes, and Physical Activity? *American Journal of Preventive Medicine*, 34(6S): S257–S266.

Bicchieri, C. (2010). Norms, Preferences, and Conditional Behavior. *Politics, Philosophy, and Economics*, 9(3): 297–313. doi:10.1177/1470594x10369276

Cacioppo, J.T., & Petty, R.E. (1989). The Elaboration Likelihood Model: The Role of Affect and Affect-Laden Information Processing in Persuasion. In *Cognitive and Affective Responses to Advertising*, A. Tybout & P. Caferata (Eds.). Lexington, MA: Lexington Books; 69–89.

Calkins, T. (2005). The Challenge of Branding. In *Kellogg on Branding*, A. Tybout & T. Calkins (Eds.). New York: Wiley; 1–10.

Chandra, A., Martino, S.C., Collins, R.L., Elliott, M.N., Berry, S.H., Kanouse, D.E., & Miu, A. (2008). Does Watching Sex on Television Predict Teen Pregnancy? Findings From a National Longitudinal Survey of Youth. *Pediatrics*, 122: 1047–1054.

Chapman, S., Ayers, J., LeTouze, O., & Renard. (2013). Branding and Social Marketing. In *Psychology of Branding*, W.D. Evans (Ed.). Hauppage, NY: Nova Science. Chapter 10.

Cialdini, R. (2007). Descriptive Social Norms as Underappreciated Sources of Social Control. *Psychometrika*, 72(2): 263–268.

Creswell, J.W., & Plano Clark, V.L. (2011). *Designing and Conducting Mixed Methods Research* (2nd ed.). Thousand Oaks, CA: Sage.

Davis, K.C., Evans, W.D., & Kamyab, K. (2013). Effectiveness of a National Media Campaign to Promote Parent-Child Communication About Sex. *Health Education and Behavior*, 40(1): 97–106. doi:10.1177/1090198112440009

Davis, K.C., Farrelly, M.C., Messeri, P., & Duke, J. (2009). The Impact of National Smoking Prevention Campaigns on Tobacco-Related Beliefs, Intentions to Smoke and Smoking Initiation: Results From a Longitudinal Survey of Youth in the United States. *International Journal of Environmental Research and Public Health*, 6: 722–740. doi:10.3390/ijerph6020722

Davis, K.C., Nonnemaker, J.M., & Farrelly, M.C. (2007). Association Between National Smoking Prevention Campaigns and Perceived Smoking Prevalence Among Youth in the United States. *Journal of Adolescent Health*, 41: 430–436.

Eldridge, S., & Kerry, S. (2012). *A Practical Guide to Cluster Randomized Trials in Health Services Research.* New York: Wiley.

Elek, E., Miller-Day, M., & Hecht, M.L. (2006). Influences of Personal, Injunctive, and Descriptive Norms on Early Adolescent Substance Use. *Journal of Drug Issues*, 36(1): 147–171.

Evans, W., Necheles, J., Longjohn, M., & Christoffel, K. (2007). The 5-4-3-2-1 Go! Intervention: Social Marketing Strategies for Nutrition. *Journal of Nutrition Education and Behavior*, 39(2): S55–S59.

Evans, W.D. (2006). How Social Marketing Works in Health Care. *British Medical Journal,* 322: 1207–1210.

Evans, W.D., Blitstein, J., Hersey, J., Renaud, J. & Yaroch, A. (2008). Systematic Review of Public Health Branding Research. Journal of Health Communication, 13(8): 351–360.

Evans, W.D., Datta, R., & Yan, T. (2014). *Paid Media and Hard-to-Reach Populations: Lessons From the 2010 Census.* New York: Russell Sage.

Evans, W.D., Davis, K.C., Umanzor, C., Patel, K., & Khan, M. (2011). Evaluation of Sexual Communication Messages. *BMC Reproductive Health,* 8: 15. doi:10.1186/1742-4755-8-15

Evans, W.D., & Hastings, G. (Eds.). (2008). *Public Health Branding: Applying Marketing for Social Change.* London: Oxford University Press

Evans, W.D., Holtz, K., & Snider, J. (2014). Effects of the Above the Influence Brand on Adolescent Drug Use Prevention Beliefs. *Journal of Health Communication,* 19(6): 721–737. doi:10.1080/10810730.2013.837559

Evans, W.D., Pattanayak, S.K., Young, S., Buszin, J, Rai, S., & Wallace, J. (2014). Social Marketing of Water and Sanitation: Systematic Review of Peer-Reviewed Literature. *Social Science & Medicine,* 110: 18–25. doi:10.1016/j.socscimed.2014.03.011

Evans, W.D., Price, S., & Blahut, S. (2005). Evaluating the truth® Brand. *Journal of Health Communication,* 10(2): 181–192.

Evans, W.D., Price, S., Blahut, S., Hersey, J., Niederdeppe, J., & Ray, S. (2004). Social Imagery, Tobacco Independence, and the truth® Campaign. *Journal of Health Communication,* 9(5): 425–441.

Evans, W.D., Uhrig, J., Davis, K., & McCormack, L. (2009). Efficacy Methods to Evaluate Health Communication and Marketing Campaigns. *Journal of Health Communication,* 14(3): 244–254.

Farrelly, M.C., Davis, K.C., Haviland, M.L., Messeri, P., & Healton, C.G. (2005). Evidence of a Dose-Response Relationship Between "truth" Antismoking Ads and Youth Smoking. *American Journal of Public Health,* 95(3): 425–431.

Farrelly, M.C., Nonnemaker, J., Davis, K.C., & Hussin, A. (2009). The Influence of the National truth® Campaign on Smoking Initiation. *American Journal of Preventive Medicine,* 36(5): 379–384.

Fekadu, Z., & Kraft P (2002). Expanding the Theory of Planned Behavior: The Role of Social Norms and Group Identification. *Journal of Health Psychology,* 7(1): 33–43.

Friedrich, L.K., & Stein, A. (1975). Prosocial Television and Young Children: The Effects of Verbal Labeling and Role Playing on Learning and Behavior. *Child Development,* 45: 27–38.

Grönroos, C. (1997). Value-Driven Relational Marketing: From Products to Resources and Competencies. *Journal of Marketing Management,* 13: 407–419.

Hansen, W.B., & Graham, J.W. (1991). Preventing Alcohol, Marijuana, and Cigarette Use Among Adolescents: Peer Pressure Resistance Training Versus Establishing Conservative Norms. *Preventive Medicine,* 20: 414–430.

Hecht, M.L., Elek, E., Wagstaff, D., Kam, J.A., Marsiglia, F., Dustman, P., Reeves, L., & Harthun, M. (2008). Immediate and Short-Term Effects of the 5th Grade Version of the keepin' it REAL Substance Use Prevention Intervention. *Journal of Drug Education*, 38: 225–251.

Hecht, M.L., Marsiglia, F.F., Elek, E., Wagstaff, D.A., Kulis, S., Dustman, P., & Miller-Day, M. (2003). Culturally Grounded Substance Use Prevention: An Evaluation of the keepin' it R.E.A.L. Curriculum. *Prevention Science*, 4: 233–248.

Hecht, M.L., Trost, M., Bator, R., & MacKinnon, D. (1997). Ethnicity and Sex Similarities and Differences in Drug Resistance. *Journal of Applied Communication Research*, 25: 75–97.

Hersey, J.C., Niederdeppe, J., Ng, S.W., Mowery, P., & Farrelly, M.C. (2005). How State Counter-Industry Campaigns Help Prime Perceptions of Tobacco Industry Practices to Promote Reductions in Youth Smoking. *Tobacco Control*, 14(6): 377–383.

Huhman, M.E., Potter, L.D., Nolin, M.J., Piesse, A., Judkins, D.R., Banspach, S.W., & Wong, F.L. (2010). The Influence of the VERB Campaign on Children's Physical Activity in 2002 to 2006. *American Journal of Public Health*, 100(4): 638–645. doi:10.2105/AJPH.2008.142968

Jordan, A., Hersey, J., McDivitt, J., & Heitzler, C. (2006). Reducing Children's Television-Viewing Time: A Qualitative Study of Parents and Their Children. *Pediatrics*, 118(5): e1303–e1310.

Judkins, D.R., Morganstein, D., Zador, P., Piesse, A., Barrett, B., & Muhopadhyay, P. (2007). Variable selection and raking in propensity scoring. *Statistics in Medicine*, 26(5): 1022–1033.

Kahneman, D., & Miller, D.T. (1986). Norm Theory: Comparing Reality to Its Alternatives. *Psychological Review*, 80: 136–153.

Kasen, S., Vaughan, R.D., & Walter, H.J. (1992). Self-Efficacy for AIDS Preventive Behaviors amon g Tenth Grade Students. *Health Education Quarterly*, 19(2): 187–202.

Khandker, S.R., Koolwal, G.B., & Samad, H.A. (2010). *Handbook on Impact Evaluation: Quantitative Methods and Practices*. Washington, DC: World Bank. doi:10.1596/978-0-8213-8028-4

Kotler, P., & Lee, N. (2008). *Social Marketing: Influencing Behaviors for Good* (3rd ed.). Los Angeles: Sage.

Lodish, L., Abraham, M., Kalmenson, S., Livelsberger, J., Lebetkin, B., Richardson, B., & Stevens, M. (1995). How TV Advertising Works: A Meta-Analysis of 389 Real World Split Cable TV Advertising Experiments. *Journal of Marketing Research*, 32(5): 125–139.

McAfee, T., Davis, K.C., Alexander, R.L, Pechachek, T.F., & Bunnell, R. (2013). Effect of the First Federally Funded US Antismoking National Media Campaign. *The Lancet*, 382(9909): 2003–2011. doi:http://dx.doi.org/10.1016/S0140-6736(13)61686-4

Miller-Day, M., & Kam, J.A. (2010). More Than Just Openness: Developing and Validating a Measure of Targeted Parent-Child Communication about Alcohol. *Health Communication*, 25(4): 293–302.

Morgan, G.A. (2000). Quasi-Experimental Designs. *Journal of the American Academy of Child & Adolescent Psychiatry*, 39(6): 794–796. doi:10.1097/00004583-2000 06000-00020

Ngoc, K.V., Mundy, G., Madan, Y., Ayers, J., Sherard, D., DeNormandie, J., & Kays, M. (2011). Using Formative Research to Promote Behavior Change Among Male Clients of Female Sex Workers in Vietnam. *Cases in Public Health Communication & Marketing*, 5 Proc: 27–47. Retrieved from http://www. casesjournal.org/volume5

Rice, R.E., & Atkin, C.K. (2013). *Public Communications Campaigns* (4th ed.). Los Angeles: Sage.

Robinson, T.N. (1999). Reducing Children's Television Viewing to Prevent Obesity: A Randomized Controlled Trial. *Journal of the American Medical Association*, 282: 1561–1567.

Rossi, P.H., & Freeman, H.E. (1993). *Evaluation: A Systematic Approach* (5th ed.). Los Angeles: Sage.

Saelens, B.E., Sallis, J.F., Nader, P.R., Broyles, S.L., Berry, C.C., & Taras, H.L. (2002). Home Environmental Influences on Children's Television Watching from Early to Middle Childhood. *Developmental and Behavioral Pediatrics*, 23(3): 127–131.

Shadish, W.R., Cook, T.D., & Campbell, D.T. (2002). *Experimental and Quasi-Experimental Designs for Generalized Causal Inference*. Boston: Houghton Mifflin.

Skovdal, M. (2011). Picturing the Coping Strategies of Caregiving Children in Western Kenya: From Images to Action. *American Journal of Public Health*, 101(3): 452–453.

Snyder, C.R., & Fromkin, H.L. (1977). Abnormality as a Positive Characteristic: The Development and Validation of a Scale Measuring Need for Uniqueness. *Journal of Abnormal Psychology*, 89, 518–527.

Stoeber, J. (2001). The Social Desirability Scale-17 (SD-17). *European Journal of Psychological Assessment*, 17: 222–232.

Terry-McElrath, Y.M., Wakefield, M.A., Emery, S., Saffer, H., Szczypka, G., O'Malley, P.M., Johnston, L.D., Chaloupka, F.J., & Flay, B.R. (2007). State Anti-tobacco Advertising and Smoking Outcomes by Gender and Race/ethnicity. *Ethnicity and Health*, 12(4): 339–362.

Wiecha, J., Sobol, A., Peterson, K., & Gortmaker, S. (2001). Household Television Access: Associations With Screen Time, Reading, and Homework Among Youth. *Ambulatory Pediatrics*, 1(5): 244–251.

Wong, F., Huhman, M., Heitzler, C., Asbury, L., Bretthauer-Mueller, R., McCarthy, S., & Londe, P. (2004). VERB—A Social Marketing Campaign to Increase Physical Activity Among Youth. *Preventing Chronic Disease*, 1(3): A10.

9

Case Studies

SOCIAL MARKETING RESEARCH IN ACTION

W. Douglas Evans

Summary Points

- Social marketing research in rich countries of the world mainly focuses on behavior change as the product, with some important exceptions, as compared to subsidized product marketing, which is characteristic of low- and middle-income countries.
- The *truth*® and Above the Influence campaigns represent contrasting and important examples of large evaluations of social marketing.
- Organizations dedicated to the advancement of behavior change programs, practice, and evidence are important to the future of social marketing research.
- This chapter illustrates the range of programs, research activities, and evidence and suggests future directions for social marketing research.

Introduction

This chapter examines a series of cases of social marketing research from across the research continuum, from formative studies to outcome evaluation, and across multiple topic areas in rich countries, or the developed world, as defined by the World Bank (2014). We highlight the distinctive characteristics of social marketing research in the developed world and contrast them with the developing world. Several case studies illustrate these characteristics and explore the methods and findings from the cases. We conclude by exploring the implications of these characteristics for social marketing research and future directions in the developed world.

Case studies of social marketing research illustrate best practices and gaps in methods and evidence and highlight areas where new research is needed. Specific published and unpublished cases from the most widely studied areas of social marketing illustrate the state of the art in social marketing research. In the developed world, the focus in recent years has been on adapting commercial marketing strategies, using innovative channels such as new and social media, and focusing on behavior change. As discussed in previous chapters in this volume, this includes the use of branding strategies (e.g., Huhman, Price, & Potter 2008; Huhman et al., 2002), use of new technologies for research and evaluation (Evans, Uhrig, et al., 2009; Harrington & Noar, 2012), and use of community-based approaches (Holden & Zimmerman, 2008).

One distinguishing characteristic of social marketing in the developed world, and thus social marketing research, is that it has primarily been focused on behavior change or, put another way, on *categories* of behavior, rather than on marketing and distribution of socially marketed products, or individual offerings *within categories.* In other words, social marketing in developing countries typically aims to get people to practice safe sex, protect themselves when being physically active, and quit smoking, for example. These reflect categories of behavior that can be undertaken in different ways and can be socially marketed in terms of the behavior rather than in terms of a *specific branded product* within the category.

By contrast, as we saw in Chapter 4, in low- and middle-income countries, specific brands of *subsidized products* such as condoms are widespread and are often socially marketed to build a viable and sustainable market to promote health using the concept of a total market approach (Pollard, 2014). This is often because the social and physical environment as well as the low-income status of the majority of potential beneficiaries of the social marketing efforts (e.g., promoting condom use or water purification product use) requires *demand creation*. A marketplace for the behavior needs to be created by generating demand for products that facilitate the behavior where demand had previously not existed (Chapman et al., 2013). The situation is different in the rich countries, such as the United States and Europe, where the social and physical environments and income levels already support the existence of markets for health behaviors and products, and the challenge is encouraging *behavior change* (adoption and maintenance of healthy behaviors).

Clearly, products can be part of the marketing mix in a developed country context. The difference between the developed and developing worlds, in this regard, is the predominance of category promotion in richer countries where a product may facilitate the behavior but is not the outcome of interest, compared to less wealthy countries in the developing world where the branded product line itself (e.g., Protector Plus condoms in Zimbabwe) is socially marketed.

For example, a recent review by the Community Guide to Preventive Services Taskforce (http://www.thecommunityguide.org/index.html) helps to illustrate this point. Robinson and colleagues (2014) conducted a review of the effectiveness of campaigns to promote use of health-promoting products (Robinson et al., 2014). The research leading to this study, summarized further in this chapter, found a wide range of social marketing efforts in rich countries, with the vast majority of the efforts focused on behavioral categories. In some cases, products facilitated engagement in the behavior (e.g., bicycle helmet use to promote safety), but only 23 studies had this characteristic, and none was specifically branded and sold to promote a product line. Rather, the category was explicitly promoted, and the product was distributed as a facilitator (Robinson et al., 2014).

The study by Robinson et al. (2014) noted that "there is ample evidence that health communication campaigns by themselves increase awareness and knowledge, and contribute to changes in attitudes and behavioral intentions of target audiences" and cited meta-analytic work supporting this conclusion, the results of which indicated that the effects of such interventions on adopting new health behaviors (e.g., seatbelt use) and reducing harmful behaviors (e.g., tobacco use) are associated with a small, but significant, relative increase in behavior change (Snyder et al., 2004).

A recently published narrative review found that health communication campaigns implemented in conjunction with other strategies (e.g., preventive health screening, community-based programs, and policy change) are more likely to produce positive changes or prevent negative changes in health-related behaviors than health communication campaigns alone (Wakefield, Loken, & Hornik, 2010). This is consistent with long-standing best practice in fields such as tobacco control (Centers for Disease Control and Prevention [CDC], 2014). Products represent another adjunct to social marketing campaigns rather than an end in themselves. In the developed world, their role is to facilitate behavior change rather than their use in fact *being the behavior that is socially marketed.*

By contrast, as described previously in this volume and elsewhere (e.g., Evans & Haider, 2008), much of the social marketing in low- and middle-income countries, the developing world, involves the sale of subsidized products to promote healthy behaviors, such as use of condoms to prevent HIV/AIDS (Agha, 2003), bed nets to prevent malaria (Armstrong Schellenberg et al., 1999), and water treatment products to purify water for drinking and other household uses (Evans et al., 2014). For the most part, social marketing campaigns and research in the developed world has focused on behavior change without the use of products.

Related to the distinction in social marketing *strategy*, one outstanding characteristic of developed world social marketing research is the use of mass media purchase patterns as a tool for designing evaluation studies such as natural experiments, as discussed in Chapters 6 and 8 (Evans, Davis, & Farrelly, 2008). The outcomes of many developed world social marketing campaigns, especially those relying on mass media, are effectiveness studies conducted in real time, in the media markets or communities where messages are delivered. For example, the national evaluation of the *truth*® campaign (described further in this chapter) was based on a quasi-experimental design in which campaign exposure was measured from both environmental measures (gross rating points, or GRPs, derived from designated market areas, or DMAs) and self-reported "confirmed awareness" of campaign ads (Farrelly et al., 2005).

As emerging economies continue to grow, they experience *epidemiological transition* (i.e., increasingly bear a dual burden of both infectious diseases common in low-income countries *and* noncommunicable diseases common in rich countries) (Wahdan, 1996), and as digital technologies transform the way social marketing is done, differences between campaigns and research in the developed and developing worlds may shrink. Opportunities to conduct research using new technologies, such as those discussed in Chapters 6 and 7, will continue to expand and spread to developing countries, making social marketing research more similar worldwide. This chapter focuses on the current state of the art in social marketing research in the developed world, noting the rapidly changing global environment in which we live. Table 9-1 summarizes several examples of major social marketing campaigns that have been evaluated in recent years and have had results published in the peer-reviewed literature.

The following sections present case studies of social marketing research and evaluation studies from across the continuum of research described in Chapter 1 of this volume. The chapter covers two major examples of campaign evaluations and their basis in formative studies and message testing and

Table 9-1 Illustrative Examples of Recent Major Social Marketing Campaigns in Developed World

Campaign	Topic Area	Research Design	Location	Target Audience
1% or Less	1% milk consumption	Observational	California	Adults, parents, and families
5-4-3-2-1 Go!	Nutrition and physical activity promotion	Experimental	Chicago	Parents and families
Above the Influence	Substance use	Quasi-experimental	United States	Adolescents and parents
Shape Up Somerville	Nutrition and physical activity promotion	Quasi-experimental	Massachusetts	Parents and families
5-A-Day for Better Health	Fruit and vegetable consumption	Observational	United States	Adults, parents, and families
Clean Your Hands	Handwashing, hygiene	Observational	United Kingdom	Adults, health care patients
Fighting Fat, Fighting Fit	Obesity prevention	Observational	United Kingdom	Adults
Freedom From Fear	Domestic violence prevention	Observational	Australia	Male perpetrators of domestic violence
Florida TRUTH	Tobacco countermarketing	Quasi-experimental	Florida	Adolescents and young adults
Food Dudes	Nutrition	Observational	United Kingdom	Children and preadolescents
Give It Up for Baby	Smoking cessation	Observational	United Kingdom	Pregnant women
HELP	Smoking cessation	Observational	Europe	Adult smokers
KNOW HIV/AIDS	HIV/AIDS awareness and prevention	Observational	United States	Young adults

(continued)

Table 9-1 Continued

Campaign	Topic Area	Research Design	Location	Target Audience
Massachusetts antitobacco campaign	Tobacco countermarketing	Quasi-experimental	Massachusetts	Adolescents (prevention) and adults (cessation)
Parents Speak Up National Campaign	Reproductive health	Experimental	United States	Parents and families
Stand	Tobacco countermarketing	Quasi-experimental	Ohio	Adolescents and young adults
The TV Boss	Children's media use	Observational	United States	Parents
truth campaign	Tobacco countermarketing	Quasi-experimental	United States	Adolescents and young adults
VERB: It's What You Do	Physical activity promotion	Quasi-experimental	United States	Preadolescent children

efficacy studies, their growth using new digital media technologies, and process and outcome evaluation. The chapter also examines the role of previous stages of research in development of later stages, such as how formative research and message testing inform outcome evaluation. Then, we turn to reviews of social marketing practice and research evidence in the United States and United Kingdom. These examples represent best research practice in the field, spanning most topic areas in the health arena. The chapter concludes by considering what these examples and emerging trends imply for the future of social marketing research.

Case Studies of the Florida TRUTH and National truth Campaigns: Formative Research and Its Role in Evaluation Design and Implementation

Florida TRUTH Campaign

Antismoking campaigns are one of the leading areas of social marketing and of social marketing research in the developed world. In the United States, major campaigns and evaluation studies began to appear in the late 1980s (Farrelly & Davis, 2008), and there was a surge of activity following the landmark master settlement agreement (MSA) between 46 states and the tobacco industry in November 1998, following successful lawsuits against major tobacco companies in Florida, Minnesota, Mississippi, and Texas (Farrelly & Davis, 2008).

Florida provides a good example. Thanks to a $11.3 billion settlement with major tobacco companies, the Florida Tobacco Pilot Program was established in 1997 with $23.2 million, and with sustained funding, to plan the program in the first fiscal year. Thus, Florida was able to adopt a commercial marketing type of approach to its antismoking social marketing. The campaign was developed by an agency that had never developed a social marketing campaign. The agency modeled its approach after other successful youth brands, such as Nintendo, Mountain Dew, and Sketchers. The goal was to understand the target audience by getting into the heads of youth. Qualitative research suggested that youth disliked antitobacco efforts that passed judgment on smokers and did not want to be told what to do (Hicks, 2001).

From this research came a number of conclusions:

- Youth had a complete understanding of the health effects of smoking.
- Tobacco was a way for youth to signal that they were in control.

- Tobacco was a tool of rebellion—precisely because it is deadly and thus a way to buck the status quo and take risks.

The research also implied that previous efforts with directive (possibly preachy) messages may have had the potential to backfire with some youth by making smoking an even more powerful tool for rebellion. It was this last notion that the agency focused on when developing the Florida TRUTH brand: The goal was to create a brand that provided an alternative outlet for this rebellion. Figure 9-1 shows an image from the campaign, which depicts tobacco industry executives as dangerous, shadowy figures, similar to a movie poster.

National truth *Campaign Formative Research*

Building on the Florida TRUTH experience, the American Legacy Foundation developed the national *truth* campaign with several agencies, including the one that developed the Florida TRUTH campaign (Healton, 2001). Like the Florida campaign, the national campaign began with a series of morbidly humorous advertisements titled "Kills 1/3" to draw attention to the fact that one-third of young people in the United States who try smoking eventually die of tobacco-related diseases.

In developing the national *truth* campaign, researchers conducted in-depth formative research both with the audience to design the campaign and with the marketers designing the campaign to understand their strategy to integrate it effectively into the process and outcome evaluation. As noted in

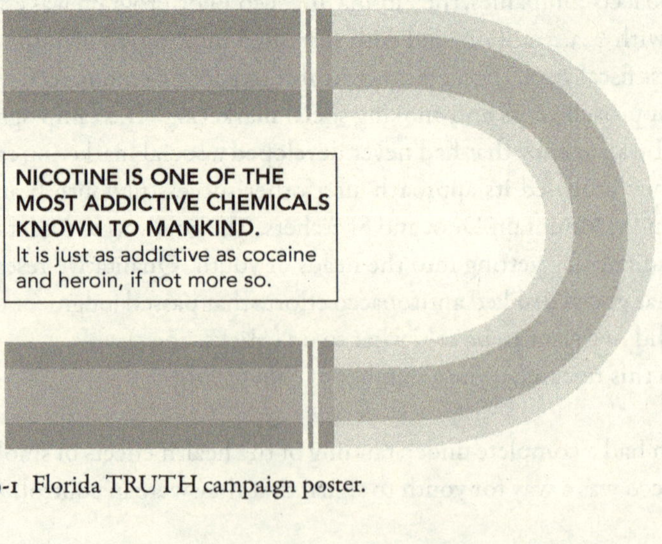

FIGURE 9-1 Florida TRUTH campaign poster.

this volume and elsewhere, well-designed social marketing depends essentially on a consumer orientation (French et al., 2010), and well-designed evaluation requires an in-depth understanding of the social marketing objectives and strategies (Evans, Davis, & Farrelly, 2008).

The national *truth* campaign and associated research were an archetypal example of this orientation. The campaign's primary objectives were to (1) expose youth to *truth* messages and promote positive reactions to those messages, (2) change attitudes and beliefs toward tobacco use and the tobacco industry, and (3) reduce tobacco use among youth. These three objectives formed the roadmap for an evaluation plan that first aimed to develop measures of youth exposure to the campaign; then to assess the relationship between campaign exposure and related knowledge, attitudes, and beliefs; and finally to assess whether the campaign was associated with reduced youth smoking prevalence.

In a series of in-person interviews conducted by *truth* campaign researchers in 2000 with the executives leading development of the *truth* campaign, the basic strategy behind its advertising emerged: build a teen-oriented brand to compete head to head with tobacco industry brands like the Marlboro man, Joe Camel, and the No Bull campaign. The *truth* campaign would build a brand similar to other brands that appeal to teenagers, such as Nike, Converse, and Mountain Dew, rather than communicate a public health and education message about health risks or other reasons not to start smoking (Evans et al., 2002). Branding was a key strategy to meet the goal of reducing the prevalence of smoking by removing its appeal and thereby changing the social norm about smoking. Branding in this case required the establishment of idealized social images to which the audience (primarily adolescents) would aspire. Motivating young people to aspire to the image embodied in the brand was perceived as the best way to reach adolescents and essential to competing with the idealized social images created by the tobacco industry. The basic idea was to use challenging, thought-provoking ad contexts and images of teens in control, rebelling against forces that would prevent them from expressing their independence (i.e., the tobacco industry).

Drawing from the executive interviews, the *truth* brand can be identified through several distinctive characteristics. First, a high level of teen influence over the brand was deemed critical. In the campaign's first months of development and immediately after its launch in February 2000, teens played a central role in planning as well as message design and development. They were viewed as controlling the brand and the methods used to deliver the message (e.g., advertising, events, gear, etc.).

A second distinctive characteristic of the *truth* brand strategy was the individuals' sense of being part of a social movement. Campaign designers intended that *truth* would become a movement to which teens were committed and of which they would feel a sense of ownership. Part of the brand identity would be the feeling that "while I may be a slightly outside-the-mainstream kid not prone to joining most establishment groups (e.g., student council, football team), I would be really interested in joining a group with a mission that fits my outside-the-mainstream values." Much like the early Vietnam antiwar protesters, *truth* teens would take up the mantle against the establishment (in this case, the tobacco industry) and create an environment that fostered camaraderie and a sense of mission. The concept of "vaccinating" youth against tobacco is central to the *truth* brand. The idea is to create protective factors to counter the attributes of open-to-smoking teens that expose them to risk of smoking.

Based on branding insights, the *truth* campaign's social marketing strategy emerged. At the same time, insights from formative research helped to shape the campaign evaluation plan. The goal of the *truth* campaign evaluation plan was to conceive and design a series of studies that would simultaneously account for these factors while being sensitive enough to detect campaign effects. In the material that follows, the primary elements of evaluation design and execution intended to address these three objectives are described, with emphasis on how the evaluation plan was shaped by specific challenges.

Implications of Formative Research for the National Truth Evaluation

Measure Exposure and Message Reactions. The first objective of the *truth* campaign was to increase youth exposure to *truth* messages and generate positive audience receptivity to those messages. Because *truth* was implemented with a fluid media schedule with new ads and "subcampaigns" (i.e., distinct messages that related to and supported the larger *truth* messages) appearing regularly, a continuous media tracking survey of youth in the United States was needed to capture awareness of and reactions to the campaign and receptivity to its messages. Because *truth* also targeted specific racial and ethnic groups, a telephone Legacy Media Tracking Survey (LMTS) was designed to provide estimates of campaign awareness and receptivity among 12- to 17-year-olds overall and separately among African American and Hispanic youth.

Awareness of the campaign was measured using a variety of metrics. Simple recall of *truth* would not be sufficient for identifying how many youth were exposed to specific messages. Thus, the LMTS included specific measures of confirmed awareness of each *truth* ad that was airing at any given time. These measures required respondents to identify specific features of the ads to confirm that they had actually seen them. The LMTS also included other, more general, measures, such as a construct that captured overall awareness of the *truth* campaign brand.

It was also important to assess how youth reacted to *truth* campaign messages. Did youth who saw campaign messages react to those messages favorably? To examine this, the *truth* campaign's evaluation plan called for measurement of a number of ad receptivity constructs, which captured the degree to which youth responded favorably or unfavorably to specific messages. These measures included whether an ad was "believable" or "gave good reasons not to smoke." The inclusion of these types of measures in the evaluation was based on the elaboration likelihood model (ELM), which asserts that attitudinal changes are a function of the level of cognitive elaboration and information-processing activity that occurs regarding a particular message (Petty & Cacioppo, 1986).

From a practical standpoint, continuous tracking of campaign awareness and receptivity to campaign messages provided real-time feedback to the campaign's media contractors, creative directors, and other stakeholders involved in designing and implementing *truth* ads. Specifically, continuous tracking (i.e., continuous data collection to monitor campaign implementation and outcomes) provided the campaign's implementation team with useful information on whether the campaign was sufficiently reaching its youth audience and whether course corrections in message content were needed.

Another function of these measures was to facilitate an examination of the relationship between exposure to the campaign and cognitive precursors to smoking. Therefore, the LMTS also included a wide range of items that measured specific knowledge, attitudes, and beliefs that were central to *truth*'s messages and believed to be predictors of the likelihood of smoking initiation. The novelty of the campaign's messages presented challenges for identifying these measures and necessitated an evaluation-planning process that was closely integrated with the campaign's creative development.

Assess Attitudinal Changes. At the time of the *truth* campaign's launch, the use of "branded" health messages that marketed the benefits of "buying into," or "having equity" in a brand such as *truth* was relatively new. Aside from several measures used in evaluations of the Florida TRUTH campaign, there were few specific measures of knowledge, attitudes, and beliefs related to these sorts of messages. Thus, new measures had to be conceptualized that not only captured the essence of *truth* messages but also were associated with the likelihood of smoking initiation.

The initial wave of the LMTS was fielded in December 1999, prior to the launch of the *truth* campaign, to determine baseline levels of tobacco-related knowledge, attitudes, and beliefs. Before the baseline LMTS was fielded, campaign evaluators participated in intensive meetings with media contractor staff to learn about the specific content of *truth* messages and then develop measures of knowledge, attitudes, and beliefs that would be influenced by the specific message content. A second wave of the LMTS was conducted 10 months after the launch of the campaign. The first evaluation study published on these data showed that the campaign had made significant progress in achieving its first two goals. Awareness of the campaign was high, as approximately 75% of 12- to 17-year-olds in the United States reported being exposed to specific ads. There were also significant changes in knowledge, attitudes, and beliefs related to *truth* messages 10 months after the launch of the campaign, and these changes were statistically associated with exposure to the campaign (Farrelly et al., 2002).

Subsequent waves of the LMTS were used to evaluate behavioral outcomes and long-term effects of the campaign (Farrelly et al., 2005; Evans, Price, & Blahut, 2005). The LMTS continued to be the primary tool for evaluating awareness of and reactions to the *truth* campaign during its first 3 years (2000 to 2003). The survey evolved as the campaign frequently introduced new ads and subcampaigns. Thus, the evaluation-planning process was iterative and ongoing in assessing campaign context and in identifying and developing needed attitudinal and behavioral measures as well as measuring recall of specific ads that were going to air over the data collection time period.

Assess Behavioral Impact. With its flexibility to be implemented multiple times a year and its ability to provide timely and continuous data on campaign awareness, receptivity, and campaign-related knowledge, attitudes, and beliefs, the LMTS was ideal for examining the first two objectives of the *truth* campaign. However, accurately measuring youth tobacco use via telephone surveys is challenging. Youth who are smokers, or have recently experimented with tobacco, are often reluctant to provide truthful responses when their parents are present in the home, which results in significant underreporting of smoking among youth in telephone surveys. Thus, the third overall objective of the *truth* campaign, reducing youth tobacco use, needed to be assessed with a more suitable method: in-school surveys. In-school surveys such as the National Youth Tobacco Survey (NYTS) and Monitoring the Future (MTF) are more appropriate for measuring substance use because they are self-administered without the presence of parents or others who could motivate youth to provide socially desirable responses to substance use questions. With its large national sample and coverage of major media markets where the *truth* campaign was advertised, MTF became the cornerstone of evaluation-planning efforts to assess the campaign's impact on youth smoking behaviors. However, the specific design of this component of the evaluation was influenced by a number of challenges stemming from the implementation of the campaign's media strategy.

The most significant factor that influenced evaluation planning of behavioral changes was the fact that Legacy decided to implement the *truth* campaign nationally with no control or comparison markets. All television markets in the United States received at least some exposure to the *truth* campaign. This implementation strategy presented a fundamental challenge to evaluating the campaign's effects on smoking behaviors. Specifically, the lack of a control or comparison group that was not exposed to the *truth* campaign was this challenge. However, the variation in level of exposure from market to market created natural quasi-experimental comparison groups across the country.

Variation in the level of exposure by market was primarily due to the market-level availability of television stations on which *truth* commercials were aired. During the launch of the campaign and into the first 2 years of implementation, Legacy's media strategy was to use national media buys dominated by advertising on broadcast network and syndicated television stations. This strategy produced a natural pattern of high variability in market-to-market delivery of the campaign. This variability stemmed from the fact that some networks on which the *truth* campaign advertised (e.g., UPN, WB) were not available in certain markets, thereby creating a wide range of exposure levels across markets. These natural quasi-experimental comparison groups across the country provided a basis for examining associations between the "dose" of *truth* campaign advertising at the market level and youth smoking prevalence.

The evaluation plan for assessing the behavioral impact of the *truth* campaign thus called for multivariable analyses that made use of the natural variation in exposure across markets over time to isolate the impact of the *truth* campaign on youth smoking behavior. This was achieved by obtaining market-level cumulative GRPs for *truth* from the campaign's media contractor. These data were linked to individual-level data on adolescents in the MTF surveys and were used to estimate the association between market-level exposure to the *truth* campaign and youth smoking prevalence.

Another important consideration in the evaluation planning process for the *truth* campaign was environmental context. At the time of the campaign's launch, there were many other factors that could have affected youth smoking prevalence apart from any effects of the *truth* campaign. For example, many states were building their own media campaigns and other interventions with funds from the 1998 MSA. State-level investments in tobacco control programs were also increasing, as were cigarette prices and taxes—these factors are also linked to youth smoking prevalence.

At the same time, *truth* had "competition." The tobacco industry was mounting national youth prevention campaigns of its own, including Philip Morris's Think. Don't Smoke (TDS) campaign. Unless the *truth* evaluation accounted for all of these factors, critics could argue that declines in youth smoking would have happened in the absence of the campaign, and that those declines could be attributed to these external factors.

The evaluation aimed to measure the effects of the national campaign on smoking behavior and its behavioral determinants. One of the main evaluation questions was "What is the dose-response effect of *truth* exposure?" However, this presented a design challenge because there was no experimental control. The evaluators' solution was to use natural variation in exposure to the campaign across media markets as a market-specific measure of the dose of *truth*. Dose by media market was then used as a control variable in analyses, as discussed in more detail in Chapters 2 and 6 and elsewhere in this volume.

The launch of *truth* coincided with the early stages of a period of declining adolescent smoking rates. Another challenge to evaluating *truth* was to analytically account for the existence of an independent trend in youth smoking and to determine what proportion of that trend was attributable to the campaign. This was a major challenge facing analysis of campaign outcomes, given (1) the absence of control (non-*truth*) DMAs without campaign exposure; (2) environmental conditions in which smoking rates were changing independent of the campaign; and (3) changes in the campaign media buying, advertisements, and other external factors varying independently over time.

However, the natural variation in *truth* exposure across DMAs presented an opportunity to use campaign dose to control for these factors and identify a dose-response effect. Farrelly and colleagues (2005) analyzed LMTS tracking data and national data on adolescent smoking rates and found that 22% of the total decline in youth smoking was attributable to the *truth* campaign. The 22% effect of *truth* on smoking is relatively large by social marketing standards (see Snyder & Hamilton, 2002, for a review of effect sizes in social marketing, which typically range from 5% to 9% for effective campaigns). The campaign's practical significance is perhaps even greater, as it represents roughly 300,000 fewer US youth smokers over a 3-year period as a result of *truth* (Farrelly et al., 2005).

Case Study of the Above the Influence Campaign: Process Evaluation of Substance Use Prevention Campaigns

Above the Influence (ATI) is a campaign under the umbrella of the US National Youth Anti-Drug Media Campaign (NYADMC). ATI is a positive, motivational brand campaign that is designed to be both aspirational and relevant to teens. In its basic form, ATI is the state of being directly opposite to and in competition with being "under the influence" (of drugs and alcohol). ATI represents an aspirational ideal that celebrates being "better than" *whatever* negative influence is presented. It taps into the pride teens take in themselves when they resist influences (peer influence, media influence, cultural influence) that make them less than what they are and what they know they can be.

The most recent version of the ATI campaign, discussed here, is the result of a rebranded campaign that launched in 2010. This effort was in response to previous versions of the campaign, which failed to reduce substance use and indeed produced iatrogenic, or "boomerang," effects in some cases (meaning that the campaign actually promoted pro-substance use attitudes in this case). A large-scale evaluation of the preceding My Anti-Drug campaign found no effects of exposure on drug use attitudes and behaviors (Hornik et al., 2008). Indeed, the Hornik and colleagues (2008) study and previous reports published by the campaign evaluator, Westat Incorporated, found evidence of the iatrogenic or boomerang effect (i.e., exposure to the campaign promoted negative outcomes)(GAO, 2006) despite the continuous 25% decline in drug use that occurred between 1988 and 2000 as reported by MTF.

Other research has found that exposure to the My Anti-Drug campaign messages was effective in reducing drug use attitudes and behaviors among youth who had a high need for sensation or "high-sensation seekers" (Palmgreen et al., 2007). In addition, recent research suggested that personal aspirations and sense of personal autonomy may be constructs that mediate the effects of ATI on improved drug use attitudes and reduced drug use behaviors (Slater et al., 2011). This is relevant to the current study because aspiration and autonomy are brand constructs, and measuring response to the ATI brand may extend understanding of the processes by which it affects drug use outcomes.

As a brand idea, ATI empowers and credits teens with making this positive choice away from the negative. This empowerment reflects a positive brand that respects and supports teens in their power to choose in favor of themselves, for themselves—in contrast to the antidrug branding that came before, which focused on rejection of a substance. ATI is "pro me."

The ATI message centers on drugs and the social context that lead to bad decisions (drug use). In this way, the ATI brand positions the competition—drugs—within the larger context of negative influences that bring teens down and limit their potential. A teen who is above the influence is smart enough to recognize the risks of negative influences and both proud and capable enough to rise above them.

The overall goals of this process evaluation research were to (1) establish a system of brand equity measurement for the NYADMC and (2) evaluate the relationship between brand equity metrics and campaign outcomes among the NYADMC target audience of 13- to 17-year-old youth. As a result of the study, specific recommendations for brand development and campaign strategy were provided to campaign developers. The specific objectives of the research were to

1. Field a module of brand equity questions in multiple waves of the NYADMC media-tracking survey;
2. Analyze resulting baseline and follow-up brand equity data;
3. Determine the effects of brand equity on NYADMC campaign outcomes; and
4. Evaluate the effects of NYADMC brand equity on drug abuse prevention knowledge, attitudes, beliefs, and behavior change over time.

This research sought to answer four specific research questions (RQs):

RQ1. What is the baseline level of NYADMC brand equity among 13- to 17-year-old respondents to the media-tracking survey?
RQ2. What change in brand equity occurred between the baseline and follow-up media tracking surveys?
RQ3. What is the relationship between NYADMC brand equity and short-term performance measures, including campaign salience, relevance, and involvement?
RQ3a. How do these relationships change from baseline to follow-up?
RQ4. What is the relationship between NYADMC brand equity and long-term outcomes, including drug-related normative beliefs and outcome expectations, intentions, and behavior?
RQ4a. How do these relationships change from baseline to follow-up?
RQ5. What differences are there in brand equity between NYADMC subgroups?
RQ5a. What differences are there in brand equity between more-open-to-use and less-open-to-use 13- to 17-year-old respondents to the media-tracking survey?

RQ5b. What differences are there in brand equity between respondents who are more engaged and less engaged?

Two hypotheses (H) were tested as well: (H1) ATI brand equity measures form multidimensional scales as observed in previous research; (H2) higher NYADMC brand equity is associated with more positive campaign-targeted attitudes and drug-related normative beliefs and expectations.

Methods

Above the Influence is grounded in social cognitive theory (SCT) and the theory of planned behavior (TPB) (Bandura, 2004; Ajzen, 1991). From SCT, the campaign posits that building self-efficacy to resist social and peer pressure to use drugs will build resistance skills. In addition, role modeling by teens who have socially desirable characteristics (e.g., are attractive, popular, successful) and are drug free will encourage emulation. This approach has been widely used in development of other behavioral and lifestyle branding (Evans & Hastings, 2008).

From TPB, the campaign envisions a sequence of drug-free attitudes, beliefs, perceived social norms, intentions, and ultimately behavior stemming from campaign exposure (Ajzen, 1991; http://www.abovetheinfluence.com/). Increased exposure will initiate a sequence of cognitive changes, leading to perceptions that external norms (descriptive and subjective norms about drug use in the teens' environment) support remaining drug free (Hornik & Yanovitsky, 2003). Teens who adopt these attitudes and beliefs will be more likely to intend to remain drug free and ultimately avoid drug use. The ATI brand is designed to spur the behavior change process modeled on TPB.

By measuring brand equity constructs that represent summative beliefs about ATI and what it promotes, this study attempts to fill a gap in previous ATI evaluations. By measuring brand equity in the campaign, we can begin a research agenda aimed at validating ATI campaign theory and expanding our understanding of the role of brand equity and its relationship to mediators of drug use prevention cognitions and behavior.

Study Design and Data Collection

The ATI campaign reaches teens through multiple media platforms (TV, print, banner ads, website, mobile and social media). To monitor responses to the campaign, a continuous-tracking study is conducted among the teen audience by OTX/Ipsos (http://www.ipsos.com/), a leading market research company. The study aims to gauge responses based on the depth of exposure and engagement with the campaign through these platforms.

The tracking study is conducted online. Respondents are recruited from a blended mix of sources, including major sample panels, social networks, and ad networks. This approach allows for high-quality data collection that includes deduplication and controlled survey participation. Online surveys are administered through OTX's standard survey environment; respondents are recruited via email from OTX's Sample Community and linked to the survey environment to complete the survey. Each interview takes approximately 15 minutes to complete. At present, 900 teens ages 13 to 17 are sampled each month. Data for the a focused analysis of ATI barnd equity and its effects on campaign outcomes were collected between June and October 2010. During this time period, the overall response rate for the tracking survey was 34%. The following reports on that specific analysis.

The brand equity scales formed a module on the tracking survey. Respondents who completed the brand equity module were randomly selected from those who stated they had recently seen, heard, or read anything about ATI ads on a previous question answered by all respondents. One-quarter (or 225 per month) of the teen sample was randomly assigned to complete the brand equity scales. Respondents were balanced according to US Census proportions by age, gender, race/ethnicity, education, county size, and region. The sample was also augmented to capture readable samples of African American and Hispanic youth to ensure representation of a diverse population.

The survey covered the following major domains: media consumption, awareness, ad/banner recognition, interaction with campaign content, lifestyle/environmental factors, demographics, brand associations/importance/relevance, brand equity, and campaign message comprehension Also included were positive and negative outcome beliefs, social normative and peer disapproval beliefs associated with general drug and alcohol use. There was also a question on self-reported exposure, and respondents were asked to estimate the number of times they had seen ATI ads (0 or more).

NYADMC Brand Equity Scales

Based on review of the ATI brand positioning and advertising plans, and on previous work by the authors on brand equity scale development and validation (Evans, Price, & Blahut, 2005; Evans, Longfield, et al., 2012), researchers developed scales to reflect ATI brand equity constructs. The scales use the same constructs and same question format as in the previous studies but were worded to reflect the specific branding attributes (e.g., quality attributes, personality) promoted by ATI. They were designed to reflect the categories of measurement validated in previous studies and tailored to the content of the ATI brand positioning and advertising.

The ATI brand equity scales were all 4-point agreement scales, ranging from strongly agree to strongly disagree with a no opinion option. For the "price premium" construct, the items were as follows:

I'd like to help ATI get the word out.
I'd defend ATI if someone were putting it down
I'd support ATI even if my friends didn't.

For the "satisfaction/loyalty" construct, the items were as follows:

If I had the chance, I would tell other kids my age to watch the ATI ads.
I'd wear an ATI T-shirt.
I'd become a fan of ATI on my social networking website.
I'd create a YouTube video to support ATI.

For the "perceived quality" construct, the items were as follows:

ATI ads are the best antidrug ads out there.
ATI gives me information that I want.
ATI helps me understand how drugs can influence me.

For the "leadership/popularity" construct, the items were as follows:

ATI is becoming more popular with kids like me.
ATI is for kids like me.
ATI is the best way for kids to learn about drugs.

For the "brand personality" construct, the items were as follows: Would you say that the young people in ATI ads generally (item stem for each of following) . . .:

Take control of their lives.
Have their own style.
Stand up for themselves.
Are self-confident.

See how drugs can influence them.
Make their own decisions.

For the "organizational associations" construct, the items were as follows:

When I see antidrug ads on TV, I can always tell which ones are from ATI.
ATI ads are always honest.
ATI gives kids facts they need.

Finally, for the "brand awareness" construct, the items were as follows: When you think of the ATI ads, you think (item stem for each of following) . . . :

Refusing drugs earns you respect.
More and more kids are above the influence of drugs.
I can stand up for myself.
I'll have more fun without drugs.
Refusing drugs is a way to express your independence.
It's cool to be above the influence of drugs.

Drug Use Outcome Measures

In this study, researchers were interested in the effects of ATI brand equity on short-term attitudes about ATI targeted specifically in the campaign advertising and strategic approach and on normative beliefs targeted by the campaign. They used the following outcome measures: ATI campaign attitudes, drug use social norms (all 4-point agreement scales), analysis procedure, and brief results.

ATI Campaign Attitudes

The following items (and response categories) were used to measure ATI campaign attitudes:

Do you have a positive image of the ATI campaign? (Yes/No)
How well do you think ATI communicates messages? (5-point scale from "strongly communicates" to "doesn't communicate")
Do you view drug-using behaviors as high risk? (Yes/No)
Do you believe you'd be better off not using drugs? (Yes/No)

Drug Use Social Norms (All Four-Point Agreement Scales)

The following items (all 4-point agreement scales) were used to measure drug use social norms:

> I would have a better time with friends if I got buzzed or high.
> I would be more like the popular kids if I got buzzed or high.
> Teens today are deciding to resist influences to do things like getting buzzed or high.

Analysis Procedure

Researchers conducted all data analysis in Stata version 10 (College Station, TX). We compared brand equity measures for the baseline and follow-up study groups and age, race, and gender by looking at agreement of key constructors of brand equity. Initially, researchers used a *t*-test to examine the relationship between self-reported ATI exposure and brand equity and normative beliefs. They conducted confirmatory factor analysis (CFA) to identify brand equity subscales and higher order brand equity scales.

Next, researchers estimated multivariable logistic regression models to analyze the relationship between brand equity and campaign outcomes. First, they regressed ATI campaign attitudes on ATI brand equity. Second, they regressed drug use social norms on ATI brand equity. All models included the following covariates: age, gender, single-parent household status, a measure of sensation-seeking drawn from previous research (Palmgreen et al., 2007), and self-reported ATI campaign exposure. Models separately examined baseline and follow-up data. Because the data were cross sectional, with different respondents in each wave, researchers did not attempt to compare baseline to follow-up data in these analyses.

Brief Results

As reported in depth elsewhere (Evans, Holtz, & Snider, 2014), there was a high level of agreement with the brand equity items for most constructs, with the vast majority of point estimates above 60% agreement and a large proportion above 70%. Some estimates increased over time, and the confidence intervals are nonoverlapping, reflecting statistical significance below the $p < .05$ level. For example, the perceived quality item "ATI ads are the best antidrug ads out there" increased by 10 percentage points, from 69.6% to 79.6%, from baseline to follow-up.

Researchers also found that, overall for the brand equity constructs, there was an increase in brand equity, both over time and as a function of increased exposure. This same effect was not observed for normative beliefs, although there were differences within time point as a function of exposure.

Researchers conducted CFA on the seven brand equity scales. Using the widely accepted Comry and Lee (1992) criteria of .5 factor loading or higher, results showed that each of the scale items loaded onto one brand equity factor. The lowest factor loading for any item was .73 for "More and more kids are above the influence of drugs" in the brand awareness scale.

Next, researchers estimated multivariable logistic regression models. They regressed each of the four ATI attitude items and the three normative ATI beliefs on each of the seven ATI brand equity factors identified in the factor analysis. The model controls for a set of covariates, including sociodemographics, and personal characteristics such as sensation-seeking and engagement with ATI that previous research suggested may be associated with drug use behavior and be related to brand associations (Palmgreen et al., 2007). Researchers observed several significant associations, and in general higher brand equity was predictive of more positive antidrug attitudes and beliefs. For example, at follow-up, the price premium brand equity factor was associated with higher odds of having a positive image of the ATI campaign (odds ratio [OR] = 1.93, $p < .002$) and believing that he or she would be better off not using drugs (OR = 2.14, $p < .001$). In addition, at follow-up, the brand awareness factor was associated with lower odds of respondents believing they would have a better time with their friends if they got buzzed or high (OR = 0.54, $p < .007$).

Overall, the ATI brand was significantly and positively associated with several important short-term and intermediate outcomes targeted by the campaign. Perceptions of the ATI brand appear to be evolving after its rebranding and relaunch of the campaign in 2010.

Task Force for Community Preventive Services (Community Guide): Systematic Reviews of the Evidence in Health Communication and Social Marketing

The Guide to Community Preventive Services, or Community Guide, conducts systematic reviews of public health interventions in several topic areas. Findings are presented to the Task Force on Community Preventive Services, which issues evidence-based recommendations for use by practitioners, researchers, policymakers, and others (The Community Guide, 2010).

Although Community Guide reviews typically focus on a particular health topic, the task force has also addressed the effectiveness of health communication and social marketing (The Community Guide, 2010). This 2010 review focused on campaigns as an intervention methodology, and the effectiveness of those interventions, in changing multiple health behaviors. As social marketing takes a 4P (place, price, product, and promotion) approach to behavior change and the concept of "product" is a critical part of the social marketing process, this review focused on behaviors that are enabled by products and were implemented in rich countries according to the World Bank definition (see World Bank, 2014 for a description).

Following standard practice, an internal working group and experts from the field established parameters for the review; these parameters were based on behavioral theory, the current state of the literature, and the broader public health framework from which the Community Guide works and through which the Task Force on Community Preventive Services draws the basis for its findings and recommendations. The task force evaluated the effectiveness of health communication and social marketing interventions based on a broad range of outcomes related to or resulting from product use that have a clear and proven link to decreased morbidity and mortality or improved health. The review followed the published Community Guide evidence review process (see http://www.thecommunityguide.org/about/methods.html).

The review focused on three categories of overarching questions. Table 9-2 summarizes questions and review criteria related to products.

Primary Questions

- Are communication campaigns that promote the use of a product and include distribution of that product effective in changing behaviors?
- Are communication campaigns that promote the use of a product, but do not distribute the product, effective in changing behaviors?

Questions Related to Social Marketing

- Are campaigns that were developed using formative research or message testing more effective than those that do not?
- Are campaigns that use audience segmentation strategies more effective than those that do not?
- Are targeted campaigns more effective than those that are not targeted?

Table 9-2 Community Guide Review Questions and Criteria Related to Products

Product	User	Repeat Purchase?	Personal Cost of Product Use (Discomfort)
Condoms	Self/partner	Yes	Moderate
Sun protective gear	Self/child	Yes	Low to none
Recreation safety helmet	Self/child	No	Low
Child safety seats	Child (self)	No	Low
Pedometers	Self	No	None
Folic acid	Self	Yes	Low to none
Smoking cessation products	Self	Yes	Moderate
Insect repellent	Self	Yes	Low
Oral health products	Self	Yes	Low

Source: The Community Guide. (2010). Health Communication and Social Marketing: Health Communication Campaigns That Include Mass Media and Health-Related Product Distribution. Retrieved on September 1, 2015, from http://www.thecommunityguide.org/healthcommunication/campaigns.html.

Questions Related to Campaign Characteristics

- Are campaigns that include a mass media component more effective than those that do not?
- Are campaigns that include an interpersonal approach more effective than those that do not?
- Is the number of components used related to effectiveness?
- Is the number of channels used related to effectiveness?
- Is the duration of the overall campaign related to effectiveness?

The review defined the topic of interest as follows: "Health communication campaigns apply integrated strategies to deliver messages designed, directly or indirectly, to influence health behaviors of target audiences" (The Community Guide, 2010).

Campaigns evaluated in this review met the following criteria:

- Included multiple channels (e.g., radio, television, print media, etc.) to convey the message.

- Included one or more messages that explicitly promote the use of specific tangible products (booster seats, condoms, folic acid supplements, helmets, insect repellent, nicotine gum, patch or lozenge, oral health products, pedometers, or sunscreen, hats, or sun protective clothing).
- Did not disseminate a message using a single medium at one point in time (media include mass media [e.g., radio, TV, newspaper, billboards, and web page advertisement] and small media [e.g., posters, brochures, and pamphlets]).
- Did not use a channel as recruitment into the study (e.g., Quitline).
- Did not use one of the following methods as the primary mechanism for product promotion (but may include them as components): interpersonal communication such as one-on-one counseling, peer outreach or education, small-group education, small-group experiment.
- Did not require registration or group membership and are not a condition of employment.
- Included at least one behavior change outcome (i.e., product use or behavior secondary to product use, like walking in the case of a pedometer study).
- Were published in English.
- Were conducted in a high-income country.
- Were published after 1980? (The team did not want to exclude based on year; it stated that there were many early campaigns addressing family planning).

Products included in this review were selected because they

- Were tangible, physical products (that were not a service)
- Facilitated behavior change directly (rather than via knowledge gain)
- Facilitated a behavior that must be repeated (rather than a one-time behavior such as getting a dental sealant)
- Were used directly by the consumer without requiring a health professional to prescribe or administer (e.g., vaccine, prescription drug)
- Had been proven to lead to public health outcomes (i.e., reduce morbidity or mortality in the population)

Other products, such as sports protective eyeware and exercise video games, were considered but excluded for one or more of several reasons: (1) No studies were published that evaluated their effectiveness; (2) they were not intended to facilitate behavior; (3) they were not distributed by a campaign; (4) they could not be independently used by the target audience (i.e., required a facilitator, such as a healthcare provider); or (5) they were not linked to any potential health impact (Robinson et al., 2014).

The results of this review were that the task force recommended the use of campaigns that apply multiple channels, including multimedia combined with free or subsidized products. Campaigns meeting these criteria were deemed effective and specifically were identified as effective in promoting (1) adoption of health-promoting behaviors, such as increased physical activity through pedometer use; (2) cessation of harmful behaviors, such as smoking using nicotine replacement therapy; and (3) protection against preventable disease or injury though products such as condoms and child safety seats (The Community Guide, 2010). Results showed that health promotion campaigns having these characteristics were effective within a range of absolute observed median change ranging from 2.7 to 14.5 percentage points, or an average of 8.4 percentage points. Strong evidence was found for other types of campaigns, but the differences were not reported in terms of absolute percentage point differences (The Community Guide, 2010).

The task force has also conducted a number of other reviews of evidence related to health communication and social marketing. These reviews have yielded mixed results and may be found at the main Community Guide Task Force findings website (http://www.thecommunityguide.org/about/conclusionreport.html).

Two examples help to illustrate the nature of these reviews and the state of current evidence for social marketing campaigns. For example, one review examined "Increasing Tobacco Use Cessation: Mass Media Campaigns When Combined With Additional Interventions." Campaigns, as evaluated for this review, were defined as mass media interventions that use brief, recurring messages to inform and motivate tobacco users to quit. Message content is developed through formative research, and the campaigns use paid airtime and print space (advertisements) or donated time and space (public service announcements). Campaigns can be combined with other interventions, such as an increase in excise tax, or additional community education efforts.

In this case, the task force recommended mass media campaigns when combined with other interventions based on strong evidence of effectiveness in

- Reducing population consumption of tobacco products
- Increasing cessation among tobacco product users

This recommendation was based primarily on the effectiveness of long-duration, high-intensity campaigns implemented and evaluated in three states

(California, Massachusetts, and Oregon) in which use of mass media was coordinated with an excise tax increase and funding for other community- and school-based education programs (The Community Guide, 2013).

In a second example, the task force review examined "Increasing Tobacco Use Cessation: Mass Media Education—Cessation Series." Cessation series for tobacco cessation are mass media interventions that use instructional segments to recruit, inform, and motivate tobacco product users to begin and maintain efforts to quit. They can be coordinated with broadcast or print promotion, community education such as distribution of self-help cessation materials, and organization of cessation groups in the community. The series can range from several weeks to several months, and techniques include nightly or weekly segments on news broadcasts that provide expert advice or peer group experiences. In this case, the task force found insufficient evidence to assess the effectiveness of cessation series based on inadequate comparison populations or groups and inconsistent results (The Community Guide, 2000).

Overall, the Community Guide has conducted nine reviews that directly related to health communication and social marketing, including the behavior change and products review discussed at the beginning of this section (Robinson et al., 2014). The identification of a specific topic area for future reviews (see http://www.thecommunityguide.org/healthcommunication/index.html) suggests this is an important future area for evidence reviews. The Community Guide will be an important part of building the future evidence base and guiding the development of social marketing research.

National Social Marketing Centre (United Kingdom): Case Studies and Social Marketing Practice and Evidence Reviews

The social marketing evidence base continues to build in other developed countries outside the United States and appears to be accelerating; national organizations focus increasingly on behavior change as a means to improve population health and well-being. The National Social Marketing Centre (NSMC) in the United Kingdom was founded in 2006 as the organization within the National Health Service (NHS) that develops national programs in the field. In 2010, the NSMC became a private entity and now conducts donor-sponsored programs across the United Kingdom and worldwide (http://www.thensmc.com/).

Social marketing is increasingly being used in behavior change interventions in the United Kingdom and many other developed nations—either as the organizing framework for an intervention or via the incorporation of social marketing elements into interventions that may not label themselves as social marketing. For example, three existing reviews were recently conducted by the NSMC, in London, and addressed specific health topics (nutrition, physical activity, and substance abuse). To identify interventions for these reviews, NSMC used the six criteria proposed by Andreasen (2002): (1) having behavior change as the benchmark for developing interventions; (2) consistently using audience research; (3) carefully segmenting target audiences; (4) creating attractive and motivating exchanges; (5) using all four Ps (price, product, place, promotion) of the marketing mix; and (6) paying careful attention to the competition faced by the desired behavior. Interventions featuring these elements were included in the reviews, which included multiple types of interventions (e.g., school-based, church-based, family-based, and multicomponent community interventions).

NSMC Reviews

- The review of the effectiveness of social marketing **nutrition** interventions found that the vast majority (24) of interventions had at least one significant positive effect on some type of nutritional behavior, with three reporting nonsignificant trends and three being ineffective (Gordeon et al., 2006).
- The review of the effectiveness of **physical activity** interventions found that, regarding levels of physical activity, 10 interventions showed overall positive effects, 8 had mixed results, and 4 had no effects (Gordon et al., 2006).
- The **substance abuse** review found that the majority of interventions to prevent alcohol, tobacco, and other drugs among youth reported positive effects in the short term, although effects tended to dissipate in medium and longer terms McDermott et al., 2005). Evidence was more mixed for smoking cessation, with a few studies showing effectiveness.
- "The Effectiveness of Social Marketing Interventions for Health Improvement: What's the Evidence?" (Gordon et al., 2006). This article describes the three reviews previously given in this list, noting that they provide evidence that social marketing interventions can be effective in improving diet, increasing exercise, and tackling the misuse of substances like alcohol, tobacco, and illicit drugs.

Other Reviews

- Milat et al.'s (2005) review of population health social marketing campaigns **targeting culturally and linguistically diverse (CLD) communities** in Australia found eight studies that provided tentative support for the potential efficacy of CLD social marketing strategies. CLD communities accessed campaign-related information from both mainstream and ethnic media channels, with Vietnamese respondents more likely to access campaign messages through ethnic radio and Chinese respondents through ethnic press.
- The importance of **socioeconomic context** for social marketing models for improving **reproductive health**: evidence from 555 years of program experience (Meekers & Rahaim, 2005). This study used a database of annual statistics about reproductive health social marketing programs that distributed and promoted the use of oral contraceptives and condoms in over 70 countries. It found that, as expected, programs implemented in lower income countries predominantly used the *nongovernmental (NGO) model*, characterized by heavily subsidized products. Although the NGO model was also the most used in middle-income countries, these countries were more likely than lower income countries to use the *manufacturer's model*, in which interventions are treated as temporary and include a realistic exit strategy.
- The performance of social marketing in **reaching the poor and vulnerable** in **AIDS** control programs (Price, 2001). The narrative review discussed the impact and effectiveness of condom social marketing programs (CSMPs) in reaching the poor and vulnerable. It noted that, despite a 30-year history, there is limited evidence regarding effectiveness of CSMPs in meeting the sexual health needs of the poor and vulnerable, particularly due to the use of sales data and couple years of protection computations in program evaluation. Recent data suggest that these programs do not initially reach the poorest, but that as programs develop and mature, inequities in condom access and use tend to diminish.

Case Study of the What's Pants Campaign in the United Kingdom: Cervical Cancer Screening Promotion for Young Women

The following discussion of What's Pants is one summary example of a detailed review conducted by the NSMC of UK-based social marketing and outcome evaluation results.

Campaign Background

"What's Pants . . . ?" was the first West Midlands NHS social marketing campaign, and the first cervical screening campaign in the United Kingdom to directly link data trends, audience segmentation, and social behavior research with the construction of a campaign (see http://www.thensmc.com/search?search=what%27s+pants).

The marketing mix used by the campaign included multiple strategies:

- radio, bus, and ambient advertising;
- direct mail, such as personalized letters and branded leaflets; and
- modified and increased service provision, with more test centers and better opening hours.

(Source: NSMC, see URL above)

Evaluation Background

What's Pants, But Could Save Your Life? generated an unprecedented increase in cervical screening uptake in the West Midlands region. According to laboratory workload data for 25- to 39-year-olds during the first quarters of both 2008–2009 (i.e., April to June), there was an 8% increase from the previous quarter (January–March) in workload across 12 laboratories, with results ranging from –1% to 21%—and a 17% increase from the same quarter in the previous year.

The overall effectiveness of the combined approach was monitored and evaluated by the West Midlands Cervical Screening Quality Assurance Reference Centre via routinely collected quarterly and annual cervical screenings. Because the target population was large and there were no identified seasonal or natural fluctuations in demand, it is possible to determine the precise impact of the project's first year.

The threshold for success was the achievement of a 12% uplift in the target 25–29 age group by the end of year 1, based on a model of limited gains in year 1, more substantial gains in year 2, and the highest gains in year 3, once the campaign had been established in the minds of the public. This would be measured by total annual returns as part of the regular monitoring processes.

At the end of quarter 1, laboratories reported a 16% increase in the gateway age group alone. The target for the project's first year was a 4% increase across all age groups by the end of year 1. The initial figures showed the program to be well on track to achieve this, with 7 of 17 PCTs reporting a halt on decreasing attendance and 8 reporting an increase—this is compared to 2007, when attendance at 15 PCTs was on the decline.

To evaluate the campaign, a feedback survey was designed and distributed by university students and sent to 7,000 people; 1,802 replied, with 34% saying unprompted that they were familiar with the campaign and 41% saying they were much more likely to be screened as a result of the campaign. The cost of treating one person with cancer is estimated to be £23,000 per level of treatment, with four levels total. The cost of the campaign was estimated to be 25p per person in the target age group, which means, in financial terms, the campaign has paid for itself.

Conclusions

Social marketing research examples discussed in this chapter illustrate each stage of the research continuum, multiple 4P strategies, methods of evaluation, and similarities and differences between social marketing in the rich and low- to middle-income countries. The large-scale ATI campaign, which initially evidenced boomerang effects, was later rebranded and now shows signs of effectiveness; and the evolution from Florida's TRUTH to the national *truth* campaigns are good examples of research across the continuum that make distinctive contributions to the social marketing practice and evidence base.

One clear trend is the increasing use of new media technologies, both in terms of changes in the campaign strategies and tactics and in terms of evaluation methods and measures. The increasing use of technology will likely accelerate in the coming years, as we saw in Chapter 7. These changes, along with the growth of wealth and epidemiological transition of many low- to middle-income countries (e.g., China, India, Indonesia, and South Africa), will lead to greater convergence of social marketing strategies and research between the lower and higher income countries.

Additional Resources: Web Based

- Centers for Disease Control and Prevention. (2015). Gateway to Health Communication and Social Marketing Practice: Research and Evaluation. Retrieved on September 9, 2015, from http://www.cdc.gov/healthcommunication/research/index.html
- The National Social Marketing Centre. (2015). Tools and Resources. Retrieved on September 9, 2015, from http://www.thensmc.com/content/tools-resources
- Task Force on Community Preventive Services. (2005). The Guide to Community Preventive Services: What Works to Promote Health.

Retrieved on September 9, 2015, from http://www.thecommunityguide.org/library/book/Front-Matter.pdf

References

Agha, S. (2003). The Impact of a Mass Media Campaign on Personal Risk Perception, Perceived Self-Efficacy and on Other Behavioral Predictors. *AIDS Care*, 15(6): 749–762.

Ajzen I. (1991). The theory of planned behaviour. *Organisational Behaviour and Human Decision Processes*, 50: 179–211.

Andreasen, A. (2002). *Marketing research that won't break the bank: A practical guide to getting the information you need* (2nd ed.). San Francisco: Jossey-Bass.

Armstrong Schellenberg, J.R.M., Abdulla, S., Minja, H., Nathan, R., Mukasa, O., Marchant, T., Mponda, H., Kikumbih, N., Lyimo, E., Manchester, T., et al. (1999). KINET: A Social Marketing Programme of Treated Nets and Net Treatment for Malaria Control in Tanzania, With Evaluation of Child Health and Long-Term Survival. *Transactions of the Royal Society of Tropical Medicine and Hygiene*, 93: 225–231.

Bandura, A. (2004). Health promotion by social cognitive means. *Health Education & Behavior*, 31(2): 143–164.

Centers for Disease Control and Prevention. Best Practices for Comprehensive Tobacco Control Programs—2014. Atlanta: U.S. Department of Health and Human Services, Centers for Disease Control and Prevention, National Center for Chronic Disease Prevention and Health Promotion, Office on Smoking and Health, 2014.

Chapman, S., Ayers, J., LeTouze, O., & Remard, B. (2013). Branding and Social Marketing. In Evans, W.D. (Ed.), *Psychology of Branding.* New York: Nova Science Publishers.

Comrey, A.L., & Lee, H.B. (1992). A first course in factor analysis (2nd ed.). Hillsdale, NJ: Lawrence Erlbaum.

The Community Guide. (2000). Mass Media—Cessation. Retrieved on September 1, 2015, from http://www.thecommunityguide.org/tobacco/index.html

The Community Guide. (2010). Health Communication and Social Marketing: Health Communication Campaigns That Include Mass Media and Health-Related Product Distribution. Retrieved on September 1, 2015, from http://www.thecommunityguide.org/healthcommunication/campaigns.html

The Community Guide. (2013). Mass-Reach Health Communication Interventions. Retrieved on September 1, 2015, from http://www.thecommunityguide.org/tobacco/index.html

Evans, W.D., & Haider M. (2008). Public Health Brands in the Developing World. In *Public Health Branding: Applying Marketing for Social Change*, W.D. Evans and G. Hastings (Eds.). Oxford: Oxford University Press.

Evans, W.D, & Hastings, G. (2008). Public Health Branding: Recognition, Promise, and Delivery of Healthy Lifestyles. In *Public Health Branding: Applying Marketing for Social Change*, W.D. Evans and G. Hastings (Eds.). London: Oxford University Press.

Evans, W.D., Davis, K.C., & Farrelly, M.C. (2008). Planning for a Media Evaluation. In *A Practical Guide to Program Evaluation Planning*, D. Holden and M. Zimmerman (Eds.), Thousand Oaks, CA: Sage Publications, Inc.

Evans, W.D., Holtz, K., Snider, J. (2014). Effects of the Above the Influence Brand on Adolescent Drug Use Prevention Beliefs. *Journal of Health Communication*, 19(6): 721–737. doi:10.1080/10810730.2013.837559

Evans, W.D., Longfield, K., Shekhar, N., Rabemanatsoa, A., Snider, J., & Reerink, I. (2012). Social Marketing and Condom Promotion in Madagascar: A Case Study in Brand Equity Research. In *Handbook of Global Health Communication*, R. Obregon, and S. Waisboard (Eds.). New York: Wiley.

Evans, W.D., Pattanayak, S.K., Young, S., Buszin, J, Rai, S., & Wallace, J. (2014). Social Marketing of Water and Sanitation: Systematic Review of Peer-Reviewed Literature. *Social Science &Medicine*, 110: 18–25. doi:10.1016/j.socscimed.2014.03.011

Evans, W.D., Price, S., & Blahut, S. (2005). Evaluating the truth® Brand. *Journal of Health Communication*, 10(2): 181–192.

Evans, W.D., Wasserman, J., Bertolotti, E., & Martino S. (2002). Branding Behavior: The Strategy Behind the truth® Campaign. *Social Marketing Quarterly*, 8(3): 17–29.

Evans, W.D., Uhrig, J., Davis, K., & McCormack, L. (2009). Efficacy Methods to Evaluate Health Communication and Marketing Campaigns. *Journal of Health Communication*, 14(3): 244–254.

Farrelly, M.C., & Davis, K.C. (2008). Case Studies of Youth Tobacco Prevention Campaigns From the USA: Truth and Half-Truths. In *Public Health Branding: Applying Marketing for Social Change*, W.D. Evans & G. Hastings (Eds.). London: Oxford University Press. Chapter 7.

Farrelly, M.C., Davis, K.C., Haviland, M.L., Messeri, P., & Healton, C.G. (2005). Evidence of a Dose-Response Relationship Between "Truth" Antismoking Ads and Youth Smoking. *American Journal of Public Health*, 95: 425–431.

Farrelly, M.C., Healton, C.G., Davis, K.C., Messeri, P., Hersey, J.C., & Haviland, M.L. (2002). Getting to the truth®: Evaluating National Tobacco Countermarketing Campaigns. *American Journal of Public Health*, 92: 901–907.

French, J., Blair-Stevens, C., McVey, D., & Merritt, R. (2010). *Social Marketing and Public Health*. Oxford, UK: Oxford University Press.

Gordon, R., McDermott, L., Stead, M., & Angus, K. (2006). The Effectiveness of Social Marketing Interventions for Health Improvement: What's the Evidence? *Public Health*, 120(12): 1133–1139.

Harrington, N.G., & Noar, S. (Eds.). (2012). *eHealth Applications: Promising Strategies for Health Behavior Change*. New York: Routledge.

Healton, C.G. (2001). Who's Afraid of the Truth? *American Journal of Public Health*, 91: 554–558.

Hicks, J.J. (2001). The Strategy Behind Florida's "Truth" Campaign. *Tobacco Control*, 10: 3–5.

Holden, D., & Zimmerman, M. (Eds.). (2008). *A Practical Guide to Program Evaluation Planning*. Thousand Oaks, CA: Sage.

Hornik, R., & Yanovitsky, I. (2003). Using Theory to Design Evaluations of Communication Campaigns: The Case of the National Youth Anti-Drug Media Campaign. *Communication Theory*, 13(2): 204–224.

Hornik, R., Jacobsohn, L., Orwin, R., et al. (2008). Effects of the National Youth Anti-Drug Media Campaign on youths. *American Journal of Public Health*, 98(12): 2229–2236.

Huhman, M., Price, S., & Potter, L. (2008). Branding Play for Children: *VERB^{Tm}* It's What You Do. In *Public Health Branding: Applying Marketing for Social Change*, W.D. Evans & G. Hastings (Eds.). London: Oxford University Press. Chapter 6.

Huhman, M.E., Potter, L.D., Nolin, M.J., Piesse, A., Judkins, D.R., Banspach, S.W., & Wong, F.L. (2002). The Influence of the VERB Campaign on Children's Physical Activity in 2002 to 2006. *American Journal of Public Health*, 100(4): 638–645. doi:10.2105/AJPH.2008.142968

McDermott, L., Stead, M., & Hastings, G. (2005). What is and what is not social marketing. *Journal of Marketing and Management*, 21: 545–553.

Meekers, D., & Rahaim, S. (2005). The Importance of Socio-Economic Context for Social Marketing Models for Improving Reproductive Health: Evidence from 555 Years of Program Experience. *BMC Public Health* 5(10): 30–37.

Milat, A.J., Carroll, T.E., & Taylor, J.J. (2005). Culturally and linguistically diverse population health social marketing campaigns in Australia: a consideration of evidence and related evaluation issues, *Health Promotion Journal of Australia*, 16(1): 20–25.

Palmgreen, P., Lorch, E.P., Stephenson, M.T., et al. (2007). Effects of the Office of National Drug Control Policy's Marijuana Initiative Campaign on high-sensation-seeking adolescents, *American Journal of Public Health*, 97(9): 1644–1649.

Petty, R.E., & Cacioppo, J.T. (1986). *Communication and Persuasion: Central and Peripheral Routes to Attitude Change.* New York: Springer-Verlag.

Pollard, R. (2014). Total market approaches to the social marketing of health services and commodities in low-income countries. *Cases in Public Health Communication & Marketing*, 8(suppl 1): S4–S18.

Price, N. (2001). The Performance of Social marketing in Reaching the Poor and Vulnerable in AIDS Control Programmes. *Health and Policy Planning*, 16(3): 231–239.

Robinson, M.N., Tansil, K.A., Elder, R.W., Soler, R.E., Labre, M.P., Mercer, S.L., Eroglu, D., Baur, C., Lyon-Daniel, K., Fridinger, F., et al. (2014). Health Communication Campaigns That Include Mass Media and Health-Related Product Distribution: A Community Guide Systematic Review. *American Journal of Preventive Medicine*, 47(3): 360–371.

Slater, M.D., Kelly, K.J., Lawrence, F.R., et al. (2011). Assessing Media Campaigns Linking Marijuana Non-Use With Autonomy and Aspirations: "Be Under Your Own Influence" and ONDCP's "Above the Influence," *Prevention Science*, DOI:10.1007/s11121-010-0194-1.

Snyder, L.B., & Hamilton, M.A. (2002). Meta-Analysis of US Health Campaign Effects on Behavior: Emphasize Enforcement, Exposure, and New Information, and Beware the Secular Trend. In *Public Health Communication: Evidence for Behavior Change*, R. Hornik (Ed.). Hillsdale, NJ: Erlbaum; 357–383.

Snyder, L.B., Hamilton, M.A., Mitchell, E.W., Kiwanuka-Tondo, J., Fleming-Milici, F., & Proctor, D. (2004). A Meta-Analysis of the Effect of Mediated Health Communication Campaigns on Behavior Change in the United States. *Journal of Health Commununication*, 9(Suppl 1): 71–96.

United States Government Accountability Office (GAO). (2006). ONDCP Media Campaign: Contractor's National Evaluation Did Not Find That Youth Anti-Drug Media Campaign Was Effective in Reducing Youth Drug Use. Report to the Subcommittee on Transportation, Treasury, the Judiciary, Housing and Urban Development, and Related Agencies, Committee on Appropriations, U.S. Senate.

Wahdan, M.H. (1996). The Epidemiological Transition. *Eastern Mediterranean Health Journal*, 2(1): 8–20.

Wakefield, M.A., Loken, B., & Hornik, R.C. (2010). Use of Mass Media Campaigns to Change Health Behaviour. *Lancet*, 376(9748): 1261–1271.

World Bank. (2014). Updated Income Classifications. Retrieved on September 10, 2015, from http://data.worldbank.org/news/2015-country-classifications

10

Lessons Learned and Future Social Marketing Research

W. Douglas Evans

Summary Points

- Social marketing research is growing along with theory and practice in the field.
- This book identifies best practices and innovations in social marketing research.
- New methods and technologies can fill important gaps in the evidence.
- More research on how best to diffuse social marketing methods into practice and how to close the research-practice loop is needed.

What Are Best Practices and Challenges in Social Marketing Research?

This volume defines and describes a framework and series of processes and methods for social marketing research. While far from exhaustive, each of the previous chapters describes and illustrates the major steps in the social marketing research continuum defined in Chapter 1 and provides examples of best practice at each stage of the continuum. In this final chapter, the goal is to summarize what we have covered, lessons learned, and what the material presented implies for the future of social marketing research.

One observation is that social marketing research is a growing field. Applications such as the use of behavioral theory in research, health branding, directly addressing the competition, gaining and applying in-depth audience insight through research, and the other social marketing benchmark criteria first laid out by Andreasen (2006) and by French and colleagues (2010) illustrate this growth. Recent reviews of the literature suggest that there may be some acceleration in the use of these best practices (Evans, Blitstein, et al., 2014), and the growth of major professional associations such as the International Social Marketing Association and meetings such as the World Social Marketing Conference also attest to the development not only of social marketing as a practice but also of the research and evidence base.

At the same time, many challenges are evident. First and foremost, the true nature of the social marketing evidence base remains somewhat unclear. Studies such as the Community Guide review discussed in Chapter 9 (Robinson et al., 2014) provide some insight into campaigns that use at least the product P and in some cases other Ps (4Ps, place, price, product, and promotion). Studies, such as that of Evans, Blitstein, and colleagues (2014), provide further insight and suggest that the evidence is robust and growing. But, well-known problems in identifying which studies actually constitute social marketing evidence persist (Gordon et al., 2006; Hastings, 2007). Mainly, these stem from differences in language, lack of consistency in descriptions of social marketing, confusion between straightforward communication campaigns (promotion P only) and 4P strategies, and lack of editorial consistency in publishing of social marketing research continue to be major issues for academic researchers and groups such as the Community Guide and National Social Marketing Centre in the United Kingdom to synthesize the evidence (Evans, 2013).

An important next step in the field is to develop more precise standards for reporting of social marketing evidence, increase the quantity and quality of research and evaluation studies published, and educate the social marketing workforce and journal editors on the importance of consistently describing campaigns and social marketing research and evaluation studies. Consistent use of the benchmark criteria terminology (French et al., 2010) and clear presentations of data that enable social marketing studies to be synthesized and compared to one another, such as expressions of absolute percentage point differences in behavioral and other outcomes of campaigns, are critical improvements that need to be made to build the evidence base (Community Guide, 2010).

What Is the Future Research Agenda?

Based on the investigation of past and present social marketing research in this volume, where is the field headed? Major changes in terms of social marketing implementation have occurred due to digital technologies, cocreation of programs by participants (and the reconceptualizing of the very idea of an "audience," and the engagement of communities in the process of behavior, systems, and environmental change (Lefebvre, 2011). Given these trends, three areas clearly stand out for the near-term development of social marketing research: (1) use of multiple modalities of new media and technologies as platforms not only for campaigns but also for research; (2) engagement of participants in the social marketing process, including research activities; and (3) attention to multiple comorbid conditions that coexist within populations and communities that can be simultaneously addressed by campaigns.

Trends in Research Using New Technologies

Evaluation using social media, mobile devices, and other Internet-connected technologies is already with us and remains at the forefront of future social marketing research. Mobile devices are now a popular medium for providing treatment support through behavioral change and intervention strategies, medication reminder, treatment information, and various adherence tools targeted to improve health outcomes though healthy behavior (Free et al., 2013). These programs increasingly are evaluated using the same Internet, mobile, and social media technologies through which they are delivered. One example of this is the *text4baby* mobile health program, discussed in Chapter 7, which delivers timely pregnancy and postpartum information to new mothers to improve maternal and child health (Evans, Nielsen, et al., 2014). Not only was this program delivered through text messages to participants' mobile phones, but also the evaluation was enabled through surveys conducted online and in mobile-friendly format for completion via the mobile phone. Texts were sent to remind participants to complete follow-up data collection that contained links that, when clicked, took the participant directly to the correct (e.g., second or third follow-up, as appropriate for that individual) survey for completion in real time on their phone. This type of methodology is increasingly common and used by most major survey research organizations today, such as the GfK Knowledge Panel (formerly Knowledge Networks; http://www.gfk.com/products-a-z/knowledgepanelr-north-america/).

Engaging Participants in Research

New technologies, including the Internet, social media, and mobile phones, expand the reach and effectiveness of public health programs (Free et al., 2013). As noted, some prevention programs have used social media as delivery channels, such as Above the Influence (ATI) and its large Facebook presence and efforts to create a social community of youth sharing narratives related to avoidance of marijuana and other drug use (Office of National Drug Control Policy; ONDCP, 2014). In the public health generally, and drug use prevention in particular, relatively little has been published demonstrating the effectiveness of social media as prevention channels. Substance Abuse and Mental Health Services Administration (SAMHSA) has funded a number of state media campaigns for prevention, some of which, including Colorado's *SpeakNow!* Campaign focused on teen drinking prevention, have used social media activities (http://captus.samhsa.gov/access-resources/substance-abuse-prevention-media-campaigns). However, these efforts are in their infancy.

A new intervention called *#STM4U*, based on the school-based Shattering the Myth prevention program (http://www.mentorfoundationusa.org/), uses the Adobe Youth Voices (AYV) platform to train youth to generate their own content and create video-based narrative stories to disseminate over social media. AYV offers a free online course, Adobe Youth Voices: Create Change. The course is designed to prepare educators to lead youth media development (https://youthvoices.adobe.com/). Many health topics have previously been included in AYV projects, including marijuana use and addiction (https://youthvoices.adobe.com/youth-media-gallery/). AYV has also been used in school settings and capitalizes on the power of digital media to allow youth to express their own stories in exportable video format, ready made for sharing over social media such as YouTube, Facebook, Twitter, and Instagram. #STM4U uses AYV to train youth in the creative process and to create video media. The intervention will consist of a self-expression component by which students will learn techniques for expressing their ideas about marijuana use. Expressive segments will be created as videos for social media.

Youth who participate in the social media activities will disseminate the video-based narratives they create throughout their social media networks using all platforms to which they are current members. They will also post to a dedicated project YouTube channel. Researchers will document all participant exposure to #STM4U social media metrics captured on the Hootsuite social media management platform (https://hootsuite.com) and through survey responses from all participants and control for potential contamination in the analyses. Researchers will use the Hootsuite platform to capture social media process (implementation) data. Outcome evaluation surveys with youth who create the videos and disseminate them will be conducted via posts to the very same social media they are using. Thus, the participants both cocreate the intervention and actively participate in the research, process, and outcome evaluation process via multiple digital media modalities.

Comorbid Conditions and Social Marketing

About 19 million new sexually transmitted infections (STIs) and 40,000 new HIV cases occur each year in the United States. Reducing the burden of HIV/STIs is a critical public health objective. Strategies need to address risky behaviors associated with infection, a task that is complicated by substance use and abuse (National Institute on Drug Abuse [NIDA], 2015). Risk behaviors associated with both public health problems tend to cluster together and increase the likelihood of incidences of HIV/AIDS (Agha, 2003). Intoxication interferes with decision-making and enhances risky sexual behaviors, and some substance use (e.g., needle sharing) is directly related to infection (Mayer, Skeer, & Mimiaga, 2012). The Monitoring the Future study showed sustained levels of substance use, and the resulting risky sex remains widespread in the United States (Johnston et al., 2009), making substance use and HIV/STI co-occurring problems (Masson et al., 2004). The risk factors associated with both problems are disproportionately high among certain populations, such as young people who frequent bars and nightclubs, where substance use and risky sex are common (Hipwell et al., 2012). But, interventions traditionally address single risk factors and not co-occurring problems.

Social marketing by its nature is capable of addressing these co-occurring risk factors. Specifically, using a *health branding* approach, as discussed in Chapter 4 and elsewhere in this volume, social marketers can create positive brand identification with healthy behaviors among a targeted audience as a behavior change strategy (Evans & Hastings, 2008; Evans, Holtz, & Snider, 2014). Health branding has two important attributes that make it an appropriate strategy for co-occurring behaviors and health risk factors. First, by creating identification with specific healthy behaviors it can address the common risk behaviors for co-occurring problems such as HIV/STI and substance abuse. A second advantage is the ability to target specific high-risk groups with a combined risk profile by promoting benefits of alternative safer behavioral choices (e.g., always carrying a condom when going out, not using drugs) that underlie the co-occurring conditions (Hecht & Lee, 2008). There are examples of effective branding of condom use and specific brands developed through social marketing programs aimed at increasing overall behavior change as opposed to maximizing product sales (Tobler et al., 2000). For example, recent quasi-experimental and correlational studies have linked drug resistance branding to improved substance abuse attitudes and reduced substance abuse behavior (Lee, 2010).

To date, however, there have been no experimental studies addressing co-occurring risk factors for HIV/STIs and substance abuse or comparing branded and unbranded messages to uncover the added benefits of branding for prevention of HIV/STIs and substance use. In addition, we know little about the causal mechanisms through which successful brands operate. Thus, new research is needed to empirically test health branding as an approach to changing social cognitive determinants of HIV/STIs and substance use. The goal of this research would be to develop and compare prevention social marketing strategies and isolate the effects of these strategies, such as branding, on changes in determinants of prevention behavior.

Diffusion of Social Marketing Research and the Research-Practice Gap

Diffusion of Social Marketing Research Methods

Despite growing evidence showing the effectiveness of social marketing when its full set of proven practices are applied (French et al., 2010), as discussed previously, there has been too little diffusion of the practices of social marketing research in the prevention and health promotion fields. Little has been done to train the healthcare workforce and scientific community to effectively use social marketing research in program development and translation. Continuing with the theme of HIV/STI and substance use programs, prevention practitioners and researchers need a training program to build branding knowledge, skills, and aptitude (KSA) and resources to support their branding efforts for behavior change.

With the enormous public health burden of HIV/STIs, and other risk behaviors such as substance abuse, effective behavior change strategies are essential. The National Institutes of Health (NIH) have made major investments in programs to prevent these risk behaviors (Fauci, 2008), but translation of effective initiatives into sustained programs with effective delivery and distribution has proven challenging (Global Health HIV Prevention Working Group, 2008). One reason for this problem is that programs are not adequately marketed, recognized, and appealing to targeted populations who could benefit from them.

This void needs to be filled by developing and testing a health branding research and education program. There are two main elements that need to be addressed. First, rigorous research needs to be sponsored and conducted to build the evidence base and establish the effectiveness of branding in multiple subject matter domains using rigorous methods. Second, educational tools need to be developed, tested, and disseminated to increase KSA in the public health and scientific workforce. These factors will be facilitated by more diffusion of research into practice and application of lessons learned to develop improved prevention programs.

PRECEDE-PROCEED and the Research-Practice Gap

Perhaps the greatest challenge and future direction for social marketing research is increasing the uptake of knowledge and lessons learned from campaign research and evaluation studies into new programs. The PRECEDE-PROCEED model is the underlying theory that supports this approach (Green & Kreuter, 2005), and increased application of it in social marketing and our research activities in the field is much needed. To quote one of the theory's creators, Larry Green, "PRECEDE-PROCEED can be thought of as a road map and theories of behavior change as specific directions to a destination" (see http://prezi.com/bdadbok_fv1w/?utm_campaign=share&utm_medium=copy&rc=exoshare).

In many ways, the model is intuitive. It postulates a process, and factors to be considered, in translating evidence into practice and a continuous improvement loop in which lessons learned from practice are then studied to increase the base of evidence, which can then be translated again into improved practice (Green & Kreuter, 2005). The PRECEDE part of the model came first (Green et al., 1980) and refers to "predisposing, reinforcing, and enabling" constructs, or individual and environmental or ecological factors that may promote or inhibit individual behavior and health. The PROCEED part of the model was added in the 1990s and later updated (Green & Kreuter, 2005); it refers to policy, regulatory, and related ecological/environmental factors in determining health and health behaviors (Green & Kreuter, 1991). This refers to the social and physical environmental factors that influence health behavior and health outcomes, what has now come to be known as the social determinants of health (Marmot, Allen, & Goldblatt, 2010).

With this in mind, the two main tenets of PRECEDE-PROCEED are that

1. Health and health risks are caused by multiple factors; and
2. Because health and health risks are determined by multiple factors, efforts to effect behavioral, environmental, and social change must

be multidimensional or multisectoral and participatory (Green & Kreuter, 2005).

PRECEDE has four phases of research activities, which refer to the investigation and diagnosis of predisposing, reinforcing, and enabling factors that can be used to design effective health programs and interventions. PROCEED has four additional phases of research activities, which refer to the evaluation (process, outcome, impact) of the PRECEDE activities when implemented. The loop is closed when these activities are integrated and there is a transfer of information to and from program implementation to evaluation, leading to improved programs in the future (Green & Kreuter, 2005). A summary graphic presentation is available online (http://lgreen.net/precede.htm).

This model and approach to intervention are closely tied to the tenets of social marketing, and social marketing research can be the vehicle to help practitioners follow the PRECEDE-PROCEED "roadmap." The PRECEDE-PROCEED evidence in a social marketing context would be the results of monitoring and evaluation activities discussed in this volume:

- Process results: Were milestones achieved as planned?
- Campaign endpoints: Were objectives achieved?
- Did the campaign achieve communication and behavioral objectives?
- Is there evidence of health impact?
- What are the predictors? Exposure level, segmentation, mediators?
  - How can these results be used to build a better future campaign?

This volume provides good examples of how social marketing research and practice have followed (albeit not necessarily by design) the PRECEDE-PROCEED model. For example, Chapter 9 addressed the original Florida TRUTH campaign to the National Legacy *truth*® campaign (now Truth Initiative). The insights were that youth need to express their "need for uniqueness" (for rebellion, independence) as adopted and applied by national *truth*. This led to a large-scale campaign that applied evidence from Florida to expand and thoroughly monitor and evaluate the new approach, which has contributed to the growth of evidence and improvement of practice in tobacco control (Centers for Disease Control and Prevention [CDC], 2014).

Also, Chapter 9 addressed the original ATI and transition to the new ATI antidrug campaigns. The original campaign was indeed unsuccessful, and considerable evaluation and follow-up analysis were conducted to determine the underlying causes (PRECEDE factors) that may have led to this result. The insight was that talking about drugs, even to promote being drug free, creates a meta-message that "everybody's doing it." This insight was adopted and applied by the most recent ATI antidrug campaign (Jacobsohn & Hornik, 2008).

Finally, Chapter 4 addressed Population Services International (PSI) condom promotion campaigns in low- and middle-income countries. Many of these campaigns to promote purchase of subsidized condoms within a total market approach (TMA) were successful but faced new environmental and other external pressures (PROCEED factors) that led them to be redesigned and rebranded. The insight was that condom use as a category of behavior, and specific condom brand appeals, needs to be refreshed as generational shifts and market dynamics change in order to be branded as part of a young adult lifestyle that promotes adoption and consistent use (Evans et al., 2012).

The interesting question for social marketing, and for social marketing research, is how the changes, adaptations, and improvements in future social marketing efforts enabled by research and process of translation of research were put into practice. Looking at the examples noted, and the many others cited in this book and elsewhere (Hastings, 2007; Lefebvre, 2011), four promising practices stand out:

- Collaborations between social marketers and evaluators
- Applying data from evaluations to campaign design
- Testing proven approaches in formative research with new populations, settings, problems
- Developing new objectives and campaign strategies using evidence from the prior campaign

So, for example, in the case of *truth*, the Florida campaign and its research and evaluation revealed a key insight that the *competition* (i.e., the tobacco industry) used a proven approach that could be adapted to a countermarketing campaign. As shown in Figure 10-1, the tobacco industry used the need for uniqueness construct (Tian, Bearden, & Hunter, 2001) to differentiate itself as the purveyor of independence and rebellion, two need states sought by teens who might consider initiating smoking. This adaptation led to the *truth* brand and many of the distinctive strategies that proved so successful on a national scale.

Through social marketing research, ATI came to the realization that it could not create a meta-message that drug use was normal and had to focus

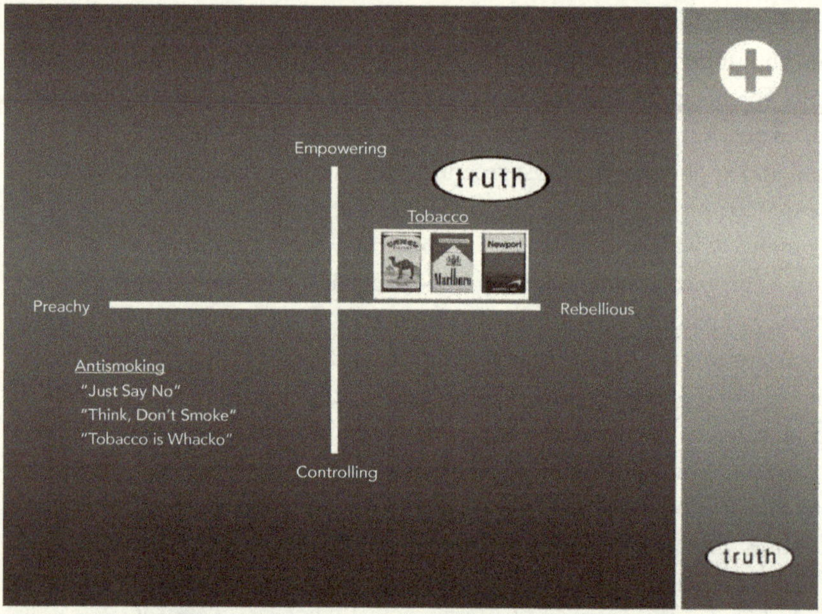

FIGURE 10-1 Brand positioning of *truth* to countermarket tobacco industry brands.

FIGURE 10-2 Population Services International condom branding examples.

on building a *relationship* with adolescents in which credible and appealing alternatives to drug use were offered (Evans, Holtz, & Snider, 2014). This occurred as a result of adapting program practice and a new rebranding effort based on previous research, leading to new evaluation efforts of the updated campaign.

Population Services International condom brands adapted to changes in marketplaces, in some cases in competition with commercial brands, epidemiological transition in low- and middle-income countries, and changing generations and product preferences. These insights, much like those used by commercial marketers, led to successful rebranding and continued success in marketing the category of condom use through renewed product offerings. Figure 10-2 illustrates some of PSI's marketing efforts.

These improvements in practice all stemmed from the strategic use of social marketing research very much along the lines of PRECEDE-PROCEED. Strategic use of this approach should be a priority for social and behavior change programs generally. Renewed efforts to build knowledge, education, and skills in the use of research for this purpose are an urgent priority for social marketing.

Additional Resources: Web Based

- For more on PRECEDE-PROCEED, visit http://lgreen.net/.
- For more on PSI and condom branding programs, visit http://psi.org.
- For more on social and health branding, visit http://rescuescg.com/.
- For more on the *truth* campaign, visit http://truthinitiative.org/.

REFERENCES

Agha, S. (2003). The Impact of a Mass Media Campaign on Personal Risk Perception, Perceived Self-Efficacy and on Other Behavioral Predictors. *Aids Care*, 15(6): 749–762.

Andreasen, A. (2006). Social marketing in the 21st Century. *Thousand Oaks*, CA: Sage Publications.

Centers for Disease Control and Prevention. Best Practices for Comprehensive Tobacco Control Programs—2014. Atlanta: U.S. Department of Health and Human Services, Centers for Disease Control and Prevention, National Center for Chronic Disease Prevention and Health Promotion, Office on Smoking and Health, 2014.

The Community Guide (2010). Health Communication and Social marketing: Health Communication Campaigns that Include Mass Media and Health-Related Product Distribution. Retrieved September 1, 2015 from http://www.thecommunityguide.org/healthcommunication/campaigns.html.

Evans, W.D. (2013) Branding Social and Health Behavior: An Education and Research Agenda. In *Psychology of Branding*, W.D. Evans (Ed.). Hauppauge, NY: Nova Science. Chapter 8.

Evans, W.D., Blitstein, J., Vallone, D., Post, S., & Nilsen, W. (2014). Systematic Review of Health Branding: Growth of a Promising Practice. *Translational Behavioral Medicine*, 5(1): 24–36. doi:10.1007/s13142-014-0272-1

Evans, W.D., & Hastings, G. (Eds.). (2008). *Public Health Branding: Applying Marketing for Social Change*. London: Oxford University Press.

Evans, W.D., Holtz, K., & Snider, J. (2014). Effects of the Above the Influence Brand on Adolescent Drug Use Prevention Beliefs. *Journal of Health Communication*, 19(6): 721–737. doi:10.1080/10810730.2013.837559

Evans, W.D., Nielsen, P., Szekely, D., Wallace, J., Murray, E., & Snider, J. (2014). Initial Outcomes From a 4-Week Follow-Up Study of the text4baby Program in the Military Women's Population: Randomized Controlled Trial. *Journal of Medical Internet Research*, 16(5): e13. doi:10.2196/jmir.3297

Evans, W.D., Rivas, J., Andrade, B., Longfield, K., Lungo, S., Sinder, J., & Wallace, J. (2012). HIV prevention through condom brand social marketing: Case study of brand equity research in Central America. *2011 International Communication Association Theme Book*. New York: Hampton Press.

Fauci, A.S. (2008). Testimony before the Committee on Oversight and Government Reform, U.S. House of Representatives. Retrieved on February 22, 2016 from http://www.hhs.gov/asl/testify/2008/09/t20080916f.html.

Free, C., Phillips, G., Galli, L., Watson, L., Felix, L., Edwards, P., Patel, V., & Haines, A. (2013). The Effectiveness of Mobile-Health Technology-Based Health Behavior Change or Disease Management Interventions for Health Care Consumers: A Systematic Review. *PLoS Med*, 10(1): E1001362. doi:10(1):e1001362

French, J., Blair-Stevens, C., McVey, D., & Merritt, R. (2010). *Social Marketing and Public Health*. Oxford, UK: Oxford University Press.

Global HIV Prevention Working Group. (2008). Behavior Change and HIV Prevention: (Re)Considerations for the 21st Century. Retrieved on February 22, 2016 from http://www.globalhivprevention.org/pdfs/PWG_behavior%20report_FINAL.pdf.

Gordon, R., McDermott, L., Stead, M., & Angus, K. (2006). The Effectiveness of Social Marketing Interventions for Health Improvement: What's the Evidence? *Public Health*, 120(12): 1133–1139.

Green, L., & Kreuter, M. (1991). *Health Promotion Planning: An Educational and Environmental Approach* (2nd ed.). Mountain View, CA: Mayfield.

Green, L., & Kreuter, M. (2005). *Health Program Planning: An Educational and Ecological Approach* (4th ed.). New York: McGraw-Hill.

Green, L.W., Kreuter, M.W., Deeds, S.G., & Partridge, K.B. (1980). *Health Education Planning: A Diagnostic Approach*. Mountain View, CA: Mayfield.

Hastings, G. (2007). *Social Marketing: Or, Why Should the Devil Have All the Best Tunes*. London: Butterworth-Heineman.

Hecht, M.L., & Lee, J.K. (2008). Branding Through Cultural Grounding: The Keepin' It REAL Curriculum. In *Public Health Branding: Applying Marketing for Social Change*, W.D. Evans & G. Hastings (Eds.). London: Oxford University Press. Chapter 9.

Hipwell, A., Stepp, S., Chung, T., Durand, V., & Keenan, K. (2012). Growth in Alcohol Use as a Developmental Predictor of Adolescent Girls' Sexual Risk-Taking. *Prevention Science*, 13(2): 118–128.

Jacobsohn, L., & Hornik, R. (2008). High Brand Recognition in the Context of an Unsuccessful Communication Campaign: The National Youth Anti-Drug Media Campaign. In *Public Health Branding: Applying Marketing for Social Change*, W.D. Evans & G. Hastings (Eds.). London: Oxford University Press. Chapter 8.

Johnston, L.D., O'Malley, P.M., Bachman, J.G., & Schulenberg, J.E. (2009). *Monitoring the Future National Survey Results on Drug Use, 1975–2008. Volume I: Secondary School Students* (NIH Publication No. 09-7402). Bethesda, MD: National Institute on Drug Abuse.

Lee, J.K. (2010). The Role of Branding in the keepin' it REAL Substance Use Prevention Curriculum. Dissertation in partial fulfillment of doctoral degree requirements at the Pennsylvania State University.

Lefebvre, R.C. (2011). An Integrative Model for Social Marketing. *Journal of Social Marketing*, 1(1): 54–72.

Marmot, M., Allen, J., & Goldblatt, P. (2010). *Fair Society, Healthy Lives: Strategic Review of Health Inequalities in England Post 2010*. London: Marmot Review Team. Retrieved on September 1, 2015, from http://www.instituteofhealthequity.org/

Masson, C.L., Sorensen, J.L., Phibbs, C.S., & Okin, R.L. (2004). Predictors of Medical Service Utilization Among Individuals With Co-occurring HIV Infection and Substance Abuse Disorders. *Aids Care*, 16(6): 744–755.

Mayer, K.H., Skeer, M., & Mimiaga, M.J. (2012). Biomedical Approaches to HIV Prevention. Retrieved on September 1, 2015, from http://pubs.niaaa.nih.gov/publications/arh333/195-202.htm

National Institute on Drug Abuse. (2015). Drug Abuse and HIV. Retrieved on February 22, 2016 from http://atforum.com/documents/HIVResearchReport.pdf.

Office of National Drug Control Policy (2014). Above the Influence Media Campaign. Retrieved on February 22, 2016 from https://www.whitehouse.gov/ondcp/ondcp-fact-sheets/above-the-influence-ATI.

Robinson, M.N., Tansil, K.A., Elder, R.W., Soler, R.E., Labre, M.P., Mercer, S.L., . . . Rimer, B.K., Task Force on Community Preventive Services. (2014). "Health Communication Campaigns That Include Mass Media and Health-Related Product Distribution: A Community Guide Systematic Review." *American Journal of Preventive Medicine*, 47(3): 360–371.

Tian, K.T., Bearden, W., & Hunter, G. (2001), Consumers' Need for Uniqueness: Scale Development and Validation. *Journal of Consumer Research*, 28: 50–66.

Tobler, N.S., Roona, M.R., Ochshorn, P., Marshall, D.G., Streke, A.V., & Stackpole, K.M. (2000). School-Based Adolescent Drug Prevention Programs: 1998 Meta-analysis. *The Journal of Primary Prevention*, 20: 275–336. doi:10.1023/A:1021314704811

Index